主编 / 孙有中　副主编 / 陈　弘　韩　锋
执行主编 / 李建军　胡　丹

澳大利亚研究

2018 年第 2 辑

总第 2 辑

Chinese Journal of Australian Studies

社会科学文献出版社
SOCIAL SCIENCES ACADEMIC PRESS (CHINA)

《澳大利亚研究》编委会

目　录

特　稿

专题论文

澳研历史回顾专栏

《李尧译文集》专栏

会议综述

Contents

Special Articles

Feature Essays

Special Column: History of Australian Studies

Special Column: Prof. *Li Yao's Translation Series of Australian Literature*

Conferences

特稿

Special Articles

2017年澳大利亚对华政策"政经悖离"现象加速发展的内外动因评析

于　镭　于飞洋*

摘要：2017年中澳关系"政经悖离"现象加速发展：特恩布尔政府一方面在政治上急剧右转，并进一步强化澳美军事同盟，以遏制中国在印太地区日益增长的力量和影响；另一方面希冀与中国加强经贸合作，以维持澳大利亚的经济繁荣与民众就业。特恩布尔对华政策的"政经悖离"既有国内政治斗争激化的内生性，亦有美国压力日益增大的外生性。澳国内右翼亲美保守势力强大，特恩布尔政府执政地位异常脆弱，这导致政府在决策时往往面临国内保守政治势力的强大压力。由于历史原因，澳自独立之日即奉行与超级大国结盟的立国之策，以获取经济利益和安全庇护。在从澳美同盟获利的同时，澳也不得不对美效忠，并甘为其驱使。澳美同盟的演变表明澳美两国的同盟关系并非主要基于两国文化、历史和价值观的相似性，而更多的是出于对政治、经济和安全利益的考量。作为中等强国，澳大利亚的国家利益与美国并不完全重合，并且

* 作者简介：于镭，聊城大学太平洋岛国研究中心首席研究员，北京外国语大学澳大利亚研究中心研究员。主要研究方向：澳美同盟，区域安全与合作等，其著述见 *International Affairs*，*Cambridge of International Affairs*。于飞洋，北京建筑大学文法学院研究生，主要研究方向：中澳文化比较。

它也不会自不量力到像美国一样，把扼制一个新兴超级力量崛起作为自己的战略目标。中国与澳大利亚的经济融合与依存仍会继续增强，这正是中澳两国关系不断深化的基础，也是澳大利亚政府领导人对华政策的基石。

关键词：澳美同盟　对华政策　印太战略　中澳关系　平衡策略

2017年，特恩布尔政府基本上延续了霍华德总理（1996～2007）在21世纪初开创的在中美两大国间寻求平衡的外交策略，并对中国“两面下注”：澳大利亚在与中国保持密切的经济和贸易合作，追求自身经济利益和经济繁荣的同时，也加大了对中国在经济、政治和安全领域的防范。特恩布尔领导的自由党－国家党联盟在2016年大选中惨胜主要反对党工党，特恩布尔以微弱优势继续组阁执政，但其对党内不同派系和议会的掌控力量遭到了极大的削弱。如果不取得党内外右翼力量的支持，特恩布尔政府根本无法在党内和议会内获得多数支持，也无法在议会中通过任何法案和提案。为了获得党内和国内右翼势力的支持，特恩布尔在国内政治、外国投资审查、外交政策等问题上不得不大幅度右转，并一再在涉华问题和对华政策上向美国和国内亲美势力妥协，从而导致中澳关系“政经悖离”的现象进一步加剧。

出于国内政党角力和国家安全的需要，并在美国的政治、经济利诱和压力下，特恩布尔政府积极强化与美国的军事和安全同盟，并推动美国在“重返亚太”战略的基础上构建更大地域范围的“印太战略”，以配合美国遏制中国崛起对美国主导的全球和区域霸权体系和权力架构构成的挑战。澳大利亚此举旨在防范中国崛起可能对澳大利亚国家安全构成的挑战，维护其在美国主导下的霸权体系中获取的各种既得利益和“美国的地区代理人”以及亚太地区“副警长”的政治地位。在美国与澳大利亚两国建制派和军方势力的双重压力下，中澳关系因此呈现出经贸往来不断增加，经济融合进一步发展，但双方在政治和安全领域的分歧益发呈现出加速扩大之势。

一　中澳经贸合作的加速与深化

2017 年中澳双边经贸关系继续保持快速增长的势头，中国连续第九年蝉联澳大利亚第一大贸易伙伴国。由于《中澳自贸协定》得到进一步落实，“贸易创造效应”和“贸易转移效应”成效显著，对两国贸易和投资的快速增长发挥了重要作用。许多澳方贸易官员和经济学家认为《中澳自贸协定》涵盖了货物贸易、服务贸易、投资、环保和贸易规则等领域，是目前亚太地区一份质量较高的自贸协定，正对两国经贸合作以及双边关系的发展产生重要而深远的影响。一些经济界人士指出《自贸协定》为两国实现高品质的经济互补提供了可靠的法律保障，也为整个亚太地区高质量的经贸安排协议发挥了良好的示范作用。《中澳自贸协定》的签署与成功实施对于推动亚太地区经济一体化的发展，促进亚太地区各经济体的深度融合做出了有益的尝试。澳大利亚国际经济研究中心曾预测《自贸协定》得到充分落实后，将分别拉动澳中两国的 GDP 增长 0.7 个和 0.1 个百分点[①]。但澳大利亚经济部门和经济界人士现在则普遍认为《自贸协定》对澳大利亚的贡献可能还会更大。[②] 特恩布尔总理对《自贸协定》的效果表示满意，强调它是关乎澳大利亚未来繁荣的重要基石之一，为澳大利亚经济的持续繁荣与发展奠定了基础。[③]

---

① The Centre for International Economics, *Estimating the Impact of An Australia-China Trade and Investment Agreement*, November 2008, http: //acbc. com. au/admin/images/uploads/Copy 3report_ fta_ modelling. pdf.

② Department of Foreign Affairs and Trade, Australia 2017, ChAFTA Outcomes at a Glance, https: //dfat. gov. au/trade/agreements/in - force/chafta/fact - sheets/Pages/chafta - outcomes - at - a - glance. aspx.

③ Malcolm Turnbull, *ChAFTA and Rebalancing of Chinese & Australian Economies: Speech to Australia - China Business Forum*, Malcolmturnbull Website, 6 August 2015, http: //www. malcolmturnbull. com. au/media/China - Business - Week.

中国海关数据表明，截至2018年初，98.5%的澳大利亚商品得以免税，或者以优惠的税率出口至中国大陆地区。《自贸协定》的进一步落实和实施为澳大利亚对华商品与服务出口的快速增长做出了巨大的贡献。2017年，中澳双边贸易总额创下1830亿澳元（约合1500亿美元）的历史新高，其中澳对华商品和服务出口总额高达1100多亿澳元，比2016年增长了五分之一。[①] 澳大利亚政府和经济界感到十分高兴的是，惠及澳大利亚广大农户和中小企业主的奶制品、葡萄酒和美容护肤品等具有澳大利亚特色的商品的对华出口额较2016年翻了一番。更令澳方倍感欣喜的是，澳大利亚对华商品出口近年来还呈现出多元化、开放化的趋势。澳大利亚不仅向中国出口优质的农业、矿业产品等传统优势商品，现在还为中国客户提供极富竞争力的服务业产品，其内容涵盖健康、教育、养老和医疗等诸多领域。

据澳大利亚外交贸易部统计，澳大利亚2017年对华六周的出口额即超过对英国的全年出口总额。澳大利亚服务业的对华出口总额已经超过了对英国、美国服务业出口总额之和。[②] 由此可见，日益繁荣的中国市场和日益壮大的中国中产阶级群体对澳大利亚经济的持久繁荣具有极为重要的意义。时至今日，中国已成为澳大利亚第一大贸易伙伴、第一大出口目的地、第一大进口来源国、第一大贸易顺差来源国、第一大农产品出口市场、第一大服务贸易出口目的地、第一大年度外资来源国、第一大移民来源国、第一大旅游收入来源国、第一大留学生来源国。[③] 这“十个第一”标志着中澳两国的经贸合作已经达到了历史新高度。不论人们的主观意愿如何，

---

① Department of Foreign Affairs and Trade (Australia), *Fact Sheets of Australia*, April 2018, https://dfat.gov.au/trade/resources/Documents/aust.pdf.

② Steven Ciobo, "UTS - Australia China Relations Institute Event", 28 June 2018, http://trademinister.gov.au/speeches/Pages/2018/sc_sp_180628.aspx? w = tb1CaGpkPX%2FlS0K%2Bg9ZKEg%3D%3D.

③ 马朝旭：驻澳大利亚大使马朝旭在《中资企业在澳大利亚》首发仪式上的致辞，中国驻澳大使馆网站，2015年12月10日，http://au.china-embassy.org/chn/sgfyrth/t1323088.htm。

中澳两国的经济融合已经无法阻挡。这是中澳两国关系势将“更加深入，更加稳固”的基础，也是不论来自哪个党派的澳大利亚政治家都不得不重视发展对华关系的最重要的因素。[①]

二　中澳政治和安全关系的“悖离”加速

在中澳双边经贸关系不断加速发展之际，中澳两国在政治、外交和印太区域的安全观和安全架构上的分歧却呈现加速扩大之势，这主要表现在以下几个方面。

首先，澳大利亚政界、安全防卫界不断渲染“中国威胁论”，指责中国“干涉澳大利亚内政”、对澳大利亚进行“政治渗透”和“安全威胁”，并危言耸听地攻击百万华人、华侨和留学生都是中国政府派至澳大利亚的“间谍”。[②] 澳大利亚一些极右翼政客也趁机喊出了“澳大利亚需要麦卡锡主义”的谬论，企图借此机会扩大影响，捞取政治利益。[③] 澳大利亚政府对此不仅不设法加以阻止，反而推波助澜地借机向议会提交了“反对外国干涉法案”，企图借此将国内政治争斗的矛头转向中国。澳方的这一系列举动不仅恶化了中澳关系发展的氛围，而且进一步动摇了特恩布尔总理的政治地位。

其次，澳大利亚政府将政治问题扩大化，不仅将澳方一些政治人物对涉华问题的个人观点上升至关乎国家对外政策和国家安全利益的高度，而且将一些原本属于商业活动的行为定性为“为外国政府和外国利益服务”，致使一些对华较为友好的政治人士被迫辞

---

① Alex Oliver, “What to Expect from Malcolm Turnbull”, *Foreign Policy*, 16 September 2015, http://foreignpolicy.com/2015/09/16/what-to-expect-malcolm-turnbull-australia-tony-abbott-prime-minister/.

② Charles Wallace, “The Art of Influence: How China's Spies Operate in Australia”, *Sydney Morning Herald*, 3 December 2017, https://www.smh.com.au/public-service/the-art-of-influence-how-chinas-spies-operate-in-australia-20171203-gzxs06.html.

③ Paul Karp 2018, “Kevin Rudd Accuses Turnbull Government of ‘Anti-Chinese Jihad’”, *Guardian*, 18 February, https://www.theguardian.com/australia-news/2018/feb/12/kevin-rudd-accuses-turnbull-government-of-anti-chinese-jihad.

职，也迫使一些华人企业家不得不运用法律工具将澳大利亚联邦政府的有关部门和一些全国性媒体诉上法庭，以维护自身的名誉和合法权益。[①] 政治问题的扩大化严重破坏了中澳两国的经贸关系和经贸合作进一步深化的氛围，直接导致两国经贸增长势头的减缓，特别是中国投资在澳大利亚的大幅度减少。澳大利亚因其部分政治人士在文化、政治和经济等领域的对华不友好言行而被中国的一些主流媒体列为 2017 年度对华最不友好国家，两国政治关系也因此被迫处于调整之中。

最后，中澳两国对亚太，乃至印太地区在后冷战时代的安全体系与安全架构的分歧进一步扩大。在后冷战时代，中国一直倡导以互信、合作和共同安全为主体的新安全观来取代旧有的以军事集团对抗为主的冷战模式。与中方的观点相反，澳大利亚政府坚持澳美军事同盟是澳对外政策的基石，也是维护印太地区安全体系和澳大利亚既得利益与地位的最重要的力量。对此，特恩布尔政府积极推动和支持美国的"印太战略"，深化澳美军事同盟，不断升级澳美在亚太和印太地区的联合军事演习规模，并竭力将澳大利亚打造成"印太战略"最为重要的军事枢纽。

相当一部分澳大利亚政治人士和学者对澳大利亚的"印太"安全观和印太区域的军事同盟体系提出异议，他们认为美国在亚太地区的庞大军事存在和构筑于冷战时期用以争夺区域霸权的军事同盟网，即"轮辐体系"（或旧金山体系）是冷战的残余，不仅与亚太地区以和平和发展为主的大趋势格格不入，而且日益产生"囚徒困境"式的负面效应。这些人士指出，在后冷战时期，美澳军

① Australian Broadcasting Company 2018，"Chinese-Australian Businessman Chau Chak Wing Sues Fairfax"，ABC News，https：//search. yahoo. com/search；_ ylt = Awr9DWaLpplbJX8AIxtXNyoA；_ ylc = X1MDMjc2NjY3OQRfcgMyBGZyA3lmcC10LTUwMi1zYgRncHJpZANlamQxNFZSQ1R0QzhIVXhYQ1l4MnRBBG5fcnNsdAMwBG5fc3VnZwMwBG9yaWdpbgNzZWFyY2gueWFob28uY29tBHBvcwMwBHBxc3RyAwRwcXN0cmwDMARxc3RybAM4MgRxdWVyeQNjaGluZXNlJTIwYm9ybiUyMGJ1c2luZXNzbWFuJTIwc3VlJTIwYWdhaW5zdCUyMGF1c3RyYWxpYW4lMjBicm9hZGNhc3RpbmclMjBjb21wYW55BHRfc3RtcAMxNTM2Nzk2NzIz？ p = chinese + born + businessman + sue + against + australian + broadcasting + company&fr2 = sb – top&fr = yfp – t – 502 – sb.

事同盟的加强和频频军演只能增加亚太地区的紧张局势，加深本地区包括中国在内的一些国家的疑虑，使他们认为美国已经将其冷战时期的军事矛头转向了这些国家。[①] 一些学者还指出，美国将日本和澳大利亚描绘成其在西太平洋地区安全架构的南北“双锚”，极大地增加了中国对美国战略意图的疑虑，因为它令中国不能不想起美国自1949年以来长期奉行的对华封锁和包围的战略。这些学者还批评美、日、澳意图构建的三方共同安全架构会议与其说是美、日、澳三国对朝鲜核能力的担心，不如说是对中国日益增长的国防能力的担忧，反映了“美澳意在将两国间的双边安全会谈扩充为以美为首的多边安全框架，旨在首先并主要防范中国”。[②] 这些学者还特别强调指出“某些国家有选择地纠集起来将另一些国家排挤出去的做法在政治上非常不明智，这完全是冷战模式”。在这些学者的眼中，日益强化的美、澳、日军事同盟不仅加剧了本地区的“囚徒困境式”的军事竞赛，而且无益于亚太地区的安全与合作。学者们强调“一个合作与包容，而不是排斥与遏制的多边架构显然是适合本地区安全的一个更好的选择”。[③]

三 中澳“政经悖离”加速的表象与影响

中澳两国在政治和安全上的观点迥异不仅影响了两国政治关系的发展，而且直接影响了两国的经贸合作，特别是中国对澳大利亚的投资。在美国和澳大利亚内部右翼势力的压力下，澳大利亚政府在两国经贸关系增长势头加速之际，对我国在澳大利亚的投资采取了加大审查力度和收紧压缩的政策。一些澳大利亚媒体指出，控制和减少中国对澳投资并非是由于澳大利亚“不差钱”，而是澳大利

---

① Franz - Stefan Gady, “Australia and US Conclude Major Military Exercise in Pacific Region”, *Diplomat*, 28 July 2015, http://thediplomat.com/2015/07/australia - and - us - conclude - major - military - exercise - in - pacific - region/.

② Purnendra Jain, “A Little Nato Against China”, *Asian Times*, 18 March 2006, http://www.atimes.com/atimes/China/HC18Ad01.html.

③ 同上。

亚某些政客将冷战思维置于国家利益之上，刻意政治化、妖魔化中国投资的结果。[①] 自 20 世纪 90 年代，特别是新千年以来，中国对澳投资日益增多，但是澳大利亚政府长期以来一直对中国投资采取单方面歧视性的双重标准。澳大利亚前总理阿伯特在 2012 年以反对党领袖身份访华时，曾公开声称我国在澳的投资“令人不安”。由于缺乏资金支持，西澳州的采矿业等行业深受影响。西澳州州长巴奈特曾对澳大利亚联邦政府的对华投资审查政策大加批评，他指出：澳大利亚外国投资审查委员会对 10 亿澳元以下的美国投资采取免检放行的政策，却对中国实行差异化的审查制度——对中国民企在 2.58 亿澳元以下的投资予以免审，对中国国企则是每一分钱投资都必须审查。[②]

阿伯特总理 2013 年上台执政后，囿于澳经济发展乏力，海外投资减少，加之中澳《自由贸易协定》的缔结，对我国在澳大利亚的投资控制有所松动。但是近年来，随着国际大宗商品市场价格的回升，澳大利亚经济形势的好转，以及美国对中澳经贸关系日益深化的忧虑和不满，澳大利亚政府再次收紧了对中国投资的审查和控制力度。虽然目前我国对澳累积投资额仅为 600 亿澳元，不到澳吸引外资总额的 1%，且远远落后于美（8968 亿澳元）、日（2192 亿澳元）[③]，但澳大利亚的保守势力对我国经济的快速发展和中澳关系的日益深化深感“不安”和“恐惧”，一再挑动政府和既得利益群体加强对我国的投资审查，重点限制我国在澳大利亚农业、矿业和基础设施等领域的投资。例如，极右翼政客、参议员、一族党党首波琳·汉森不断地在澳大利亚媒体散布危言耸听的言论：“共

① James Laurenceson 2016, “Hawks Have Poor Record on Chinese Security Threats”, *Australian Financial Review*, 9 August, viewed 20 August 2016, http://www.afr.com/news/world/asia/ausgrid-hawks-have-poor-record-on-chinese-security-threats-20160808-gqnf5s.

② Graeme Powell 2013, “Barnett Says Chinese Investors Discriminated Against”, Australia Broadcasting Corporation, 5 June, viewed 8 May 2014, http://www.abc.net.au/news/2013-06-05/barnett-says-firb-rules-discriminate-against-china/4733904.

③ Australian Department of Foreign Affairs and Trade 2018, *United States Fact Sheet*; *Japan Fact Sheet*.

产党中国为什么想拥有我们的电网？你们不担心吗？警钟一直在长鸣！”[①] 这些右翼势力“逢中必反”，时常纠集起来，致函总理和财政部部长，甚至是澳相关并购的企业领导人，千方百计地阻挠我国的商业投资。

客观分析，澳大利亚政府加强对我国投资的审查和限制既有国内政党斗争和政治氛围右转的因素，也有美国等西方利益集团不断施压的外部因素，例如，在获悉我国企业租赁澳北部重镇达尔文港后，美国前总统奥巴马怒不可遏，曾当面要求特恩布尔“以后必须提前通知美国中国在澳大利亚的类似投资”。对于奥巴马的不悦，特恩布尔一再保证“必要时，澳国防部和联邦政府都会随时接管达尔文港”。[②] 华盛顿智库战略预算评估总裁卡莱皮纳维奇在澳最大媒体《澳大利亚人报》上撰文，一语泄露了奥巴马不悦的“天机”：“该交易最坏之处在于它在美国倾力实施‘重返亚太’战略时，损害了美国对澳美同盟的信任”。[③] 在受到奥巴马的严厉批评后，澳政府即以安全为由，连续否决我国数起大型企业的并购活动。在澳大利亚某些政治势力看来，否决中国对澳大型投资虽然与澳大利亚的国家安全无涉，但确是为了防止中国在澳美特殊关系间再钉入一枚离间的楔子。[④]

由于国内外的压力，也由于特恩布尔自己对亚太地区形势的研判，以及对澳美同盟根深蒂固的思维定式，特恩布尔上台执政不久

---

① Sean Nicholls 2016, “Pauline Hanson's Message to Scott Morrison: ‘Don't Sell Ausgrid’”, *Sydney Morning Herald*, 30 July, http://www.smh.com.au/federal-politics/political-news/pauline-hansons-message-to-scott-morrison-dont-sell-ausgrid-20160729-gqgwjp.html

② Peta Donald 2015, “Let Us Know Next Time: Obama to Turnbull on Darwin Port Lease”, Australian Broadcasting Company, 19 November, http://www.abc.net.au/worldtoday/content/2015/s4355269.htm.

③ Jonathan Pearlman 2015, “US Alarm Over Aussie Port Deal with China Firm”, *Strait Times*, 19 November, http://www.straitstimes.com/asia/australianz/us-alarm-over-aussie-port-deal-with-china-firm.

④ “The Elephant in the Room on US-Australia Relations”, ABC News, 13 June 2014, http://www.abc.net.au/news/2014-06-13/switzer-the-elephant-in-the-room-on-us-australia-relations/5522366.

便鲜明地表明了对美国主导下的全球和亚太区域秩序的支持。这一点在澳大利亚《国防白皮书》和澳大利亚政府对南海问题的表态中都有清晰的体现。新一期《国防白皮书》40 多处提到亚太地区所谓的“基于规则的秩序”，并明确无误地将中国定义为亚太现存秩序的挑战者。特恩布尔政府还在《外交白皮书》中对中国与邻国的海洋领土纠纷表示高度关注，指责中国在东海和南海的维护国家主权的行为给亚太地区带来“不确定性”和紧张的地区形势。

白皮书的这些表述无疑将中国列为其批评对象，并公开在事关中国主权的敏感问题上对中国进行攻击。这些态度和立场表明特恩布尔政府已经公开转向支持美国的印太战略，并愿意追随美国共同遏制中国在印太地区的崛起。在南海仲裁结果问题上，特恩布尔总理和外长毕晓普的讲话内容与美国政府的讲话如出一辙，并公然要求中国政府接受海牙仲裁庭超出其权力范围的裁决。① 澳大利亚政府此举不仅表现出对中国国家主权和核心利益的挑战，而且也全然忘记它自己就曾拒绝接受国际法庭对其与邻国领土纠纷的裁决结果。这种对国际法律的双重标准一方面反映了澳大利亚政府和政客的虚伪，另一方面也说明了在美国政府态度明确的情形下，澳大利亚只能跟进，无心也根本无力抗拒。正如澳大利亚国立大学著名学者修·怀特所言，澳大利亚国防白皮书和澳大利亚对南海问题的立场表明，时至今日，堪培拉依然只是华盛顿对外战略的海外执行机构。

四 特恩布尔政府“右转”的内生与外生动因

根据一年多来对澳大利亚政局的演变分析，澳大利亚对华政策出现较大幅度的右转既有国内政治角力的内生因素驱动，也有美国压力的外部因素驱动。首先，澳大利亚国内政党竞争致使国内政治

① Eoin Blackwell, “Julie Bishop Stands by South China Sea Stance after Sharp Criticism from China”, *Guardian*, 13 July 2016, http://www.huffingtonpost.com.au/2016/07/12/australia-warns-china-to-heed-hague-ruling-on-south-china-sea_a_21430941/.

角力激化，特恩布尔不得不右转，并将国内政治斗争“外溢化”，以求摆脱政治困境。澳大利亚 2016 年的大选结果出乎特恩布尔的意料，执政的自由党 - 国家党联盟不仅未能利用大选扩大自身的政治优势，反而导致特恩布尔政府成为事实上的“跛鸭”，严重削弱了特恩布尔本人对党内外势力的掌控和影响能力。为了赢得 2018 年的议会补选胜利，并为 2019 年的大选作准备，特恩布尔不得不迎合党内和国内的右翼势力，以换取他们的政治支持。

而国内政治气氛的右转反过来又进一步恶化了国内的政治氛围，迫使特恩布尔不得不与他早年经商时与中国建立的密切的经济关系作“切割”。特恩布尔因而主动提出“反外国干涉法”的动议，以自证清白。[①] 但是，特恩布尔的举动不仅未能消除其与中国关系密切的印记，反而进一步恶化了澳大利亚的国内政治气氛，导致一些极右翼政治势力趁机兴风作浪，对中澳本质上基于互利互惠的经贸关系开展了并不符合实际情况的批评和攻击。[②] 一些极右势力甚至宣传澳大利亚需要“麦卡锡主义”，以便进一步遏制国内左翼政治力量。特恩布尔的政治“投机”不仅未能带来他希冀的结果，反而导致党内右翼力量进一步增强，最终迫使其交权下台。

其次，自冷战以来，澳大利亚国内政治一直偏右，保守势力相当强大。东欧剧变、苏联垮台更加助长了保守势力的气势，弗朗西斯·福山的“历史终结论”在澳大利亚受欢迎的程度甚至远远超越了美国。90 年代的“台海危机”、21 世纪初的“中美撞机”等事件中，澳大利亚政府曾单独跳出西方阵营，成为公开发声“一边倒”地支持美国的唯一一个西方国家。澳大利亚也曾在台湾、西藏、新疆等中国“核心利益”问题上公开挑战中国的观点，并

---

① David Crowe 2018, “Overhaul for Foreign Interference Laws in Bipartisan Deal”, *Sydney Morning Herald*, 7 June, https://www.smh.com.au/politics/federal/overhaul - for - foreign - interference - laws - in - bipartisan - deal - 20180607 - p4zk29.html.

② David Crowe 2018, “Tougher Foreign Interference Laws can't Come Soon Enough”, *Sydney Morning Herald*, 31 May, https://www.smh.com.au/politics/federal/tougher - foreign - interference - laws - can - t - come - soon - enough - 20180531 - p4zipb.html.

采取实质性行动挑战中国的对台政策。澳大利亚政府和军方的种种对华不友好行为都在一定程度上反映了澳大利亚右翼力量的强大。21 世纪以来，中国的综合国力迅速增强，中澳经贸合作日趋紧密，澳民众对中国的认知程度日益加深。但澳政界、安全防务界乃至政治学术界的保守势力仍旧强大，不时发出有悖中澳关系发展的声音。例如，“遏制中国”“妖魔化中国”的论调在上述政治和学术圈子里时隐时现。在中国加快国防现代化的步伐后，澳保守势力不断宣传“中国威胁论”，声称只有巩固和扩大澳美同盟，在印太区域建立由美、日、印组成的“民主之钻”，共同遏制中国，才能维护美国在印太地区的霸权体系，才能维护澳大利亚的安全和既得的政治、经济利益。①

为此，澳大利亚政府和军方在四个方面采取措施，以巩固和加强美澳同盟：一是美军在澳大利亚的军事基地的规模越来越大，战略性指向也越来越有针对性。二是美澳在亚太区域的联合军事演习越来越机制化，规模不断实现新的突破，冷战时期都很少出现的逾万人的联合军演在今日的亚太和印太地区却频频出现。三是美、日、澳在亚太区域军事联动的趋势越来越明显，并且将之进一步扩大到印度洋地区，呈现出印太合流的态势。四是尽管澳大利亚目前的经济形势不容乐观，财政困难加剧，特恩布尔政府却不断地削减医疗、教育等社会福利支出，以支持军费的大幅度增加。

特恩布尔在大选后多次声称：“我们生活的亚太地区比以往更富挑战，我们必须将国防开支增加到国内生产总值的 2%。”② 尽管特恩布尔没有具体言明他心中所谓的“挑战”究竟是什么，澳大

① Hugo Seymour 2018, *Trilateral Diplomacy*: *Australia's Indo – Pacific Strategy*, Australia Institute of International Affairs, 3 April, https://www.internationalaffairs.org.au/australianoutlook/trilateral-diplomacy-foundations-in-an-australian-indo-pacific-strategy/.

② Andrew Greene 2016, “Malcolm Turnbull Sticks to Tony Abbott's Defence Spending Pledges in Long-awaited White Paper”, Australian Broadcasting Company, 24 February, http://www.abc.net.au/news/2016-02-23/defence-white-paper-turnbull-sticks-to-abbott-pledges/7194480.

利亚随后发表的新一期《国防白皮书》明确表明了“这就是对中国国防现代化的不安”。[①] 白皮书声称到 2021 年，澳大利亚将花费巨资用于扩充军备，购战机，造潜艇，以强化澳大利亚作为美军“印太”军事“南锚”的军事地位。澳最大的广播电台——澳大利亚广播公司为此评论说：政府铁心大幅度增加军费，即使损害宏观经济健康也在所不惜。[②]

最后，特恩布尔政府顾忌美国压力，迎合美国战略目标，巩固澳美军事同盟是澳不断右转的最重要的外部驱动力。[③] 澳大利亚建国百年，始终将“与超级大国结盟”的策略视为立国之本、强国之径。这一立国之策在澳有着深厚的理论与实践基础，长期以来，它不仅深受澳政坛左、中、右各派追捧，而且在澳普通民众中也有着深厚的民意基础。澳美同盟不仅为澳带来安全和政治利益，同时也为其带来了丰厚的经济利益。

自我国于 2009 年跃升为澳第一大贸易伙伴以来，澳国内各界持续辩论中美两国究竟谁在经济领域对澳更为重要。出乎许多中国专家学者的意料，澳大利亚各方经过比对中美两国对澳经济生活的影响指数，普遍倾向于认为美在现阶段仍然是澳“最重要的经济伙伴”。截至 2017 年底，美对澳投资存量高达 9000 多亿澳元，是中国对澳投资存量的 14 倍，这意味着美国资本已经深入到澳大利亚经济生活的各个方面。[④] 美国投资人和美国资本实际上是许多澳大利亚大型矿山和企业的最大的股东，对澳经济繁荣与发展以及普

---

① 同上。

② Greg Jennett 2016，“Defence White Paper：Australia Joins Asia's Arms Race with Spending on Weaponry and Military Forces to Reach ＄195b”，25 February，Australian Broadcasting Company，http：//www.abc.net.au/news/2016－02－25/defence－white－paper－released－increased－spending/7198632

③ “Remarks by the Vice President and Australian Prime Minister Turnbull at a Press Conference”，White House，22 April 2017，https：//www.whitehouse.gov/briefings－statements/remarks－vice－president－australian－prime－minister－turnbull－press－conference/.

④ Department of Foreign Affairs and Trade（Australia），*Fact Sheets of the United States*，and *Fact Sheets of the People's Republic of China*，April 2018，viewed 9 August 2018，https：//dfat.gov.au/trade/resources/Documents/usa.pdf.

通民众的就业影响巨大。例如，澳大利亚最大的本土品牌汽车“HOLDON”实际上就是美资企业，其在澳存在历史悠久，仅在阿德莱德一地就雇用了 3000 多名当地工人。因此，当该汽车厂宣布破产关闭时，在全澳引起了极大的震动。

正是由于美国资本对澳经济和社会生活的重大影响，澳大利亚外长毕晓普才会在国会和媒体上一再提醒议员和选民，美国才是澳大利亚“唯一最重要的经济伙伴”，是澳大利亚对外关系的基石。[①] 中澳近年来经贸合作的不断深化以及中国在澳投资领域的日益扩大触及了西方一些国家，特别是美国资本的既得利益，致使一些美国政要，如前总统奥巴马和前国务卿希拉里·克林顿都曾当面对特恩布尔发出严词警告，希望澳大利亚即便是在经济上也不要与中国走得太近。[②] 美国一些政府机构和情报部门，如中央情报局等也借机对澳大利亚国家安全发出警报，向特恩布尔政府施加压力。[③] 没有美国政府的认可和坚持，任何澳大利亚政治领导人都无法稳定执政是澳大利亚公开的秘密。堪培拉政治圈至今仍然盛传陆克文总理的下台与美国幕后作用关系密切。特恩布尔政府因此在政治上不得不右转，并加强与美国的政治和军事同盟；在经济上，则加强对中国投资的审查和限制，以保护西方一些国家，特别是美国在澳大利亚的既得利益。

五　结语

美澳同盟是美国在亚太，乃至印太地区维护美国主导的霸权

---

① Julie Bishop, *US - Australia: The Alliance in an Emerging Asia*, Minister for Foreign Affairs, 22 January 2014, viewed 5 April 2016, http: //foreignminister. gov. au/speeches/Pages/2014/jb_ sp_ 140122. aspx? ministerid = 4.

② Peta Donald 2015, “Let Us Know Next Time: Obama to Turnbull on Darwin Port Lease”, *Australian Broadcasting Company*, 19 November, http: //www. abc. net. au/worldtoday/content/2015/s4355269. htm.

③ Jonathan Pearlman 2015, “US Alarm Over Aussie Port Deal with China Firm”, *Strait Times*, 19 November, http: //www. straitstimes. com/asia/australianz/us - alarm - over - aussie - port - deal - with - china - firm.

体系与秩序，以及由此而产生的地缘政治、经济和战略利益的重要支柱。美澳两国政府在国内建制派和右翼势力的推动下，对进一步巩固和强化美澳军事同盟，维护印太地区霸权表现出空前的积极性和热情。澳大利亚自立国以来一直奉行的与全球体系中的超级大国结盟的立国之策不仅有着深厚的西方理论基础，而且有着深厚的历史背景、广泛的民意基础以及行之有效的实践结果。从西方国际关系权力架构理论的视角分析，这也是中美综合国力，特别是军事和高科技实力在现阶段依然悬殊的必然结果。因此，任何澳大利亚政治领导人都很难在短时间内改变这一政策取向，这是澳大利亚的国家利益和政策思维定式所共同决定的，很难因政府领导人的更迭，及其个人好恶而轻易改变。可以预见在今后相当长的一段时期内，澳仍将继续扮演美国“铁杆”追随者的角色。

但是，与美国强化军事同盟，并不一定意味着澳大利亚一定会立即在中美之间选边，也不意味着澳一定会马上介入中美之间的纠纷，这也是澳大利亚的国家利益所决定的。作为中等强国，澳大利亚的国家利益与美国并不完全重合，并且它也不会自不量力到像美国一样，把扼制一个新兴超级力量的崛起作为自己的战略目标。[1]中国是澳大利亚的第一大贸易伙伴，并且极有可能在不远的将来取代美国成为澳大利亚的第一大经济伙伴。由此可以预见，中国与澳大利亚两国间的经济融合与依存度仍会继续提升，而这正是中澳两国关系不断深化的基础，也是澳大利亚政府领导人很难轻易改变对华政策的基石。为了自己的既得利益，澳大利亚仍会延续 21 世纪以来的外交方略，继续在中美间奉行平衡策略，以使两头获利，获得利益最大化。

① William Tow, “Australia, the US and a China Growing Strong”, *Australian Journal of International Affairs*, Vol. 55, No. 1, 2001, pp. 37 – 54.

An Analysis on the Paradoxical Development of Sino – Australian Relations

Yu Lei, *Yu Feiyang*

Abstract: 2017 witnessed the acceleration of the paradoxical development of Sino-Australian relations: the Turnbull government had on the one hand politically turned right and intensified Australian-American military alliance to contain China's rise in power and influence in the "Indo-Pacific" region; on the other hand, it aspired to maintain an intensified economic cooperation and trade with China in the hopes of keeping Australian prosperity and employment. The paradoxical development might be attributed at one level to Australia's domestic politics and at another level to increasing American pressure. The powerful right-wring forces in Australia and the weakened Turnbull government led to the changed Australian China policy. Australia has pursued a strategy of aligning with a superpower since its independence in trade for economic benefits and protection. In return, Australia has to be committed to the alliance as well as the interest of the United States, which reveals the alliance is more based on shared political, economic and security interest rather than shared culture, history and value. As a middle power, Australia differs the United States in the fundamental interest and can hardly prioritize the containment of China in its strategic objectives. The momentum of economic integration and interdependence between these two nations remains strong, which bases Sino-Australian relations and makes it hard for any radical change in Australian China policy.

Keywords: Australia-America Alliance; Australian China Policy; Indo-Pacific Strategy; China-Australia Relationship; Balanced Strategy

澳大利亚焦虑症话语下的中国*

〔澳〕格瑞格·麦卡锡　〔澳〕宋宪琳 撰**
董　汀 编译***

摘要： 中国对于当今澳大利亚的贸易关系、资本流动、教育以及全球秩序等方面都具有重要的意义。然而，澳大利亚关于中国的公共话语却陷入两种舆论的相互冲突之中：一种舆论是关于两国经济互补性的，另一种就是关于"恐惧"和"焦虑"。中国的发展导致澳大利亚社会出现了两种不同的反应：一种认为中国的经济壮大"标志着其加入资本主义的世界体系"而应受到鼓励，而另一种则认为中国的发展是一种"威胁"，需要加以防控。本文探讨的就是这样一个矛盾的话题，可称之为"中国焦虑症"(Changst)。作者们认为正是由于按照发展主义的逻辑(Chakrabarty，2000) 和运用西方资本主义和欧洲中心主义历史的同质化而误读了中国。这种误读认为中国发展只能复制西方的资本主义模式，但是中国独特的资本流动形式打乱了西方的发展逻辑，因而导致焦虑。同样，这种话语认为中国社会及其教育体系处在准现代化时代，大批中国

---

* "China in Australia：The Discourses of Changst", *Asian Studies Review*, 12 Mar. 2018, pp. 323 - 341.

** 作者简介：格瑞格·麦卡锡 (Greg McCarthy)，澳大利亚西澳大学政治与国际关系学系政治学教授、第二任北京大学必和必拓澳大利亚研究讲席教授 (2016 ~ 2018)。宋宪琳 (Xianlin Song)，西澳大学孔子学院前外方院长，亚洲研究学副教授。

*** 董汀，法学博士，2018 年获北京大学博雅博士后项目资助，开始在北京大学国际关系学院工作，研究领域包括中澳关系在内的亚太地区国际政治与经济关系。

学生留学海外又让人“恐惧”其文化受到“污染”。本文通过六个澳大利亚的案例分析来探讨这种焦虑情绪，揭示中国与澳大利亚的交往如何产生了强烈而毫无根据的焦虑。

关键词：中国发展　发展主义　中国投资　中国留学生　“恐华”

2017 年 6 月，澳大利亚广播公司（ABC）与费尔法克斯媒体集团（FairfaxMedia）共同制作了一期专题节目，将一些澳大利亚华人社区领袖和华人企业家参与该国常规政治的行为和社会活动描化为“替中国在澳扩展影响力”，还把矛头指向中国留学生，暗指他们为中国政府安插在澳大利亚的“间谍”，宣称“澳国家自由与主权受到威胁”[①]，成为一些西方媒体建构的“中国影响力渗透论”的一部分。澳联邦政府官员亦纷纷公开指责中国[②]，身陷“政治献金案”的工党参议员邓森（Sam Dastyari）最终被迫辞职。[③] 澳大利亚安全情报机构（Australian Security Intelligence Organisation，ASIO）的年度报告声称，外国政府在澳的“间谍活动”达到了前

① “Power and Influence：The Hard Edge of China's Soft Power”，June 5，2017，http：//www. abc. net. au/4corners/power – and – influence – promo/8579844. 这期节目号称由两家公司经过历时 5 个月的调查制作而成，不仅在播出前通过社交媒体广推预告片，还经由数家澳媒大型“剧透”预热，如：“China's Operation Australia”，https：//www. smh. com. au/interactive/2017/chinas – operation – australia/soft – power. html；“Australian Sovereignty under Threat from Influence of China's Communist Party”，http：//www. abc. net. au/news/2017 – 06 – 04/australian – sovereignty – under – threat – from – chinese – influence/8583832（译者注，浏览时间：2018 年 4 月 10 日）。

② “‘Chinese Are Spying on Us’：Veteran Mandarin Dennis Richardson Bows Out”，https：//www. theguardian. com/australia – news/2017/may/12/chinese – are – spying – on – us – veteran – mandarin – dennis – richardson – bows – out；“China's Soft Power：Julie Bishop Steps Up Warning to University Students on Communist Party Rhetoric”，Oct. 16，2017，http：//www. abc. net. au/news/2017 – 10 – 16/bishop – steps – up – warning – to – chinese – university – students/9053512（译者注，浏览时间：2018 年 4 月 10 日）。

③ “Sam Dastyari Resigns from Parliament，Says He is ‘Detracting from Labor's Mission’ Amid Questions over Chinese Links”，http：//www. abc. net. au/news/2017 – 12 – 12/sam – dastyari – resigns – from – parliament/9247390（译者注，浏览时间：2018 年 4 月 10 日）。

所未有的程度。[1] 随着这种不安情绪的激增，2017 年 12 月初，特恩布尔（Malcolm Turnbull）总理宣布要对有关间谍及外国干预的国家安全立法进行改革，以限制外国势力对澳政治进程和政府决策的干预[2]，并随后在联邦议会讲话中表示，“澳方应严肃对待媒体有关中国对澳进行渗透的报道，通过议会和法律来维护澳国家主权”。[3] “中国渗透”史无前例地成为澳大利亚的政治热点议题，引发了广泛而激烈的辩论。[4] 民调显示，有超过三分之二的公众支持立法。[5]

① “ASIO Annual Report 2016-2017”, Oct. 3, 2017, https://www.asio.gov.au/sites/default/files/Annual%20Report%202016－17.pdf（译者注，浏览时间：2018 年 4 月 10 日）。

② “Press Conference with Senator the Hon. George Brandis QC, Attorney－General and Senator the Hon. Mathias Cormann, Minister for Finance”, https://www.pm.gov.au/media/press－conference－senator－hon－george－brandis－qc－attorney－general－and－senator－hon－mathias（译者注，浏览时间：2018 年 4 月 10 日）。

③ “Malcolm Turnbull, Speech Introducing the National Security Legislation Amendment (Espionage and Foreign Interference) Bill 2017”, https://www.pm.gov.au/media/speech－introducing－national－security－legislation－amendment－espionage－and－foreign－interference.《中国外交部发言人耿爽就澳大利亚领导人有关言论答记者提问》，2017 年 12 月 8 日，http://au.china－embassy.org/chn/zagx/t1517868.htm（译者注，浏览时间：2018 年 4 月 10 日）。

④ 例如，澳大利亚查里斯特大学（Charles Sturt University）教授汉密尔顿（Clive Hamilton）著作《无声的入侵：中国如何把澳大利亚变成木偶国》（Silent Invasion: How China is Turning Australia into a Puppet State）指责“中国正在利用虚假的历史定位自己，以在将来控制澳大利亚”。https://www.pressreader.com/new－zealand/the－press/20180224/281934543433359；澳大利亚工党前元老级参议员，现任天空新闻台（Sky News Live）的政论员理查德森（Graham Richardson）撰文批判其观点，https://cn.theaustralian.com.au/2018/03/01/3435/；美国国防部亚太事务助理部长薛瑞福（Randy Schriver）撰文支持澳大利亚政府的立场，“Australia has ‘Woken up’ the World on China's Influence: US Official”, https://www.smh.com.au/politics/federal/australia－has－woken－up－the－world－on－china－s－influence－us－official－20180226－p4z1un.html；《陆克文特稿：马尔科姆·特恩布尔对华政策的新麦卡锡主义》，https://cn.theaustralian.com.au/2018/02/26/3356/；澳大利亚著名国防战略家休·怀特（Hugh White）认为，“中国影响的问题是真实的，但这个问题容易被夸大，我们此刻就面临如此这般反应过度的重大危险”，https://www.quarterlyessay.com.au/essay/2017/11/without－america；澳大利亚悉尼大学副校长公开谴责特恩布尔政府的恐华言论将危及澳大利亚大学产业，“Sydney Uni's Michael Spence Lashes Government over ‘Sinophobicblatherings’”, http://www.afr.com/news/policy/education/sydney－unis－michael－spence－lashes－government－over－sinophobic－blatherings－20180128－h0pjc4；（译者注，浏览时间：2018 年 4 月 10 日）。

⑤ “Bennelong ReachTEL Poll: Voters Shift Away from John Alexander but Endorse China Scrutiny”, https://www.smh.com.au/politics/federal/bennelong－reachtel－poll－voters－shift－away－from－john－alexander－but－endorse－china－scrutiny－20171213－h03wja.html（译者注，浏览时间：2018 年 4 月 10 日）。

学界则分裂成两大极化阵营，包括澳大利亚首任驻华大使费思芬（Stephen FitzGerald）、世界知名汉学家白杰明（GeremieBarmé）和澳前外交官梅卓琳（Jocelyn Chey）等重量级人物，联名发表公开信提交议会，批评澳大利亚政府对中国的指控，敦促延迟立法①，另有持相反观点的 35 名中国问题研究人员写信支持澳政府的做法，推动议会通过特氏立法改革。②

但我们也看到，在这种喧嚣的舆论对立中，有澳大利亚学者进行了严肃、冷静的反思。2018 年 3 月，西澳大学两名跨文化研究学者在澳大利亚亚洲研究学会的网刊《亚洲研究评论》撰文，使用六个案例，铺陈各方具体观点，尝试解答澳大利亚作为一个以中国为最大贸易伙伴的丰饶岛国，同时又是西方价值观序列中的美国盟国，缘何产生出对华“全方位”的“焦虑”。

本着“知己知彼”的考量，译者翻译整理了这些案例，为方便中国读者聚焦事实，生发出自有路向的思考，译文省去了原作的理论部分③，特此说明。

---

① “An Open Letter from Concerned Scholars of China and the Chinese Diaspora”, Mar. 26, 2018, https://www.policyforum.net/an-open-letter-from-concerned-scholars-of-china-and-the-chinese-diaspora/; “Review of the National Security Legislation Amendment (espionage and foreign interference) Bill 2017 Submissions”, No. 44, https://www.aph.gov.au/Parliamentary_Business/Committees/Joint/Intelligence_and_Security/EspionageFInterference/Submissions（译者注，浏览时间：2018 年 4 月 10 日）。

② “China's Influence in Australia: Maintaining the Debate”, Mar. 27, 2018, https://www.policyforum.net/chinas-influence-australia-maintaining-debate/; “Review of the National Security Legislation Amendment (espionage and foreign interference) Bill 2017 Submissions” No. 50, https://www.aph.gov.au/Parliamentary_Business/Committees/Joint/Intelligence_and_Security/EspionageFInterference/Submissions（译者注，浏览时间：2018 年 4 月 10 日）。

③ 两位作者使用印度裔历史学家查卡拉巴提（Dipesh Chakrabarty）的发展主义理论和黎巴嫩裔人类学家赫德（Ghassan Hage）的“白色幻想”理论来诠释澳大利亚的对华焦虑情结。发展主义理论认为以欧洲文明为发展终点的本体目的论逻辑建立在种族歧视的基础上，一维机械地理解应该被多元化定义的资本发展路径。“白色幻想”理论指出，在澳大利亚存在三种形式的种族歧视，“数量种族主义”、“既有种族歧视”和基于“共同性”的种族歧视。作者认为，焦虑的根源在于澳大利亚从西方资本主义和欧洲中心主义历史的同质化逻辑出发，无法完全理解中国独特的资本流动形式和社会、政治制度。

一 经济利益“焦虑”：明显的双重标准

（一）矿业领域并购

2007 年 11 月，英澳矿业巨头必和必拓（BHP Billiton）发出 3∶1换股收购力拓（Rio Tinto）的意向。2008 年 2 月，中国铝业联合美国铝业，向力拓提出以 140 亿美元增加 9% 的股权。澳大利亚竞争和消费委员会（Australian Competition and Consumer Commission，ACCC）批准了必和必拓的要约，却驳回了中铝的竞购。时任财长韦恩·斯旺（Wayne Swan）要求外国投资审查委员会（Foreign Investment Review Board，FIRB）根据“国家利益”原则对中铝的标书进行审查。同时，总理陆克文（Kevin Rudd）下令制定更加具体的监管规则，以更有力地“制约”中国国有企业。[①] 2008 年 2 月 17 日，财长宣布执行新的外商投资准则[②]，尽管政府声称这些规则是普遍适用条款，却显然直指中国国有企业，特别是中国铝业的这桩交易。[③] 财政部的高级官员乔斯克（Joske）承认，

---

① Wilson，J.，“Resource Nationalism or Resource Liberalism? Explaining Australia's Approach to Chinese Investment in its Minerals Sector”，*Australian Journal of International Affairs*，65（3），2011，pp. 283 – 304；Wong，L.，“The ‘Liability of Foreignness’：Chinese Investment in Australia”，*Transnational Corporations Review*，4（4），2012，pp. 46 – 75.

② 新规则首次阐述了“国家利益”的六条原则，包括：投资者的业务运作是否独立于相关的外国政府；投资者是否遵守法律和一般企业行为准则；投资是否会有碍竞争，或导致不适当的行业集聚或控制；投资是否会影响澳大利亚政府收入或其他政策；投资是否会影响国家安全；投资是否会影响澳大利亚企业的运作或管理，包括其对经济和社会的贡献。规则规定，对国有企业要通过其是否属于其母国政府，是否像私营企业一样行事以及对市场的控制程度来判断交易行为是“基于市场”还是“基于战略”。规则针对矿业投资提出了“15/50”的新准则，即外资对澳大利亚矿业企业的持股比例不得超过 15% 或在新项目上的投资不超过 50%，低于这一标准的投资可以被认为是符合市场规律的，否则“基于战略”的风险较高，可能不予批准。https：//cdn. tspace. gov. au/uploads/sites/79/2016/01/FIRB – Annual – Report – 2006 – 07_ Appendix_ A. pdf（译者注，浏览时间：2018 年 4 月 10 日）。

③ Nyland，C.，Forbes – Mewett，H.，& Thomson，S. B.，“Sinophobia as Corporate Tactic and the Response of Host Communities”，*Journal of Contemporary Asia*，41（4），2011，p. 616.

这种行为确实源自政府“根深蒂固的不安”，他们认为所有的中国国企都是国家的战略部门。① 美国驻堪培拉大使馆也回应了这一说法，表示“制定新的规则主要是因为中国对战略物资领域的投资越来越多，引人担忧”。②

2009 年 3 月 18 日，澳大利亚参议院批准了一项由反对党及独立议员联合提出的申请，由参议院经济委员会对外国特别是中国国有企业在澳投资展开调查。③ 这项动议最早由绿党领袖鲍勃·布朗（Bob Brown）提出，他宣称中国是一个“警察国家”，“如果中国铝业成功收购力拓，澳大利亚的矿产资源将被共产主义控制”。④来自国家党的参议员乔伊斯（Barnaby Joyce）也附和道，“我们十分担忧其他主权国家要成为我国主权资产的所有者”。⑤ 在国内资金的支持下，乔伊斯参议员还利用电视广告发起抵制，声言“外国人要买走我们的财富”⑥，“中国绝不会允许澳大利亚政府购买他们的矿山”。独立参议员尼克·色诺芬（Nick Xenophon）表示，“我们应该卖牛奶而不是奶牛，所以我们应该卖矿产而不是矿山”。紧接着，时任反对党领袖马尔科姆·特恩布尔（Malcolm Turnbull）指责陆克文政府“亲华”，并宣称这一竞购涉及“共产主义国家”，一定要被阻止。⑦ 此外，《澳大利亚人报》报道称，59% 的民众反对中铝对力拓增持 9% 的股份。⑧ 2009 年 6 月，力拓的大股东投票

① Garnaut, J.,“Rudd Policy on China ‘set by BHP’”, http://www.smh.com.au/business/rudd-policy-on-china-set-by-bhp-20091014-gxqm.html.

② Cai, P.,“A Mission to Serve, Protect and Profit”, http://www.smh.com.au/business/a-mission-to-serve-protect-and-profit-20131025-2w7ae.html#ixzz495HdzXHT.

③ “Senate to Eye Rios's Chinalco Deal”, *Sydney Morning Herald*, http://www.smh.com.au/business/senate-to-eye-rios-chinalco-deal-20090318-91xy.html.

④ Grubel, J.,“Rio Names New Chairman as Chinalco Row Escalates”, http://uk.reuters.com/article/uk-riotinto-chairman-idUKTRE52G2C720090317.

⑤ “Australian Senate Moves Cast Shadow Over Rio Shares”, *International Business Times*, http://www.ibtimes.com/australian-senate-move-casts-shadow-over-rioshares-239319.

⑥ Coorey, P.,“Joyce Turns to Television to Undermine Chinalco Bid,” http://www.smh.com.au/business/joyce-turns-to-television-to-undermine-chinalco-bid-20090316-8zxq.html.

⑦ Ibid..

⑧ Findlay, C.,“Public Opinion on Chinalco's Investment in Rio Tinto”, http://www.eastasiaforum.org/2009/04/19/public-opinion-on-chinalcos-investment-in-rio-tinto/.

否决了中国铝业的竞购。

在这一过程中，也有与政府和大部分民众不同的观点。关于国家资源主权问题，有学者认为，第一，矿产资源属于澳大利亚，部分资源必将出售或出租给外国投资者。第二，与必和必拓的收购不同，中国铝业只是要增持一小部分股份，只会在力拓增加两个董事席位，更何况力拓不是澳大利亚全资公司。第三，中铝无意压低铁矿石价格。作为一家铝冶炼公司，中铝根本不是铁矿石客户。澳大利亚竞争和消费委员会也承认这一点。第四，充足的证据表明中国的国有企业并非国家战略部门，而是具有很强竞争力和自主市场决策权的企业。[①] 还有学者经过调查和大量采访发现，中铝竞购反对者通过媒体开展精心策划的反华运动，把中国与澳大利亚相异的资本道路和两国不同的价值观捆绑在一起，宣称中国的投资是来自“不容异议的共产主义政权”和一个“中国公司”[②]，制造“恐华”舆论。[③] 来自维基解密的文件也证明，必和必拓的董事会主席唐·阿格斯（Don Argus）和首席执行官马里厄斯·克劳伯斯（Marius Kloppers）也是这场反华活动的参与者。[④]

（二）房地产领域并购

2014 年，悉尼房价大幅攀升，价格高企被怪罪到中国人头上。[⑤] 瑞信在一份报告中虚称，“有钱的中国投资者”买空了澳大

① Findlay, C., “Public Opinion on Chinalco's Investment in Rio Tinto”, http://www.eastasiaforum.org/2009/04/19/public-opinion-on-chinalcos-investment-in-rio-tinto/.

② Nyland, C., Forbes-Mewett, H., & Thomson, “S. B. Sinophobia as Corporate Tactic and Theresponse of Host Communities”, *Journal of Contemporary Asia*, 41 (4), 2011, p. 616.

③ Nyland, C., Forbes-Mewett, H., & Thomson, “S. B. Sinophobia as Corporate Tactic and Theresponse of Host Communities”, *Journal of Contemporary Asia*, 41 (4), 2011, p. 619.

④ Uren, D., “Chinalco's Rio Raid Rattled the Government,” http://www.theaustralian.com.au/archive/business/chinalcos-rio-raid-rattled-the-government/storyfn8sc6jr-1226381969530; Wong, L., “The ‘Liability of Foreignness’: Chinese Investment in Australia”, *Transnational Corporations Review*, 4 (4) 2012, pp. 46-75.

⑤ Glynn, J., “China Driving Australian House Prices”, http://blogs.wsj.com/economics/2014/08/14/china-driving-australian-house-prices-report/.

利亚新房市场五分之一的存量，总价值高达 50 亿澳元。今后六年，这一数字会增长至 600 亿澳元。在房地产拍卖市场上，“手持现金”的中国投资者们击败了澳大利亚本土的首次置业者。[①] 这一报告被广泛引用，多是重复中国人违规大肆投资的说辞。[②] 媒体使用“从中国涌入的现金”和“毫无监管的资金洪流”等情绪化字眼来描述中国投资。[③]

这种情绪也波及政界，澳大利亚联邦经济常务委员会专门展开了对外国投资者购买房产的调查，任命自由党议员凯莉·奥德怀尔（Kelly O'Dwyer）为调查小组主席并举行了听证会。调查报告称，澳大利亚房地产市场增长的一大部分来自非澳居民的中国投资者，主要是陆克文和吉拉德劳动党政府市场监控和保障不力，撤资规则松懈所造成的。[④] 尽管这是一份政治动机十分明显的报告，但仍旧掀起了澳国内反华高潮。继议会报告之后，时任财长霍奇（Joe Hockey）宣布出台了新规则，对房地产领域非法海外投资采取更加严厉的惩罚措施。[⑤] 财长公开表明，第一桩撤资令就是针对一家中国公司，该公司在派珀角（Point Piper）地区非法购置了一栋价

① Tevfik, H. &Boey, D., "Credit Suisse, Investment Strategy Nine", 2014, https://doc.research-and-analytics.csfb.com/docView? language=ENG&format=PDF&document_id=806613320&source_id=emcms&serialid=%2bD5bspsQMXTV63jZFe1GyW1wamG1kqtL0CQYnK8.

② Hyam, R., &Janda, M., "Chinese Property Investment to be Examined as House Economics Committee Reviews Foreign Investment Laws", http://www.abc.net.au/news/2014-03-17/house-of-reps-to-look-at-foreign-real-estate-investor-rules/5325190.

③ Keane, B., "Chinese Real Estate Invasion? Not According to the Data, Fellas", http://www.crikey.com.au/2014/03/10/chinese-real-estate-invasion-not-according-to-the-data-fellas/.

④ O'Dwyer, K., "House of Representatives Standing Committee on Economics: Foreign Investment in Residential Real Estate. P. V, 25, 46", http://www.aph.gov.au/Parliamentary_Business/Committees/House/Economics/Foreign_investment_in_real_estate/Tabled_Reports.

⑤ 新法规采取更为严格的惩罚措施，主要包括：对非法投资的外国个人，处以最高 12.75 万澳元罚款（过去为最高 8.5 万澳元），或者 3 年有期徒刑；对非法投资的外国公司处以最高 63 万澳元的罚款；协助外国投资者违规操作的第三方（如房地产中介、移民中介、律师等）也将面临惩罚；外国投资者购置住宅的申请费用。http://jbh.ministers.treasury.gov.au/media-release/034-2015/（译者注，浏览时间：2018 年 4 月 15 日）。

值3900万澳元的豪宅。[①] 霍奇称，这只是（政令的）冰山一角。[②] 他的继任者斯科特·莫里森（Scott Morrision）也延续这一政策，并利用媒体报道宣传涉华交易撤资令的胜利。尽管莫里森财长宣称政府已有力贯彻措施，涉华撤资金额已高达数十亿澳元，但截至2016年2月，实际发生的撤资只有27起，涉及多个国家，总额也并不惊人。[③]

事实上，澳大利亚财政部的证据显示，中国人仅购置了澳大利亚房产总量的2%。毕马威与悉尼大学的一项联合研究结果也印证了这一数字，并指出统计样本主要是商品住宅。[④] 瑞信报告中的不实表述是对外国投资审查委员会统计数字的误读所致。外委会列出的是中国投资提案，而非实际批准项目，许多提案半路夭折或未通过审批。按照实际成交计算，美国才是澳大利亚房地产最大的海外投资来源。[⑤] 独立研究结果也表明，中国对澳大利亚地产的投资并非如媒体宣传般的过度和非法。[⑥] 此外，在房地产拍卖市场上，亚洲面孔常被误认为均来自中国内地，他们实际上可能是新加坡、马

① 澳大利亚现行政策规定，外资购房应有利于增加本地房屋存量，非澳大利亚居民不能购买二手房。外资购房需向外国投资审查委员会提出申请。据报道，这套豪宅是中国公司利用旗下子公司使用离岸注册的空壳公司购入，未曾报备，存在违规。http：//www.chinadaily.com.cn/hqcj/xfly/2015－04－01/content_13475734.html；http：//www.acbnews.com.au/html/2015/azjujiao_0304/12800.html（译者注，浏览时间：2018年4月15日）。

② AAP.，"Joe Hockey Forces Chinese Investor to Sell ＄39m Sydney Mansion"，http：//www.theguardian.com/australia－news/2015/mar/03/joe－hockey－forces－chinese－investor－to－sell－39m－sydney－mansion.

③ Macken，L.，"Treasurer Scott Morrison Orders Forced Sale of ＄10m of Property"，http：//www.domain.com.au/news/treasurer－scott－morrison－orders－forced－sale－of－10m.

④ "Chinese Investment in Residential Real Estate just Two Percent"，https：//sydney.edu.au/news－opinion/news/2015/09/14/chinese－investment－in－residential－real－estate－amounts－to－just－2－.html（译者注，上网时间：2018年4月20日）。

⑤ Rogers，D.，"Racism Hides True Culprit of Housing Discrimination"，http：//www.abc.net.au/news/2014－02－25/rogers－chinese－investors－myth－vs－reality/5281538.

⑥ Ferguson，D.，&Zhi Dent，H.，"Demystifying Chinese Investment in Australia：April 2016"，https：//home.kpmg.com/au/en/home/insights/2016/04/demystifying－chineseinvestment－in－australia－april－2016.html.

来西亚或中国香港人。[①]

尽管存在大量有力反证，中国买家导致澳大利亚房价高企的说法一直盘旋在反华公共舆论中。2015 年罗伊民调显示，70% 的澳大利亚民众认为政府允许“过多”的中国投资进入澳大利亚，而只有 34% 的民众认为投资过多的国家是美国。[②]

（三）农业领域并购

澳大利亚占地最大的产棉区卡比农场（Cubbie Station）因陷财政危机，2009 年宣告破产。2012 年，山东如意集团[③]联合澳大利亚传统毛纺织公司伦普利（Lempriere），欲以 2.4 亿澳元收购卡比农场。[④]时任财长韦恩·斯万（Wayne Swan）将此申购交由外国投资审查委员会，接受例行的国家利益审查，后者经严格审核后批准了这一交易。

参议员乔伊斯（Barnaby Joyce）立即声称这一决定是“血腥的耻辱”[⑤]，要求财长解释将澳最大产棉农场出售给中国公司为何竟会符合澳大利亚的国家利益。[⑥] 他宣称，山东如意集团的大股东是由中国中央政治局任命的[⑦]，还发起了反华运动来抵制这次收购。[⑧] 澳

---

① Keane，B.，“Chinese Real Estate Invasion? Not According to the Data，Fellas”，http：//www.crikey.com.au/2014/03/10/chinese－real－estate－invasion－not－according－to－the－data－fellas/.

② Lowy Institute Poll.（2015），https：//www.lowyinstitute.org/publications/lowy－institute－poll－2015.

③ 该集团为一家上交所的上市民营企业，民营资本占 70%，日本伊藤忠商社占有剩余的 30% 股份。

④ Cranston，M.，“Cubbie Station too Pricey for Australian Purses”，http：//www.afr.com/news/politics/national/cubbie－just－too－pricey－for－australian－purses－20120903－j1vam.

⑤ Kerin，L.，“Barnaby Joyce says Cubbie Sell off a Disgrace”，http：//www.abc.net.au/news/2012－09－01/barnaby－joyce－says－cubbie－sell－off－a－disgrace/4237742.

⑥ Grattan，M.，& Willingham，R.，“Coalition Trades Blows over Cubbie Station”，http：//www.smh.com.au/federal－politics/political－news/coalition－trades－blows－over－cubbiestation－20120904－25cnjhtml.

⑦ Grattan，M.，& Willingham，R.，“Coalition Trades Blows over Cubbie Station”，http：//www.smh.com.au/federal－politics/political－news/coalition－trades－blows－over－cubbiestation－20120904－25cnj.html.

⑧ Botterill，L.C.& Cockfield，G.，“From“Unstable”to“Stable”Minority Government：Reflectionson the Role of the Nationals in Federal Coalition Governments”，*Australian Journal of Politics &History*，61（1），2015，53－66.

大利亚公民委员会主席彼得·威斯摩尔（Peter Westmore）称这是个“大问题”，因为一家显然与他国政府有联系的公司竟要收购澳大利亚价值最高、面积最大的灌溉农场。[①] 他的观点代表了政府右翼，也得到了左翼绿党的呼应，后者因为出售农场会造成水资源损失而反对这桩交易。[②] 当地媒体使用“昆士兰将被共产主义中国买下”这样的标题，把这桩交易描绘成专制国家的收购。[③]

面对歇斯底里的反华情绪，财长斯万将乔伊斯的所言所行称为“恐外”。[④] 联邦财政部前部长肯·亨利（Ken Henry）表示，“我不知道怎么说才能不冒犯某些人，但是关于外国投资，令我惊奇的一点是，一桩交易总要有出于自愿的卖家”。“我经常听到农林地居民表达对外国人购买土地的愤怒，但是他们正是出售这些土地的人啊。”他还说，“大量证据表明，中国的对外直接投资主要还是受市场利益驱动，而非出于国家战略目的”。[⑤] 有学者表示，卡比农场的出售应该放到更大的背景中去看待，中国投资澳大利亚农业，与其他任何国家的类似行为没有区别，更何况中国的投资总额并非最多。[⑥]《卫报》澳大利亚网络版记者直陈，澳大利亚 87.5% 的土地是由澳大利亚人所有的，迄今为止，美国是澳大利亚土地最大的境外所有者，拥有土地价值达 8.8 亿澳元，其次是加拿大，为

---

① Westmore, P.,“Foreign investment: Cubbie Station Sale Exposes Weak Foreign Ownership Rules”, http://www.newsweekly.com.au/article.php? id = 5338.

② McRobert, K.,“Don't Sell Our Farms: Greens”, http://www.theland.com.au/story/3587459/dont - sell - our - farms - greens/.

③ Stolz, G.,“Foreign Ownership Register Reveals the Great Haul of China”, http://www.couriermail.com.au/news/queensland/foreign - ownership - register - reveals - the - great - haulof - china/story - e6freoof - 1226518480103.

④ Cai, P.,“Barnaby Joyce ‘Beating Xenophobic Drums’: Wayne Swan”, http://www.smh.com.au/business/barnaby - joyce - beating - xenophobic - drums - wayne - swan - 20131025 - 2w5vj.html.

⑤ Cullen, S.,“Ex-treasury Boss Defends Foreign Investment”, http://www.abc.net.au/news/2012 - 09 - 05/ex - treasury - boss - defends - foreign - investment/4244792.

⑥ Lawrence, G.,“Farms and Finance: Barnaby may not like Cubbie Sale, but Our Agriculture is Outfor Tender”, https://theconversation.com/farms - and - finance - barnaby - may - not - likecubbie - sale - but - our - agriculture - is - out - for - tender - 9626.

5.53亿澳元，新加坡3.8亿澳元，第四位才是中国，为2.05亿澳元。[①] 还有民调发现，澳大利亚人普遍反对外国资本进入本国农业领域，但在卡比收购案中过激的反华情绪，显然是澳媒负面报道的结果。[②]

同样的故事也在基德曼公司（The Kidman Estate）上演，2015年，这家澳大利亚主要的牧业公司覆盖西澳、南澳、北领地和昆士兰，它有总面积超过10万平方公里的牧牛场挂牌出售。与所有的潜在买家一样，中国公司也参与了竞价。外国投资审查委员会例行审查结束后，时任财长莫里森（Scott Morrision）宣布政府拒绝所有竞价，这一交易不能按“现有形式”推进，因为标的与“国家利益”相悖，所售地块中有一部分紧邻旧导弹试射基地。他还说，由于涉及的地块面积巨大，占澳大利亚土地总面积的1.3%，政府将考虑“替代方案”。[③] 总理特恩布尔（Malcolm Turnbull）在当年马尼拉亚太经合组织会议上，向中国代表团强调这是出于国家安全考虑的决定，因为“基德曼出售的土地面积巨大，而且其中很大一部分在伍默拉（Woomera）禁区”。[④] 澳大利亚贸易部长安德鲁·罗博（Andrew Robb）质问拒绝竞购背后的市场逻辑，暗指拒绝竞购是受到了政治利益驱动。他坦言，澳大利亚“农业领域一直依靠外国投资，因为本国没有人会往这个

① Evershed, N., “How Much of Australia's Farmland is owned by Foreign Companies?”, https://www.theguardian.com/australia - news/datablog/2015/feb/12/how - much - of - australias - farmland - is - owned - by - foreign - companies.

② Laurenceson, J., Burke, P. F., & Wei, E., “The Australian Public's Preferences over Foreign Investment in Agriculture”, *Agenda: A Journal of Policy Analysis & Reform*, 22 (1), 2015, pp. 45 - 60.

③ Grattan, M., “Morrison Blocks Chinese Acquisition of Historic Kidman Cattle Empire”, https://theconversation.com/morrison - blocks - chinese - acquisition - of - historic - kidmancattle - empire - 50960.

④ Vickery, K., “Turnbull Government Refuses Sale of S. Kidman and Co Landholding to Overseas Investors”, http://www.news.com.au/national/politics/turnbull - government - refusessale - of - s - kidman - and - co - landholding - to - overseas - investors/news - story/6d282f3a013cd5e4a65701dea8e0045f.

行业投钱”。[①]

2016年初，中国大康集团修改了竞标方案，向不包括禁区地块的土地出价。当年4月20日，莫里森财长又一次以国家利益为由拒绝了中国的竞价，未做任何解释。其时恰好是2016年财政预算发布前夕和联邦竞选初始。坎贝尔（Campbell）代表基德曼家族发言表示，政府的决定“令人意外”。[②]

倡导自由市场的自由党议员大卫·利昂杰姆（David Leyonhjelm）认为莫里森的决定是“恐外的”，“这是种族主义的暗流涌动，他们担心的主要是中国投资”。[③] 澳大利亚《时代报》一篇言辞激烈的社论称这是一个“沙文主义”的决定，“散发着哗众取宠的恐外臭气。如果潜在买家是英国或美国企业，事情肯定就会不同”。[④] 南澳州州长魏杰（Jay Weatherill）也表示，“如果投资者是英美国家，我不认为还会展开这般讨论。为什么中国就要被特殊对待?”[⑤]

2016年12月，经外国投资审查委员会批准，澳大利亚矿业女富豪吉娜·莱因哈特（Gina Rinehart）的汉考克勘探公司（Hancock Prospecting）与上海中房置业（CRED）联手收购了基

① Hartcher, P., Massola, J., & Lynch, J., “Kidman Cattle Stations: Andrew Robb Criticises Scott Morrison's ‘Political’ Decision to Block Sale”, http://www.smh.com.au/federal-politics/political-news/kidman-cattle-stations-andrew-robb-criticises-scott-morrisons-political-decisionto-block-sale-20151120-gl3vkb.html.

② Barbour, L., Vidot, A., &Gunders, J., “Scott Morrison Knocks Back Sale of S. Kidman & Co. due to ‘National Interest’”, http://www.abc.net.au/news/2016-04-29/sale-of-s.-kidman-&-co-contrary-to-national-interest':-morrison/7370926.

③ Owens, J., &Loussikian, K., “Morrison Blocks Sale of S. Kidman Pastoral Holdings to Chinese”, http://www.theaustralian.com.au/business/morrison-blocks-sale-of-s-kidmanpastoral-holdings-to-chinese/news-story/84fc445e8d0f809fd549ceaef4a91ddd.

④ “Kidman Sale Rejection Demands Clarity”, *The Age*, http://www.theage.com.au/comment/the-age-editorial/kidman-sale-rejection-demands-clarity-20160502-gojq13.html.

⑤ Wills, D., “SA Premier Jay Weatherill Slams Federal Government Block of Kidman Sale to Chinese Buyer”, http://www.ntnews.com.au/news/northern-territory/sa-premier-jayweatherill-slams-federal-government-block-of-kidman-sale-to-chinese-buyer/news-story/6c8de786d1c80cd650dab27ef829c33e.

德曼价值 3.86 亿澳元的土地，其中，汉考克公司占有三分之二的股份。[①]

二 国防利益“焦虑”：建构的主权威胁

上述案例中，所有担忧都是源自以西方为标准，对中国资本“与我不同”的一维认知。再加上他们认为中国是一个共产主义国家，“统一策划中国企业所有的境外活动”。这种认知就被“出售战略资本给这类国家会丧失主权”的说法所加强。达尔文港出租引发的反华话语就是很好的例证。

达尔文港位于澳大利亚西北海岸，隶属北领地首府达尔文。2015 年 11 月 13 日，北领地首席部长宣布，经审核，中国岚桥集团（landbridge）以 5.06 亿澳元获得达尔文港 99 年租期。美国政府迅速就此表示了关切。[②] 11 月 17 日，美国前副国务卿理查德·阿米蒂奇（Richard Armitage）宣称，他对这一决定感到“震惊”，达尔文港的出租令美国措手不及。[③] 据报道，11 月 18 日，奥巴马总统当年在马尼拉召开的亚太经合组织会议上向特恩布尔总理提出此事。[④] 11 月 26 日，澳大利亚参议院通过一项动议，展开对达尔

---

① 在此之后，澳大利亚外国投资审查委员会修订了外资进入澳大利亚农业市场的法律规范。新版法规要求所有农业土地在出售前必须要向澳大利亚潜在买家进行不少于 30 天的公示期，公示期结束后方可公开销售，接受国际买家的竞价。http：//firb. gov. au/about/publication/register - of - foreign - ownership - of - agricultural - land - report - of - registrations - as - at - 30 - june - 2017/（浏览时间：2018 年 4 月 15 日）。

② 2011 年，澳、美达成为期 25 年的军事协议，美国海军陆战队以轮训方式进驻达尔文港。2012 年时任美国国防部长利昂·帕内塔（Leon E. Panetta）坦言这一举动能使美国海军陆战队迅速在亚太地区展开部署。Leon E. Panetta，Speech at Shangri - La Security Dialogue，June 2，2012，http：//archive. defense. gov/Speeches/Speech. aspx？SpeechID = 1681（浏览时间：2018 年 4 月 15 日）。

③ Kehoe，J.，& Tingle，L.，“US‘stunned’by Port of Darwin Sale to Chinese”，http：//www. afr. com/news/politics/us - stunned - by - port - of - darwin - sale - to - chinese - 20151116 - gl0omf.

④ Coorey，P.，& Tingle，L.，“‘Let Us Know Next Time’：How Obama Chided Turnbull over Darwinport Sale”，http：//www. afr. com/news/politics/let - us - know - next - time - how - obamachided - turnbull - over - darwin - port - sale - 20151118 - gl1qkg.

文港租赁交易的调查。12 月，澳大利亚时任国防部部长丹尼思·理查森（Dennis Richardson）接受询问时表示，租约在签署前已经得到包括内阁国家安全委员会在内的政府高层会商一致。[①] 他表示国防部进行了完善的尽职调查，考虑到了交易所有可能的风险和安全威胁。他认为中国海军会利用这一租约的说法是“危言耸听”和“愚蠢的”。[②]

澳大利亚战略政策研究所（Australia Strategic Policy Institute）[③]的两名研究员称，尽管岚桥集团是民营企业，但不可否认它“有可能接受中国政府的命令进行间谍活动，监控达尔文港的进出情况”。他们援引证据说，“这个集团刚成立了自己的民兵队，其董事长叶成也曾是共产党的高层官员”。[④] 悉尼大学研究中国问题的学者雅各布森（Linda Jacobsen）指出，第一，岚桥集团确实有民兵队，但这在中国十分正常，每一家大型企业，包括大学和医院，都有警卫和消防员。在澳大利亚，他们就是安保人员，这里被蓄意误译为“民兵”；第二，叶成确实是中国第十二届全国政协委员，但政协是一个中共领导的多党政治协商的机构，成为政协委员不代表叶本人是高层决策官员；第三，按照澳大利亚法律规定，如果出于国防目的，澳大利亚联邦政府或国防部可以随时介入并

① 租借达尔文港的权力属于澳北领地行政区，无须经过外国投资审查委员会批准。按照澳大利亚法律，出售类似国家重大战略资产时，必须要经包括国土部、财政部、国家安全机构等在内的政府高层部门一致审查批准。The Senate, Economics References Committee, Foreign Investment Review Framework, p. 32, https://www.aph.gov.au/Parliamentary_Business/Committees/Senate/Economics/Foreign_Investment_Review/~/media/Committees/economics_ctte/Foreign_Investment_Review/Report/report.pdf（浏览时间：2018 年 4 月 16 日）。

② McDonald, S., Doran, M., & Greene, A., "Port of Darwin: Concerns about Lease to Chinese Company 'Alarmist' and 'Absurd'", says Defence Secretary Dennis Richardson, http://www.abc.net.au/news/2015-12-15/dennis-richardson-says-port-of-darwin-lease-concerns/7029642.

③ 该研究所是一家由澳大利亚政府设立，由前国防部高级官员担任领导的智库。

④ Barnes, P., & Jennings, P., "Opinion Piece: NT Deal Shows FIRB Must be Given New National Security Credentials", http://www.afr.com/opinion/nt-deal-shows-firb-must-be-given-newnational-security-credentials-20151112-gkxvz4".

控制达尔文港。[①]

《澳大利亚人报》公布了一项美国在澳大利亚进行的民调结果，43% 的民众认为将达尔文港出租给中国有“很大风险”，46% 的人认为有“一定风险”，只有 11% 的澳大利亚人认为“没有风险”。[②]

三　文化“焦虑”：象牙塔中的“我们”与“他者”

与资本和政治体制的物理世界分割不同，文化的“焦虑”源于西方坚守的文明优越感，它所关涉的心灵世界更加复杂多异。要理解这种更为深刻的忧虑，有必要先了解一下留学生在澳大利亚大学中的重要作用。1989 年，时任教育部部长道金斯（John Dawkins）改革高等教育体系，设立了双重学费标准。国内的学生根据递延税收缴纳学费，而留学生则需提前缴纳高昂学费。双重收费标准的引入，加上政府资助的减少，改革等于鼓励学校大幅招收留学生以满足自身预算需要。2013 年的统计数字显示，澳大利亚每 5 名大学生中就有 1 名留学生，是经合组织国家中留学生比例第二高的国家，仅次于卢森堡。其中，中国学生数量最多，比例高达 36% 。[③] 年内，留学生为澳大利亚创造了 43 亿澳元的收入，约占公立大学资金总额的五分之一。[④]

先来看针对留学生的“焦虑”。2015 年 4 月，澳大利亚 ABC 电视台王牌时事栏目“四角”播出了一期题为“学位骗局”的节目，引发了全国性讨论。节目谴责澳大利亚高等教育过度依赖留学

---

① Jacobsen, L., “Darwin Port Row Shows Australia doesn't Understand China”, http://www.theaustralian.com.au/opinion/darwin-port-row-shows-australia-doesnt-understandchinese-society/news-story/9ec885e0131c6a3afd5e156a28da9f9b.

② Everingham, S., “PM Shrugs off Revelation US Conducted Secret Polling on Darwin Port lease”, http://www.abc.net.au/worldtoday/content/2016/s4421482.htm.

③ OECD, Education at a Glance 2013, https://www.oecd.org/edu/eag2013%20(eng)-FINAL%2020%20June%202013.pdf.

④ Donovan, S., “Australian Unis Left Vulnerable by Reliance on Overseas Student Fees: Study”, http://www.abc.net.au/worldtoday/content/2015/s4303120.htm.

生收入而降低了自身标准[①]，指责留学生，特别是中国留学生，“在签证、资格欺诈、抄袭和代理回扣方面助长了黑市繁荣”。老师们也倍感压力，他们不得不降低标准让学生顺利毕业，以保证学校的收入。节目警告说，如果这些学生毕业后，进入医疗或工程行业，终将影响到澳大利亚人的安危。民众、政府和院校纷纷发表各方意见，但大部分争论默认节目论点正确，仅围绕如何解决中国留学生的这种问题展开。

有观点称，并非所有的留学生都应受到指责，要将中国留学生和其他国家的留学生区分开来。[②] 也有观点认为，公众谴责留学生导致学术标准降低完全是一面之词，他们忽视了一个基本事实，那就是大规模扩招才是造成现状的最重要原因。ABC 电视台的节目把中国留学生描画成要么是毫无道德原则的中介机构之牺牲品，要么是“通过伪造文件，剽窃或购买论文来蒙混过关的骗子”，完全不提及在澳留学生的正面案例。留学生，特别是中国留学生，是高度相异的个体群，不能简单按照种族进行划分。[③]

再来看高等教育体制内部。随着澳大利亚大学国际化程度的提高，校方普遍开始强调“批判性思维”以证明西方教育的优越性，并视之为将留学生文明化至更高层级的文化使命。“西方”和“儒家”被固化为“价值”和“缺陷”的简单二元对立[④]，不具有“批判性思维”的中国学生自然就被贴上“与理想的西方学生相异”的标签。来自与澳不同语言和文化背景的“中国学生”，被认

① ABC，Four Corners：Degrees of Deception，http：//www. abc. net. au/4corners/stories/2015/04/20/4217741. htm.

② Wilson，W.（2015，22 April），University Scandal，http：//www. theaustralian. com. au/.

③ Bexley，E.，& Vu，T.，“Biased Reports on International Students not Helpful”，https：//theconversation. com/biased – reports – on – international – students – not – helpful – 40752.

④ Ryan，J.，& Louie，K.（2007），“False Dichotomy? ‘Western’ and ‘Confucian’ Concepts of Scholarship and Learning”，*Educational Philosophy and Theory*，39（4），404 – 417.

为来自所谓准现代化的教育体系，是“先天不足”的学生群体。[①] 尽管这种“我们”和“他者”的表示方法带有浓厚的“定居殖民主义”色彩，但是这种建立在发展主义基础上，认为欧洲文明高于一切的逻辑无法动摇。澳大利亚大学里的“中国学生”别无选择，只能接受以欧洲价值为标准的知识范式的同化，接受被建构为“历史的终结”的文明的同化，而放弃自身所谓落后的文化和逻辑。

四 译者后记

译者认为，上述案例涉及跨国企业行为（并购、租赁）和个人行为（置业、教育），覆盖了技术层面的探索（外资投资法规的规范）和价值观层面的思考（“我们”与“他者”的区隔），篇幅所限，作者不可能为每个案例提供更为详尽的语篇资料、背景知识和动态跟踪，然而其现有的陈列，已经使得澳大利亚对华“焦虑”情结的根源不辩自明，即澳大利亚存在对中国和自身认知的双重失误。一方面，澳部分政界与媒体人士，以西方为标准，视相异者皆为敌。他们不致力于全面了解真实的中国，不使用事实说话，单凭印象和偏见服务于自己政党或幕后金主。他们视之为敌的，是一个自我想象出来的对手。

另一方面，澳大利亚对华焦虑者们把自己树立成终极价值观的捍卫者。这种高高在上的姿态掩盖了一个主观真理：最优秀的软实力，应当是最具包容性的。如何本着“己欲立而立人，己欲达而达人”的原则去承认对方的利益，容小别而求大同？如何做到不狭隘，不僵化，以“他国之心，予忖度之”的路向，求得不同国家，不同价值观的互成？这些问题也许更加值得思考。揽镜自鉴，

① Song, X., “Changing Social Relations in Higher Education: The First Year International Student and the ‘Chinese Learner’ in Australia”, In H. Brook, D. Fergie, M. Maeorg, & D. Michell (eds.), *Universities in Transition: Foregrounding Social Contexts of Knowledge in the First Year Experience*, Adelaide: University of Adelaide Press, 2014, pp. 127 – 156.

全面认知对方国家，“由己及人”的利益互惠与价值观共情，这些领于“治国平天下”八纲之首的“格物致知，诚意正心”[①] 之精妙深意，我们自己有着何种程度的体认？前特恩布尔总理高级顾问，费尔法克斯媒体集团亚太版编辑高安西（John Garnaut）在他声援特氏政府的文章最后也不得不承认，不能只是老调重弹地呼喊“危及主权”，只有用明确的证据和合情合理的论点赢得辩论才是真正的胜利。[②]

China in Australia: The Discourses of *Changst*

Greg McCarthy, *Xianlin Song*

Translated by Dong Ting

Abstract: China matters significantly to contemporary Australia in terms of trade relations, capital movements, education and global order. Australian public discourse on China, however, inhabits two conflicting parallel universes, one a narrative of economic complementarity, the other of fear and anxiety. The spectre of the development of China haunts Australian society in and among these two spheres: one in which China's economic development is to be encouraged as "a sign of it joining the capitalist world system", and the other in which China's ascent is regarded as a "threat" to be contained. The paper examines this problematic discourse, calling it *Changst* [China angst], arguing that it is

① 《礼记·大学》：“古之欲明明德于天下者，先治其国；欲治其国者，先齐其家；欲齐其家者，先修其身；欲修其身者，先正其心；欲正其心者，先诚其意；欲诚其意者，先致其知，致知在格物。物格而后知至，知至而后意诚，意诚而后心正，心正而后身修，身修而后家齐，家齐而后国治，国治而后天下平。”

② John Garnaut, "How China Interferes in Australia and How Democracies can Push Back", Mar. 9, 2018, *Foreign Affairs*, https://www.foreignaffairs.com/articles/china/2018-03-09/how-china-interferes-australia（浏览时间：2018年4月20日）。

permeated with a developmentalist logic (Chakrabarty, 2000) that misreads China through the homogenising history of both capitalism and Eurocentrism. This reading of China as but a copy of Western capitalism evokes anxiety because its distinctive forms of capital flow disrupt the comforting teleology. Equally, when Chinese society, including its education system, is perceived as not-yet modern, this induces fear of cultural contamination from the outpouring of Chinese international students. The exploration of this anxiety is conducted via six Australian case studies, showing how China's engagement with Australia produces intense but unwarranted angst.

Keywords: Development of China; Developmentalism; Chinese Investment; Chinese Students; "Sinophobia"

专题论文

Feature Essays

The End of the British World and the Redefinition of Citizenship in Australia, 1950s－1970s

Jatinder Mann*

Bio: Jatinder Mann is an Assistant Professor in History at the Hong Kong Baptist University. He is working on a project on "The end of the British World and the redefinition of citizenship in Australia, Canada, and New Zealand, 1950s-1970s". Jatinder is the sole editor of *Citizenship in Transnational Perspective: Australia, Canada, and New Zealand* (New York: Palgrave Macmillan, 2017). He is also the author of *The Search for a New National Identity: The Rise of Multiculturalism in Canada and Australia, 1890s- 1970s* (New York: Peter Lang Publishing, 2016). Jatinder has published numerous articles in front-ranking, interdisciplinary journals.

In the 1950s Australia very much identified itself as a British country and an integral part of a wider British World, which had the United Kingdom (UK) at its centre. However, by the 1970s this British World had come to an end, as had Australia's self-identification as a British nation. During this period citizenship in Australia was redefined in a significant way from being an ethnic (British) based one to a more civic

* 作者简介：贾廷德·曼（Jatinder Mann），香港浸会大学历史学助理教授。

founded one-which was more inclusive of other ethnic groups and Aborigines. This article will argue that this redefinition of citizenship took place primarily in the context of this major shift in national identity. After having established the context of the end of the British World in Australia (with a focus on the UKs application for entry into the European Economic Community (EEC) and the British withdrawal from 'East of Suez') it will explore the *Citizenship Act of 1969* and the *Australian Citizenship Act of 1973* to illustrate the way in which citizenship became more inclusive of other ethnic groups in the country. It will then study the awarding of the right to vote for Aborigines in 1961 and the 1967 constitutional referendum to highlight the way in which citizenship in Australia also began to incorporate Aborigines at this time.

No one has explored the redefinition of citizenship in Australia between the 1950s and 1970s in relation to ethnic and Indigenous groups in the context of the end of Britishness. This is what my article will do.

Theoretical Background

Before exploring these several themes it will be useful to briefly discuss the theoretical background to citizenship in Australia during the 1950s and 1970s—namely the distinction between normative (citizenship as status) as opposed to substantive citizenship (citizenship as rights and obligations). T. H. Marshall formulated 'citizenship' as a designation given to those who are full participants of a community. Through this he enlarged citizenship to incorporate civil rights, as well as political and social.[①] According to Wayne Hudson and John Kane though, 'What most Australians understand by citizenship is a mixture of legal and

① Kim Rubenstein, *Australian Citizenship Law in Context* (Pyrmont, NSW: Lawbook Co., 2002) 10.

political citizenship … The history of legal and political citizenship in Australia, however, is problematic. '①

This relates to the fact that in the 1950s citizenship in Australia was very much normative—it did not entail extensive rights and obligations. And to complicate things even more British migrants were able to attain this status on much easier terms compared to non-British migrants. Aborigines, though possessing the 'status' of Australian citizens were deprived of rights, which are usually associated with citizenship through a swathe of restrictive legislation—both on the federal and state levels. David Dutton argues that 'The legal meaning of Australian citizenship has never been singularly defined, and must even now, be sought in the common law, and a multitude of Commonwealth and state statutes dealing with immigration, passports, the franchise, jury service, employment in the public service, and social security. '② Nevertheless, citizenship in Australia was by the 1970s considerably more substantive compared to the 1950s and all migrants were put on an equal basis in terms of attaining this citizenship. Ann-Mari Jordens neatly encapsulates this redefinition, 'Over 30 years, the presence of large numbers of non-British migrants in Australia slowly eroded the conception of Australian citizenship from a status based on British ethnicity and culture to one based on equality of rights and responsibilities. '③

Although, I will argue that a shift in national identity rather than increasing multi-ethnicity was the main reason for this redefinition.

---

① Wayne Hudson and John Kane, "Rethinking Australian Citizenship" in Hudson, Wayne and Kane, John (Eds), *Rethinking Australian Citizenship* (Cambridge: Cambridge University Press, 2000) 2.

② David Dutton, *Citizenship in Australia: A Guide to Commonwealth Government Records* (Canberra: National Archives of Australia, 1999) 17.

③ Ann - Mari Jordens, *Alien to Citizen: Settling migrants in Australia*, 1945 - 1975 (St. Leonards, NSW: Allen & Unwin, 1997) 189. However, there was still protection for British subjects who were on the electoral roll as late as 1983 to remain on the roll even if they were not citizens.

Turning to Aborigines and citizenship the most that one can really say about when Aboriginal groups became Australian citizens is that, primarily during the 1960s, Aboriginal groups gradually secured the substantive citizenship rights that up to that point had been withheld from them at the State and Commonwealth levels, as State and Commonwealth statutes that limited their citizenship rights were slowly repealed. ①Susan Dodds maintains that 'In considering ways of thinking about Australian Aboriginal citizenship, the history of European engagement with Indigenous Australians acts as a constant reminder of the gap between abstract idealisations of liberal democratic citizenship and the reality of colonial and post-colonial Australian social policy.'②

Context of the end of the British World

Having established this theoretical background, the article will now turn to exploring the context of the end of the British World as the major reason for the redefinition of citizenship in Australia between the 1950s and 1970s. In the post-Second World War period Australia was very much a British society and an integral part of a wider British World. An excellent and very appropriate example is the *British Nationality and Australian Citizenship Act of 1948*. Although this act established the concept of Australian citizenship for the very first time—it emphasised *British Nationality* over *Australian Citizenship*. Furthermore, the status of British subject was preserved and white immigrants③from the British Commonwealth were given preferential

---

① John Chesterman and Brian Galligan, "Indigenous Rights and Australian Citizenship" in Rubenstein, Kim (ed.), *Individual, Community, Nation: Fifty Years of Australian Citizenship* (Melbourne: Australian Scholarly Publishing, 2000) 67.

② Susan Dodds, "Citizenship, Justice and Indigenous Group - Specific Rights - Citizenship and Indigenous Australia", *Citizenship Studies*, vol. 2, no. 1, 1998, 106.

③ The White Australia Policy which had been established in 1901 and was primarily aimed at preventing Asian immigration to Australia, was very much alive and well at this time.

treatment in terms of naturalisation. ①The Suez Crisis of 1956②is a further demonstration of Australia's identification as an integral part of a wider British World. Throughout the episode the Australian government fully supported the UKs position of overturning President Nasser's decision to nationalise the Suez Canal. Australia offered unequivocal support for the UK as it considered itself a British country. The UK was still the centre of a wider British World, and therefore backing the UK was still regarded as supporting the 'mother-country'. ③

However, in the early 1960s the first signs that Australia's Britishness was beginning to wane started to emerge. The first application of the UK government for entry into the EEC in 1961 marked the beginning of the unravelling of the belief that Australia was part of a wider British World. It came as such a psychological shock to the Australians as they had previously received repeated assurances from the British that there was no question of them making a choice between Europe and the Commonwealth. The Australian government though became increasingly concerned by the lack of communication from London during 1960 and 1961, when the UK was reconsidering its position towards the EEC. Despite repeated requests for information, the

---

① For more on the *British Nationality and Australian Citizenship Act of 1948* see Jatinder Mann, 'The Evolution of Commonwealth Citizenship, 1945 - 1948 in Canada, Britain and Australia', *Commonwealth and Comparative Politics*, vol. 50, no. 3, July 2012, 293 - 313.

② This was a crisis precipitated by the nationalisation of the Suez Canal by Egyptian President Gamal Abdul Nasser in July 1956, which in turn led to the UK and France, who had substantial commercial interests in the canal, entering into a clandestine agreement with Israel to invade Egypt in October 1956, thus giving the two powers the opportunity to in turn send troops into the canal zone on the pretext of 'separating the warring parties'.

③ For more on the prevalence of Britishness in Australia at this time see Jatinder Mann, *The Search for a New National Identity: The Rise of Multiculturalism in Canada and Australia, 1890s-1970s* (New York: Peter Lang Publishing, 2016), Chapter 4. It should be emphasized however that Australia's Britishness was not a sign of inferiority, rather Australian Britons saw themselves as superior to those in the 'mother - country'. It was argued that the extreme Australian climate, the exigencies of colonial life and a better diet had produced a stronger and fitter British population in the antipodes.

British refused to indicate which way they were thinking until a more solid agreement had been secured with the Six (this was the six original members of the EEC-France, Germany, Italy, Belgium, The Netherlands and Luxembourg. The latter three were collectively known as Benelux) . ①

There were increasing rumours and speculation about a reversal of British policy in early 1961. This led to a sudden interest in European economic matters by the Australian government. John McEwen, Minister for Trade announced to the Cabinet in February that although the entire picture was not clear, it appeared as if the UK was shifting closer and closer towards something along the lines of full membership of the EEC. Menzies expressed the deep concerns of the Australian people about this eventuality. He specifically drew attention to the political and strategic effects Britain's decision would have on the Commonwealth. If Britain were to join the EEC how would it then consider Australia, Canada and the rest of the Commonwealth?②

But unlike the UK, Australia did not have an alternative geographic grouping to redirect its interests. Therefore, the Australian government decided to use whatever means it could to ensure that British entry into the EEC would not lead to a fundamental shift in Australia's long-standing political and economic ties to the UK. Menzies' subsequent tough probing of the British government illustrated the level of Australia's concerns. The issue of Britain and Europe, rather than being seen as just a temporary conflict of interest between Australia and Britain, had initiated a re-evaluation of the very concept of 'British interests'. Menzies increased the pressure by stating that the UK had a very hard choice between the Commonwealth and Europe. On 31 July 1961,

① Stuart Ward, *Australia and the British Embrace* (Carlton South, Vic.: Melbourne University Press, 2001) 69, 70.

② *Ibid.*, 71, 79.

British Prime Minister Harold Macmillan announced the decision of his government to seek membership in the EEC. [①]Macmillan's EEC statement resulted in a diverse range of responses in Australia. The *Sydney Morning Herald* represented the general feeling however, announcing that the British action was one of the most historic statements of the century. [②]

If the UK's application for membership in the EEC initiated the breakdown of Britishness in Australia, its resolve in 1967 to end its military role ' East of Suez ' was the culmination. This move was significant in itself as it illustrated the end of the UK's military world role. To commentators in both the UK and Australia it appeared that the decline of one of the last symbols of the Anglo-Australian relationship would result in the demise of Australia's long-standing British self-identification. This was due to British race patriotism in Australia being founded on the idea that Britons in Australia and the UK had a community of interest, which the British decision to withdraw from ' East of Suez' acted blatantly against.

But quite some time before the UK announced its move, there had been increasing problems in the British-Australian strategic relationship, which had led to Australia progressively becoming a part of the United States (US) sphere. Nevertheless, this had not affected Australia's Britannic identity in any significant way as it had always (with a few noteworthy exceptions) preserved a differentiation between sentiment and interest, particularly when it came to foreign policy. Moreover, although the UK had not yet become a member of the EEC, its failed bid in 1961 - 1963 had most definitely resulted in Australia questioning

① Ward, *Australia and the British Embrace*, 81, 85, 86, 88.

② *Sydney Morning Herarld*, 2 August 1961 cited in Ward, *Australia and the British* Embrace, 89.

their future relationship and had led to initiatives to broaden Australian trade. ①

Expectedly there were Australian protests to the British over their announcement. Alexander Downer, Australian High Commissioner in London, tried to persuade the British government that it would be a travesty of history if the UK were to be simply a European power. But largely, Downer's emotive reaction was not typical of most Australians' views in 1967, or indeed of those of the new Holt government. Although Paul Hasluck, the Foreign Minister, did suggest to Prime Minister Harold Holt that connections of familial ties and common wartime experiences should be emphasised in communications with the UK, this was only a small component of the overarching Australian plan. Even the most ardent disciples of the British heritage had been compelled to accept the existence of this new world. ②

The end of Britishness and the question of whether an Australian nationalism could be located to replace it coalesced in the late 1960s under Prime Minister John Gorton. Although Holt asked important questions, Gorton's public addresses on this subject were an illustration of the confusion and problems faced by national leaders in the late 1960s. The Whitlam government has often been associated with an unexpected emergence of a more autonomous and confident Australian nationalism, however Gorton can be regarded as a predecessor of this drive, particularly in his arts policy initiatives. By establishing the Australian Council for the Arts, facilitating the re-emergence of the Australian film industry and laying the basis for the introduction of an Australia Film and Television School, Gorton was linking himself and his

---

① Jatinder Mann, " 'Leavening British Traditions': Integration Policy in Australia, 1962 - 1972", *Australian Journal of Politics and History*, vol. 59, issue 1, March 2013, 49.

② Ibid., 49 - 50.

government with an emerging faith in Australia's cultural uniqueness. [①]

The Sunday Australian captured the substance of the ' new nationalism' in early 1972: ' A splendid opportunity exists to build a multi-national society, rich and diverse in its origins but cohesive in its identity... Australia must be a country in which our people are concerned with a common purpose and a sharing of common identity'. [②]This talk of Australia as a multi-national society but with a particular focus on national cohesion, along with somehow also possessing a clear idea of community and identity combined the key concepts and contradictions of the ' new nationalism' .

The decline of the idea that Australia was a part of a wider British World was helped by the long drawn-out way in which the UK entered the EEC, which occurred in 1973, a dozen years after the original application. It was also assisted by the realisation by Australian leaders that the nation's trading future was in Asia, which for the majority of its past had been its psychological enemy. A white British Australian identity was no longer wanted and no longer appropriate as the nation attempted to come to terms with its presence in a changed world. In the early 1960s, then, the concept of Australia as a ' British ' country started to lose credibility and relevance. Later in the decade the ' new nationalism' , which emphasised a domestic Australian identity, arose as a possible replacement for Britishness. But this entire period was one of questioning and uncertainty. Thus, apart from an emphasis on national cohesion and uniquely Australian creative effort, there was not much substance to the ' new nationalism' . [③]This was the context in

① Mann, "Leavening British Traditions", 53.

② National Library of Australia (NLA), MS 6690/Series 12/Box 40/File 22: Immigration Advisory Council, Extract from *Sunday Australian*, 13 February 1972, " Pride and prejudice", 8.

③ Mann, "Leavening British traditions", 54, 55, 62.

which nationality and citizenship legislation was amended during the 1960s and 1970s.

The Citizenship Act of 1969

The *Nationality and Citizenship Act* was changed in 1955, 1969 and 1973. The amendments of 1955 were minimal as views took another decade to begin to shift. ①The significant changes in 1973 have quite rightly been given considerable attention by scholars. However, the 1969 changes were also important and in some ways laid the foundation for the subsequent changes in 1973. Hence, I will focus on them next. ②The *West Australian* in late 1967 suggested amending Australian naturalisation ceremonies so that applicants would only be required to swear allegiance to the Queen of Australia. It justified this move in the goal of increasing rates of naturalisation and highlighted that non-British migrants had no basis for cherishing British ties. ③G. E. Hitchins, Commonwealth Director of Migration in a letter to Peter Heydon, Secretary of the Department of Immigration early the following year actually recommended amending the Oath of Allegiance to remove the reference to the 'Queen, her heirs and successors' and simply asking the applicant to declare their loyalty to 'Australia and the Constitution' as well as contemplating

---

① Alistair Davidson, *From Subject to Citizen: Australian Citizenship in the Twentieth Century* (Cambridge: Cambridge University Press, 1997), 88.

② Some of the changes in the *Citizenship Act of 1969* were most certainly inspired by amendments to Canadian legislation a few years earlier-this is not surprising as the original *British Nationality and Australian Citizenship Act of 1948* was modeled on the *Canadian Citizenship Act of 1946*. The idea of citizens of other Commonwealth countries swearing an oath of allegiance to the Queen of Canada was a case in point. National Archives of Australia (NAA), A446 1965/46671: Cable from Department of External Relations (following from Ottawa) to Department of Immigration, 26 January 1967, 126.

③ NAA, A446 1957/66699: Extract from *West Australian*, "Seeking More Citizens", 11 December 1967.

whether the renunciation of former allegiance was really required and considering a reduction in the qualifying period for naturalisation to perhaps three years. He added that there was some opposition by certain migrants to swearing allegiance to the Queen whereas they would not be against declaring loyalty to Australia. ①

A Departmental Committee to review the *Nationality and Citizenship Act 1948- 1967* also made some recommendations on amendments. In particular with the purpose of placing more importance on Australian citizenship it recommended that the title of the Act be revised from *Nationality and Citizenship Act* to *Australian Citizenship Act*. This would follow Canada's Act. In addition, in furtherance of the Minister's opinion that more emphasis should be placed on ' Australian Citizenship' than in the past, it suggested the inclusion of a new Section (similar to one in the *Canadian Citizenship Act*) allowing that when Australians were asked to state their national status, it would be acceptable to declare ' Australian citizen' . ②In terms of practicalities an Inter-Departmental Committee stated that the impact of this on other federal legislation could be handled with a clause in the Act itself, but State governments would need to introduce legislation individually to make sure that the basic description ' Australian citizen' met their legislative provisions regarding British subjects. ③Heydon in turn commented on some of the recommendations of the Committee in a letter to the Minister for Immigration in May 1968. He maintained that:

---

① NAA, A446 1957/66699: G. E. Hitchins, Commonwealth Director of Migration to Peter Heydon, Secretary, Department of Immigration, 28 February 1968, 1.

② NAA, A446 1967/72349: Departmental Committee to Review the Nationality and Citizenship Act 1948 - 1967 - Possible Amendments Discussed, and Recommendations of Amendments, 1, 3 - 4.

③ NAA, A446 1967/72349: Nationality and Citizenship Act 1948 - 1967 - Inter - Departmental Discussions, 1 - 2.

> The time may well come when our laws generally will cease to give such a privileged position to settlers from other Commonwealth countries-and will attach significance instead to the status of Australian citizens, the prerequisites for which will be common to all settlers; but while our laws remain as they are, our nationality legislation should be attuned to them. ①

He added that the Committee's report stated that a British subject with resident status had all the key rights and obligations of citizenship, and in particular he could not be deported after five years (crime-free) residence; to give them the right to apply for citizenship after five years did no more than to give 'de jure' acknowledgement of a current 'de facto' context. ②

The legal consequences of emphasising Australian *Citizenship* over a *British Nationality* were discussed within the Attorney-General's Department in late 1968:

> I understand that the proposal that a section be inserted to the effect that whenever Australians are required to state their national status, it would be sufficient to state "Australian citizen" was taken from the Canadian Citizenship Act 1946 which has an equivalent section. While this Act declares Canadian citizens to be British subjects, it does not specifically provide for British nationality… It would seem to me that before the Attorney-General could make any public statement as to the proposed changes there must be some clarification of the Commonwealth's intention as regards nationality

① NAA, A446, 1967/72349: Heydon to The Minister for Immigration, May 1968, 2 – 3.

② Ibid. .

and Australian citizens being British subjects.[1]

This highlighted the differences between the initial citizenship legislation adopted by both Canada and Australia in the post-Second World War period, which related to Britishness operating in a bicultural society in the former and a predominantly monocultural one in the latter.[2]

Clyde Cameron, the member for Hindmarsh expressed the Australian Labor Party (ALP) Opposition's view on the Liberal-National Coalition government's proposals in late 1968:

> The Opposition, generally speaking, and subject to a further examination of this proposal-we will not have an opportunity to examine it further until the Bill is introduced next year-is generally in accord with what is now proposed. However, I raise at once some doubt as to the advisability of giving to any person, not matter what the circumstances that may exist, the right to be naturalised after only 3 years in this country.[3]

This opposition to reducing the period a non-British migrant had to wait before being naturalised is interesting as the ALP position would change quite drastically in just a few years. Cameron added though that ' I

---

① NAA, A432 1968/3377: A. C. C. Menzies, Senior Assistant Secretary (Advisings) to The Secretary, Attorney - General's Department, 18 October 1968, 2.

② It also again illustrated the impact of revisions to Canadian citizenship legislation on the Australian situation. In fact the Australian Department of Immigration thanked the Canadian High Commission in Canberra for providing information on the revisions to the Canadian Citizenship regulations the following month. NAA, A446 1965/46671: G. A. Cole, for Secretary, Department of Immigration to A. R. Menzies, High Commissioner for Canada, 1 November 1968.

③ Clyde Cameron, M. P. (Commonwealth Parliamentary Debates (CPD), House of Representatives, 12 November 1968), 2730.

am pleased indeed that the Government proposes to drop this old Union Jack idea of calling ourselves British subjects… I do not like the word "subject" . '① This on the other hand was a much more traditional ALP position.

Newspapers also reacted generally very positively to the proposals. According to the *Age*: 'the decision…will, in effect, reduce from five to three years the time which alien immigrants of good character, and with a reasonable command of English, must wait before they become eligible for citizenship. '② *The Melbourne Herald* maintained that 'For many foreign-born migrants, the proposals announced last night for easing the conditions of naturalisation will be a practical form of welcome to Australia. '③ The *Sydney Morning Herald* argued that 'Those who have willingly committed themselves to Australia are entitled to expect that everything will be done to remove unnecessary barriers against obtaining full citizenship rights … But the legislation continues to recognise the privileged position of migrants from Britain and Commonwealth countries over those from Europe. '④

The Daily Telegraph asserted that 'A migrant who needs more than three years to decide to become a citizen is hardly worth having anyway-and putting those who do want citizenship into a kind of limbo for five years could be psychologically harmful. '⑤ *Il Globo*, an Italian-Australian publication triumphantly declared that 'Australian citizens will have to consider themselves above all "Australian", and "British subjects" in a secondary sense only…Our paper has fought ceaselessly for years for such

① Clyde Cameron, M. P. (Commonwealth Parliamentary Debates (CPD), House of Representatives, 12 November 1968), 2730.

② NAA, A446 1978/75530: Extract from *Age*- "Rewarding the Triers", 14 November 1968.

③ NAA, A446 1978/75530: Extract from *Melbourne Herald*- "Short Cut Citizens", 13 November 1968.

④ NAA, A446 1978/75530: Extract from *SMH*- "Becoming a Citizen", 14 November 1968.

⑤ NAA, A446 1978/75530: Extract from *Daily Telegraph*- "Migrants", 14 November 1968.

a justified reform. '①

Billy Snedden, the Minister for Immigration in his second reading speech on the Bill highlighted that 'The Bill…proposed some changes which are fundamental to our national status and the concept of Australian citizenship, as well as to the rules under which our citizenship may be acquired. '② There was a diverse range of responses to the Bill in Parliament, although most approved of the general principle of the legislation. The Liberal Member for Sturt, Ian Wilson commented that 'There is no doubt there is a growing sense of Australian nationality amongst the people of this country… I applaud the decision to give primacy to the expression "Australian citizen" . '③

Former ALP Minister for Immigration and the one responsible for the introduction of the first *British Nationality and Australian Citizenship Act of 1948*, Arthur Calwell criticised the reduction in the period of naturalisation for non-British migrants: 'I think that our gift of naturalisation is so great and so valuable that it should not be lightly regarded… If is necessary to attract all sorts of good people to Australia from all countries I do not think that we should cheapen the value of our citizenship by making it available too easily to a lot of people who want it. '④

So, the decline of Britishness in Australia led to shifts in citizenship

① NAA, A446 1978/75530: Extract from *Il Globo*- "Thanks to Minister Snedden-Australian Citizens to be 'less British'", 19 November 1968, 2.

② NAA, A446 1969/70341: Citizenship Bill, 1969-Second Reading Speech by the Hon. B. M. Snedden, Minister for Immigration, 2.

③ Ian Wilson, M. P. (CPD, House, 1 May 1969), 1597, 1598.

④ Arthur Calwell, M. P., (CPD, House, 13 May 1969), 1602. The provisions of the *Citizenship Act of* 1969 relating to an Australian Citizen having the *status* of a British subject rather than *being* a British subject were not proclaimed until 20 February 1973. This was because many State laws referred to people who *were* British subjects, it was essential therefore that each State should amend its laws before the federal provisions could be enacted. South Australia was the last to do this and thus the remaining provisions of the Act could be proclaimed. NAA, A446 1978/75531: Citizenship Circular 1/73 by H. J. Grant (for Secretary), 9 February 1973, 1 - 2.

policy towards naturalised citizens. With British race patriotism no longer having the hold it once had on the national self-imagination of Australians and a 'New Nationalism' being adopted, Australian governments felt they could make some initial moves towards equalising the status of naturalised citizens compared to their natural-born counterparts.

The *Australian Citizenship Act of 1973*

The *Australian Citizenship Act of 1973* was the next major reform of Australian Citizenship and Nationality legislation. As mentioned above it built on the reforms of the *Citizenship Act of 1969.* One of the major things the Bill introduced was a suggested new Oath (or Affirmation) of Allegiance: it firstly removed the renunciation of allegiance which had been a source of considerable emotional turmoil for some migrants and secondly allegiance was now to be sworn to the Constitution of Australia-specific mention of the Queen was not made. The Bill also provided for a transitional period of two years (after the new Act commenced) during which:

> Commonwealth citizens, Irish citizens, and South African and Pakistani citizens already resident in Australia, will be able to become Australian citizens after one year's residence; and… aliens who have lived in Commonwealth countries or served under those countries' Governments may have such residence or service accepted as part of the new qualifying period of three years' residence for the grant of Australian citizenship. ①

① NAA, A446 1978/75532: Citizenship Circular 4/73 by G. E. Hitchins (for Secretary) on "Australian Citizenship Bill 1973", 12 April 1973, 2.

Though the Bill did not adjust the context in which citizens of Commonwealth countries, whether they became Australian citizens or not, carried on having the status of British or Commonwealth of Nations subjects and hence had benefits including the vote and ability to be employed in the public service under Parliamentary legislation. ①Nevertheless, it was emphasised that the Bill would remove (after a transitional period) the past previous discrimination between citizens of Commonwealth nations and others, particularly by requiring the same period of residence for all; and providing everyone with the chance to attend citizenship ceremonies. ②

In his second reading speech on the Bill, Al Grassby, the Minister for Immigration emphasised the main thrust of the legislation, which was to establish equality between all migrants:

> The guiding principles for the Government in the vitally important matter of the grant of Australian Citizenship is that there should not be discrimination between different groups of settlers seeking to join the family of the nation. Wherever they were born-whatever their nationality-whatever the colour of their complexion-they should all be able to become Australian citizens under just the same conditions…So it is that this Bill provides for all, regardless of origins, the same requirements as to residence, good character, knowledge of the language and of the rights and duties of citizenship, and intention to live here permanently. ③

① NAA, A446 1978/75532: Citizenship Circular 4/73 by G. E. Hitchins (for Secretary) on "Australian Citizenship Bill 1973", 12 April 1973, 2.

② NLA, MS 7798/Series 3/Box 40: Papers of Al Grassby-Notes on "Discrimination in Citizenship Legislation and Policy of Previous Government".

③ NAA, A446 1978/75532: Second Reading Speech on Citizenship Bill 1973 by the Hon. A. J. Grassby, Minister for Immigration, 1, 2.

The Opposition however opposed all main features of the Bill. Philip Lynch, former Minister for Immigration and Deputy Leader of the Opposition fired the opening salvo:

> The Opposition rejects the major provisions of this Bill for a number of fundamental reasons. The legislation seeks to remove the position of preferment which British migrants have enjoyed since the inception of Australia's immigration program… our early arrivals with relatively limited exceptions, came almost solely… from the British Isles … The Government seems intent on ending that special relationship… I have… indicated that the Opposition is opposed to the proposal to delete all references to the Queen from the oath of allegiance taken by migrants at citizenship ceremonies. It is equally opposed to the Government's proposal to omit the renunciation of allegiance to another country. '①

But Grassby did also receive support from his side of the house. Maxwell Oldmeadow, the member for Holt rose to support the Bill and stated that he and his side of the house did not share the alarm expressed by Lynch. There were no disincentives to British migrants. He also drew attention to the fact that Grassby had stated that renunciation of former citizenship served no legal purpose. Though his most salient comments were: ' A nation which has come of age, which has confidence in its future and has successfully emerged from the shadows of colonialism neither requires nor will accept such a sacrifice… Australian citizenship must always be preserved and solidified by its highest common factors. '②

① Phillip Lynch, M. P. , (CPD, House, 9 May 1973), 1899, 1900, 1901.

② Maxwell Oldmeadow, M. P. (CPD, House, 9 May 1973), 1902, 1903.

The Opposition however was not finished, Alexander Forbes, the member for Barker piped in with a reference to British migrants: "Just who does the Minister for Immigration think he is kidding? Since when did people who are placed in a privileged position object because there was discrimination in their favour?"① He scathingly added now with a reference to non-British migrants that " Citizenship is an act of identification with the adopted country and with the values and mores of its inhabitants … Persons who cannot accept these things have not sufficiently identified as to be ready for citizenship. "②

But the government was not to be cowed on the Bill. The ALP member for Bowman, Leonard Keogh made a lively riposte to Forbes:

> As the honourable member for Barker (Dr. Forbes) was making his speech this evening I expected him to break out at any time into a verse from " Rule Britannia " . My colleague, the honourable member for Liley (Mr. Doyle) said to me when he walked into the chamber that he felt sure that he must have been in Rhodesia listening to Ian Smith … The Immigration policy of the Government seeks to rid the nation of the inconsistencies, inequalities and discrimination that we believe should no longer be allowed to exist when we are seeking to bring people from various countries and to welcome them as citizens in their own right in Australia. ③

Therefore, Keogh criticised the Imperial hangings on of the Opposition at the same time as stressing the positive moves the government was trying to make to remove the discrimination between

① Alexander Forbes, M. P. , (CPD, House, 9 May 1973), 1908.

② *Ibid.* .

③ Leonard Keogh, M. P. , (CPD, House, 9 May 1973), 1911, 1913.

different types of migrants. Grassby picked up on this theme in his reply to MPs responses to his second reading speech:

> The Opposition has attempted tonight to turn back the tide of history. It has rejected the concept of Australian citizenship as the badge of a free, strong and independent people… How could any Minister responsible for immigration and citizenship go out to the million here and now and the tens of thousands still coming and draft them off like so many sheep and cattle, saying: "You go to the one year pen; you go to the 3-year pen; you to the 5-year pen… Italians, Dutch, Germans, Greeks and Lebanese to the right and wait for 3 years; Tongans, Zambians, Canadians, British and Indians to the left and wait for one year if you are light enough and 5 years if you are not". ①

Grassby pleaded to all members of Parliament to look at the citizenship legislation in a non-partisan way instead of on the level of petty party politics. The Bill simply recommended that all discrimination be removed from the conditions for the grant of Australian citizenship to migrants. ②

In another speech on the *Australian Citizenship Bill of 1973* Grassby attempted to draw links between the current citizenship legislation and its predecessor in 1969:

> The present leader of the Opposition when Minister for Immigration introduced a Citizenship Bill in 1969 which showed a progressive outlook by recognising the growing importance of the

① Al Grassby, M. P., (CPD, House, 9 May 1973), 1925, 1926.

② Ibid., 1926.

status of Australian citizen. That Bill specifically provided that an Australian when asked to state his nationality had only to say "I am an Australian citizen" … "What this Government now puts to this House in the present Australian Citizenship Bill is that it is time we progressed still further towards reality by ending the artificial discriminations in the present Act, in the matter of requirements for Australian citizenship. "①

However, his call fell on deaf ears. Though the Bill passed the House of Representatives relatively easily due to the government's majority in that house. It faced a much tougher time in the Senate where the Opposition held the balance of power. Grassby was forced to accept some amendments to his legislation, in particular migrants having the choice to swear allegiance to the Australian Constitution *or* to the Queen.

So, I have shown above the way in which the end of the British World led to a redefinition of citizenship in Australia between the 1950s and 1970s in relation to ethnic groups. The article will now turn to Aborigines and the redefinition of citizenship in Australia between the 1950s and 1970s. Again with the end of the British World in Australia, and a move towards a ' New Nationalism ', Australia's Aboriginal population was regarded as something that made it unique. This new focus drew attention to the inequalities that existed between White Australians and Aborigines. Therefore, governments became more receptive to introducing changes which began to incorporate Aborigines more into ideas of citizenship.

---

① NLA, MS 7798/Series 3/Box 40: Speech by Minister for Immigration, The Honourable A. J. Grassby on Australian Citizenship Bill 1973, 2.

Awarding of the right to vote for Aborigines in 1961

There was considerable pressure on the government from various lobby groups to give Aborigines the vote for the federal franchise. One of the most vocal lobbyists was Lady Jessie Street who was affiliated with the Anti-Slavery League of the UK and in many ways dedicated her life to improving the status and conditions of Aborigines. In a letter to Prime Minister Robert Menzies in early 1960 she placed the refusal of the Australian government to give Aborigines the vote in a broader international context:

> Canada is giving their Indians the vote; I enclose a copy of the Canadian Bill… It seems that the Governments of Australia, South Africa, the U. S. A. and Portugal are the only ones who have not changed their attitude and still deny political rights to their coloured people…In view of these developments I am writing to ask you to consider reviewing our Australian policy towards our Aborigines. I believe that all adult Aborigines should be given full political rights… I feel most humiliated that Australia should be regarded as so backward in her treatment of her native people. ①

E. C. Gare, President of the Western Australian Native Welfare Council who also wrote to Menzies and made some very effective constitutional arguments in late 1960, added to this pressure:

> My Council has requested me to submit for the consideration

① NLA, MS 2683/Series 10/Box 27/File 7: Jessie Street to Robert Menzies, Prime Minister of Australia, 9 March 1960, 1, 2.

> of your Cabinet, a proposal that an amendment be made to the Commonwealth Electoral Act for the purpose of allowing Australian Aborigines to enrol and vote for the Federal Parliament… As the Commonwealth Government is prohibited from making special laws for the people of the Aborigine race it would seem that race should come within the jurisdiction of all laws common to other Australians and there should be no discrimination against Aborigines in any way by special law. If this argument holds, it is unconstitutional to exclude aborigines from voting for Commonwealth Parliament. ①

Alexander Downer, in his capacity as Acting Prime Minister conceded that there appeared to be no constitutional impediment to the revision of the *Commonwealth Electoral Act* suggested by Gare. ②

Gare though followed up his letter with a further one to Menzies in April 1961 in which he maintained that "the Commonwealth has a duty to see that all persons born in Australia are full and free citizens of the Commonwealth and entitled to vote for Commonwealth elections irrespective of any State law as to State Electoral enrolment." And he hoped that "early action can be taken to amend the Commonwealth Electoral Act so as to remove this injustice against Aborigines."③ Again Downer replied to him in his capacity as Acting Prime Minister a few months later:

> As previously stated, I am advised that the Constitution places no bar on the Commonwealth Parliament allowing the enrolment

① NAA, A463 1966/793: E. C. Gare, President, W. A. Native Welfare Council Inc. to Robert Menzies, 22 November 1960, 1. This was a reference to Section 51 (xxvi) of the constitution, which stated that the Commonwealth had the right to make special laws for all races, other than the Aboriginal race in any State.

② NAA, A432 1960/3289 PART 2: Alexander Downer, Acting Prime Minister to Gare.

③ NAA, A463 1966/793: Gare to Menzies, 8 April 1961.

> and voting of aborigines. Whilst I would not agree that the provisions of the Commonwealth Electoral Act which at present prevent certain aborigines from voting are contrary to section 51 (xxvii.) of the Constitution, I would agree that there is nothing in section 51 (xxvii.) to prevent the Commonwealth from extending the Commonwealth franchise to all aborigines, if it should be desired to do this as a matter of policy. ①

In actual fact the government at the instigation of the Minister for the Interior had already agreed that a select committee be appointed to look into and report back on whether the right to registration and the franchise currently awarded by the *Commonwealth Electoral Act 1918-1953* on individuals mentioned in section 39 of that legislation should be expanded with or without conditions, restrictions or qualifications to all aboriginal groups of Australia; aboriginal groups of Australia grouped in specific categories, and if so, what categories; and if so, the adjustments, if any, that should be made to the clauses of that legislation regarding to registration or the franchise. ②

After gathering evidence and deliberating for several months the *Report of the Select Committee on Voting Rights of Aborigines* was tabled in Parliament on 19 October 1961. The major recommendations were that the *Commonwealth Electoral Act* should be revised to allow for: all aborigines of voting age to be awarded the franchise; registration should be voluntary but exercising the franchise should be compulsory for Aborigines who were registered; early administrative action should take place to make registration and exercising the franchise compulsory for Aborigines in New South Wales and Queensland as these Aborigines had

---

① NAA, A432 1960/3289 PART 2: Downer to Gare, 4 July 1961, 1.

② NAA, A463 1966/793: Background Note on "Select Committee on Voting Rights of Aborigines" by Mr. J. McCusker, 8 August 1961, 2-3.

long been a part of the Australian community; and Aborigines who were entitled to be registered and to exercise the franchise should be informed of their right. [①]

Press reaction to the report was generally extremely positive, with *The Canberra Times* remarking that "Few Parliamentary reports have had more human warmth than that of the Select Committee on Voting Rights for Aborigines which has recommended that the right to vote at all Commonwealth elections be accorded to all Aboriginal and Torres Strait Islander subjects of the Queen."[②] The *Sydney Morning Herald* hoped "that the Federal Government will accept the committee's view and, in due course, legislate accordingly."[③]

The Age added that Aborigines "Unlike women … have no suffragette movement to press their case, but joint committee of the House of Representatives has surveyed their case with a calm, unprejudiced eye, and recommended without qualifications they should enjoy the same voting rights as white Australians."[④] The *West Australian* related the report to the situation in Western Australia: "Though the committee was confined to consideration of the franchise, its conclusions in reaching unanimous finding that all aborigines and Torres Strait Islanders be given the right to a Federal vote carry the conviction that all natives should have full citizenship."[⑤]

Increasing overseas interest in the plight of the Aborigines was communicated in a telegram from the Department of External Affairs to all posts at the beginning of 1962:

---

① NAA, A463 1966/793: Outward Cablegram from Department of External Affairs to All Posts, 19 October 1961.

② NAA, A1838 557/1 PART 2: Australia and Foreign Affairs-Digest of Press Opinion on Report of Parliamentary Committee on Voting Rights for Aborigines, 25 October 1961, 3.

③ *Ibid.*, 4.

④ *Ibid.*, 1.

⑤ *Ibid.*, 3.

> Overseas interest in the Aborigines is still small, but it has increased during the past year, and could rapidly increase still further, particularly in countries whose policies are greatly influenced by racial discrimination. As the number of colonial dependencies diminishes, the scope of anti-colonist attacks will become increasingly restricted, and political agitators in Asia, Africa and Latin America are likely to indulge instead in emotional criticism of other countries' domestic policies, especially where these appear to involve discrimination by white people against coloured people. ①

Thus, overseas interest in the Australian government's policies towards its Aborigines was becoming a growing concern.

The Cabinet considered the Report of the *Select Committee on Voting Rights of Aborigines* and agreed that the *Electoral Act* should be revised to: give Aborigines and Torres Strait Islanders, of voting age, the right to register and exercise the franchise; making exercising the franchise after registering, but not registering itself, compulsory for them; and make the exercise of pressure or undue influence, in relation to registration, an offence on top of the current offence in relation to exercising the franchise. ②The *West Australian* in April 1962 emphasised the significance of the legislative changes based on this decision: 'The Bill to extend Federal voting rights to all Australian aborigines is a landmark in post-Federation history…It can now be only a matter of time before natives in all parts of Australia are given the right to vote at State as well as Federal

① NAA, A1838 557/2 PART 3: Savingram from Department of External Affairs to All Posts, 12 January 1962, 2.

② NAA, A4940 C3496: Cabinet Minute-Decision No. 52, 13 February 1962.

elections. '[①] But a contrary, much more critical view was taken by Jessie Street the following month:

> Gestures are being made of appointing Select Committees, amending laws and regulations…to give the appearance of removing discriminations against aborigines, but the basis of these discriminations, sections 127[②] and 51 (xxvi) remains. While aborigines have not the constitutional status and rights of full citizens they will be victims of discrimination. [③]

Repeal and amendment of these sections was the basis of the 1967 referendum. It is no coincidence that this took place just as the "New Nationalism" was replacing Britishness as the basis of Australian national identity. As mentioned above, this major shift in national identity, with Aboriginality being regarded as something that made Australia unique, Australian governments became more willing to act to extend the rights associated with citizenship that Aborigines had been denied for so long.

The 1967 Referendum

There is some considerable historiographical debate surrounding the significance of the 1967 referendum. The referendum ultimately sought to

---

① "Natives' Voting Rights", *West Australian*, 20 March 1962, 6. Western Australia and the Northern Territory did indeed give Aborigines the State or Territory votes that same year.

② This referred to the section of the Australian constitution, which declared that Aborigines should not be counted in the census.

③ NLA, MS 2683/Series 10/Box 28/ Folder 16: Comments on Report from the Select Committee of Voting Rights of Aborigines by Jessie M. G. Street, April 1962, 4. Margaret Thornton who argues that 'Enfranchisement certainly did not guarantee instantaneous admission to the community of equals' supports this. Margaret Thornton, "Legal Citizenship" in Hudson, Wayne and Kane, John (Eds), *Rethinking Australian Citizenship* (Cambridge: Cambridge University Press, 2000) 118.

repeal Section 127 of the constitution and repeal the words 'other than the Aboriginal race in any State' from Section 51 (xxvi). According to Tim Rowse, "The common narration of the 1967 referendum is to exaggerate its benefits, declaring it to be the moment when Aborigines attained 'citizenship' …This is strictly speaking, a misconception."① Nevertheless, Rowse does concede that the amendment of the Constitution in the 1967 referendum is regularly reflected upon by Aborigines of a younger generation as the point at which Aboriginal people were "granted citizenship". ②Bain Attwood and Andrew Markus go even further and maintain that "The 1967 referendum to alter Australia's Constitution is now seen as an event that marked a major turning point in Aboriginal-European relations in Australia."③ Christine Flether even goes as far as saying that "The 1967 constitutional referendum was the turning point in Aboriginal affairs—a watershed in their cultural and political freedoms."④ My own opinion is that though its practical effect is certainly debatable, its symbolic value was extremely important.

Government moves towards considering constitutional amendments regarding Aborigines began in early 1965 with a Cabinet Submission by Billy Snedden, the Attorney-General:

> There would assuredly be international approbation of any

① Tim Rowse, "Diversity in Indigenous Citizenship", *Communal/Plural*, Vol. 2, 1993, 49.

② Tim Rowse, "Indigenous Citizenship" in Hudson, Wayne and Kane, John (Eds), *Rethinking Australian Citizenship* (Cambridge: Cambridge University Press, 2000) 92.

③ Bain Attwood and Andrew Markus, "Representation Matters: The 1967 Referendum and Citizenship" in Peterson, Nicholas and Sanders, Will (Eds), *Citizenship and Indigenous Australians: Changing Conceptions and Possibilities* (Cambridge: Cambridge University Press, 1998), 118.

④ Christine Fletcher, "Living Together but not Neighbours: Cultural Imperialism in Australia" in Havemann, Paul (ed.), *Indigenous Peoples' Rights in Australia, Canada & New Zealand* (Auckland: Oxford University Press, 1999), 336.

> move to repeal section 127, as it savours of racial discrimination. Its repeal could remove a possible source of misconstruction in the international field… I think also that the average elector would feel that either the Commonwealth should have the power in section 51 (xxvi) in relation to all races, including people of the aboriginal race or ought not to have the power at all; and I believe the failure to include a proposal to delete the underlined parts might well prejudice the success of a referendum that wants the repeal of section 127. ①

However, the Cabinet only agreed to the abolition of Section 127 of the Constitution being put to referendum simultaneously as the question of the nexus②. ③

This led to pressure being applied on the government by Faith Bandler, New South Wales State Secretary of the Federal Council for the Advancement of Aborigines and Torres Strait Islanders (FCAATSI) on 30 April 1965④. FCAATSI⑤was the leading organisation calling for constitutional amendments regarding Aborigines,⑥ and Faith Bandler was a particularly passionate and conscientious advocate of the organisation:

---

① NAA, A5840 507: Submission No. 660-Constitutional Amendments: Sections 24 to 27, 51 (xxvi.), 127 by B. M. Snedden, Attorney - General, 22 February 1965, 12, 14.

② The nexus referred to the constitutional arrangement in which there had to be roughly double the number of Senators in the House of Representatives in the Australian Parliament.

③ NAA, A5840 507: Cabinet Minute-Decision No. 841, 7 April 1965.

④ For more on Faith Bandler see Marilyn Lake, *Faith: Faith Bandler, Gentle Activist* (Sydney: Allen & Unwin, 2002).

⑤ For more on FCAATSI see Susan Taffe, *Black and White Together, FCAATSI: The Federal Council for the Advancement of Aborigines and Torres Strait Islanders* 1958-1973 (St. Lucia, Queensland: University of Queensland Press, 2005).

⑥ For an exploration of the impact of FCAATSI's campaign efforts on Australian public opinion see Murray Goot & Tim Rowse, *Divided Nation: Indigenous Affairs and the Imagined Public* (Carlton, Vic.: Melbourne University Press, 2007) 55 - 59.

> A Referendum to amend the Commonwealth Constitution will be held later this year and the Government has already agreed to include in this the repeal of Section 127 which discriminates against Aborigines by excluding them from the census. However there is another section of the Constitution which also discriminates against Aborigines and the Government is still hesitant as to whether or not to include repeal of Section 51 Clause xxvi in the forthcoming Referendum. ①

Snedden attempted to secure Cabinet agreement to have the words "other than the aboriginal race in any State" removed from the Constitution again on 23 August 1965. ②But the Cabinet once again refused to support this. ③The *Sydney Morning Herald* a few months later questioned whether the proposed referendum went far enough as "it will still leave the Commonwealth Government without any direct responsibility for Aboriginal advancement outside the Northern Territory, and it will still leave power of 'discrimination' in the hands of the various States."④

Mrs. L. Lippmann, Convenor of the Legislative Reform Committee of FCAATSI in a letter to Snedden early the following year commented that it appeared likely that proposals for the inclusion of the amendment of Section 51, Placitum xxvi of the Constitution would be put before Parliament. And she emphasised the importance of this

① NLA, MS 2693 Series 10/Box 27/File 9: Letter from Mrs. Faith Bandler, N. S. W. State Secretary, The Federal Council for Advancement of Aborigines and Torres Strait Islanders (FCAATSI), 30 April 1965.

② NAA, A5827 VOLUME 31: Cabinet Submission No. 1009-Constitutional Amendments: Sections 24 - 27, 127 and 51 (xxvi.) by B. M. Snedden, Attorney-General, 23 August 1965, 5.

③ NAA, A5827 VOLUME 31: Cabinet Minute-Decision No. 1175-Submission No. 1009-Constitutional Amendments: Sections 24 - 27, 127 and 51 (xxvi.), 30 August 1965, 2.

④ "Does Referendum Go far Enough", *Sydney Morning Herald*, 17 November 1965, 2.

initiative, which would enable FCAATSI and other organisations working for the advancement of Aborigines to vociferously campaign for the referendum proposals. ①Her enthusiasm was most likely due to Menzies' successor as Prime Minister, Holt taking office just a few weeks earlier. He was considered more receptive to including the second proposal on Section 51 (xxvi) and consequently announced a few weeks later that the government had decided not to hold the proposed referendum (which included only the one proposal) that year. ②

It was left to the new Attorney-General, Nigel Bowen to raise the issue again at the beginning of 1967. He argued in a Cabinet Submission that:

> The Government announce that it will hold a referendum to seek legislative power for the Commonwealth with respect to aborigines by omitting the words "other than the aboriginal race in any State" from section 51 (xxvi.) and, if the referendum is successful, will hold discussion with the States to formulate a joint policy whereby the States will be responsible for administration, but the Commonwealth will have a role of policy participation. ③

The Cabinet finally agreed to this course of action the following month. ④Holt announced the government's intention to include two proposals concerning Aborigines in a constitutional referendum very soon

---

① NAA, A432 1967/3321 PART 1: Mrs. L. Lippmann, Convenor, Legislative Reform Committee, The Federal Council for Advancement of Aborigines' and Torres Strait Islanders (FCAATSI) to B. M. Snedden, Attorney-General, 2 February 1966.

② NAA, A432 1967/3321 PART 1: Referendum-Statement by the Prime Minister, Mr. Harold Holt, 15 February 1966, 1.

③ NAA, A406 E1967/30: Cabinet Submission on 'Constitutional Amendment: Aborigines' by Nigel Bowen, Attorney-General, January 1967, 8.

④ NAA, A5840 79: Cabinet Minute-Decision No. 79, 22 February 1967.

after: "Our intention, Mr Speaker, is to put through the necessary legislation relating to these proposals as soon as practicable…I expect it to be introduced in this House within the next week or two…We proposed to have the measures passed by the two Houses as expeditiously as possible."① The Leader of the Opposition, Gough Whitlam expressed the Opposition's support for both measures. ②The *Sydney Morning Herald* explained the government's shift in position as a reaction to the persuasive arguments made by William Wentworth, a government backbencher who had introduced a Private Members Bill along similar lines the previous year. ③

FCAATSI immediately swung into action. It published several information pamphlets to promote a "Yes" vote for the two Aboriginal proposals in the upcoming referendum. ④It is no exaggeration to say that FCAATSI's extensive campaigning was the reason for the success of the Aboriginal proposals in the referendum on 27 May 1967. An illustration of this is an expose on Faith Bandler in *The Australian Women's Weekly* in May 1967. She maintained that "A Yes vote will mean that the Aboriginal people can come under Commonwealth law…Aborigines are the only Australians who live under six separate laws, one for each State …The eyes of the world are on Australia and her handling of black Australians…Not only Asia is watching but Africa and the whole Western

---

① Harold Holt, M. P., (CPD, House, 23 February 1967), 115.

② Gough Whitlam, M. P., (CPD, House, 1 March 1967), 264.

③ "Aborigines", *Sydney Morning Herald*, 28 February 1967, 2.

④ NLA, MS 8256/Series II/Sub – Series II/Box 175: "YES" vote-Information (1) Referendum-Federal Council for the Advancement of Aborigines and Torres Strait Islanders, 31 March 1967, 1, 2; NLA, MS 8256/Series II/Sub – Series II/Box 175: "YES" vote-Information (3) Referendum-Federal Council for the Advancement of Aborigines and Torres Strait Islanders, 31 March 1967, 1, 2; NLA, MS 8256/Series II/Sub – Series II/Box 175: Vote "YES" on both questions-Referendum Day-Voting is Compulsory, 27 May 1967.

world."[①]

The general press reaction to the Aboriginal referendum proposals was overwhelmingly positive.[②] Bandler drew attention to the public confusion though on the Aboriginal issue in The *Sydney Morning Herald* a few days before the referendum. She pointed out that many Australians thought a "Yes" victory on the Aboriginal question in the referendum would give Aborigines the vote-whereas in actual fact they already had this. Bandler laid the blame for this confusion firmly at the federal government and political parties' doorsteps, as they had not played much of a role at all in the campaign. She suggested that perhaps the government thought the Aborigines question would assist it in also securing support on the nexus question. Bandler showed this through the fact that the fifteen-page pamphlet, which the Commonwealth government handed out to all voters, included only two and a half pages on the Aborigines question.[③]

In the actual event there was an overwhelming majority in support of the constitutional amendments in regard to Aborigines-over 90 per cent (the biggest Yes vote in the history of federal plebiscites ever), whereas the nexus proposal failed dismally.[④] Nevertheless, The *Sydney Morning Herald* pointed out that it was depressing that the largest No vote was recorded in parts of Australia where the question had real impact—in

---

① NLA, MS 8256/Series 11/Sub - Series II/Box 175: Says a friend of the Aborigines: "Let's tell the world there's only one Australian, and his color doesn't matter at all" by Kay Keavney, Australian Women's Weekly, 10 May 1967.

② "Appeal For Yes Vote To Realise 'Dream'", *Sydney Morning Herald*, 13 May 1967, 9; "Holt Puts Yes Cases", *Sydney Morning Herald*, 16 May 1967, p. 1; "The Yes Case", *Age*, 17 May 1967, 5; "A Good Look at the Aborigines", *Sydney Morning Herald*, 17 May 1967, 6; "The Final Week", *Sydney Morning Herald*, 22 May 1967, 2; "Holt, Whitlam End 'Yes' case", *Canberra Times*, 25 May 1967, 12; "YES Vital to Help Aborigines", *Age*, 26 May 1967, 3; "No. 2: Aborigines", *Sydney Morning Herald*, 26 May 1967, 4; "Shoulder to the Wheel", *Age*, 26 May 1967, 5.

③ "Public Confusion Evident on Aboriginal Issue", *Sydney Morning Herald*, 24 May 1967, 4.

④ "Record Yes on Second Issue", *Sydney Morning Herald*, 29 May 1967, 1.

other words, in places where there were Aborigines to resent and to be prejudiced about: 'The No vote was worst in the three States—Western Australia, South Australia and Queensland—that have been most criticised for their treatment of the remaining Aboriginal population.'①

In the time after the 1967 referendum the federal government was reluctant to act on its new authority to legislate for Aborigines. ②The federal government set up an Office of Aboriginal Affairs after the 1967 referendum. But there was small substantive change until the change of government in 1972. ③Hence, Attwood and Markus conclude 'that the government's belated decision to conduct the referendum was a rather uninterested, even cynical, one that had little if anything to do with any program of change in Aboriginal affairs, and much more to do with maintaining the status quo, shoring up the government's position at home, and bolstering Australia's image abroad.'④ But as well as allowing the Whitlam government in 1972 to enter the policy field the successful referendum also put pressure on the subsequent Fraser government to stand up to the Queensland and Western Australia state governments. In this sense, its practical impact was important in the longer term.

So, the move away from an ethnic (British) based citizenship to a more civic based one led to the Commonwealth Government making some initial moves towards incorporating Aborigines into ideas of national citizenship. However, emphasis should be placed on *initial*, as it was in the 1980s that Aboriginal activism forced governments to make more substantial reforms, especially in terms of land rights.

In conclusion, this article has shown how the end of the British

---

① "The Referendum", *Sydney Morning Herald*, 29 May 1967, 2.

② John Chesterman and Brian Galligan, *Citizens without Rights: Aborigines and Australian Citizenship* (Cambridge: Cambridge University Press, 1997), 186.

③ Christopher Cunneen and Terry Libesman, *Indigenous People and the Law in Australia* (Sydney: Butterworths, 1995), 42.

④ Attwood and Markus, "Representation Matters", 125.

World led to a redefinition of citizenship in Australia between the 1950s and 1970s. The UK's first application for entry into the EEC in 1961 and the announcement of its military withdrawal from 'East of Suez' in 1967 were particular highlights, which signaled the end of the British self-identification of Australia. Through focusing on the *Citizenship Act of 1969* and the *Australian Citizenship Act of 1973* the article has demonstrated the way in which non-British migrants were put on a much more equal basis to their British counterparts in being able to attain Australian citizenship and exercise the benefits of Australian citizenship, such as employment in the Public Service. It has also illustrated the way in which the awarding of the right to vote for Aborigines in 1961 and the 1967 Referendum which removed the constitutional discriminations against them actually allowed Aborigines to exercise the rights of Australian citizenship which they had theoretically held since 1948.

摘要：20世纪50年代，澳大利亚经常把自己当作大英帝国体系中的一个重要国家。然而到了20世纪70年代，这个大英帝国体系已经不复存在，澳大利亚作为英国的自我认同也一并消失。在这一时期，澳大利亚公民身份需重新定义，从以英国血统为基础到更加多元化地包括其他种族和澳大利亚原住民，这是一个重要的转变。本文认为，公民身份的重新定义主要是在澳大利亚国家身份转变的背景下发生的。本文将首先确认澳大利亚的英国身份已经结束这一背景，随后探讨《1969年公民身份法案》和《1973年公民身份法案》的内容，以此说明澳大利亚的公民身份变得更加多元。最后，本文将研究1961年原住民获得选举投票权和1967年宪法公投两起事件，强调这一时期的原住民也开始被纳入澳大利亚公民的范围。

关键词：大英帝国　公民身份　澳大利亚　原住民

Chinese Kangaroos: Thoughts on Four Decades of a Bilateral Relationship

Jocelyn Chey*

From the late 1970s through to the 1990s, I collected Chinese kangaroo figurines. Some were given to me and some I bought for myself since during that whole period, I was working and travelling in China. When some friends contributed to my collection, by the time I was appointed Consul-General for Australia in Hong Kong in 1992, I had a dozen little figurines that I put on display in my office. They were not valuable in monetary terms, but to me they represented one important thing: that, since the establishment of diplomatic relations in 1972, people in China had begun to know more about my country as evidenced by its unique icon, the kangaroo. Remembering this collection, I decided to collect some perspectives on the development of cultural relations between China and Australia, in which I played a minor role, as a series of "kangaroo tails". (The pun is intended.) These tales are more than anecdotes. They demonstrate how cultural exchanges and cross-cultural communication inspire creativity and innovation and ultimately, empathy and understanding. This is the goal that drives all of us, translators, scholars, cultural ambassadors and

---

* 梅卓琳（Jocelyn Chey），西悉尼大学教授，任教于西悉尼大学中澳艺术与文化研究院。

humble workers in universities and cultural institutions.

Just about all the figurines in my collection were "wonky" . The first one I acquired was made by Director Chen of the Pottery and Porcelain Bureau of the Ministry of Light Industry. He presented it to me when I left Beijing in 1978 (he himself retired in that year) . He had hosted a visiting group of Australian potters and led a delegation to Australia under our official cultural exchange program. Director Chen was an amateur potter and this model was a souvenir of his visit to Australia. He made it in a mould as is common for figurative pottery and he told me he had trouble fitting the tail into the mould so he had curled it around the kangaroo's front legs like a cat's tail. He pointed this out to me and said that, although he had not observed such a pose while in Australia, he hoped it might be an occasional characteristic. Unfortunately, it is not. (See Fig 1 below) The kangaroo tail is in fact thick and fairly inflexible. It sticks out behind and often serves as a prop or a fifth leg.

Fig. 1 Two of the collection of "Chinese kangaroos" . Photo courtesy of *Mingbao yuekan*

The kangaroo can truly be called an icon of Australia, being unique to that continent. Over the last two hundred years it has also been endowed in the popular imagination with several traits that are regarded as typically Australian. It was regarded as something very strange when first seen by early European explorers and settlers. There is some speculation that the Dutch may have recorded images of kangaroos as early as the 17th century. Dutch explorer Dirk Hartog reached the West Coast of Australia in 1616 and there may have been other ship contacts even earlier. Mapmaker Cornelis de Jode (1568-1600) showed the southern continent in a map of the world dated 1593 in which it is possible that the strange creature at the bottom right of the decorative shield is intended to represent the kangaroo since there are two young animals held in a sort of pouch on the chest of the beast. (This heraldic art continues the tradition of medieval exotic images of the world outside European civilisation.)①

When Lieutenant James Cook sailed round Australia and New Zealand in the late 18th century, the strange plants and animals his party discovered were of great interest to the general public and the scientific community in England and Europe. Cook took home a kangaroo skin and George Stubbs (1724-1806) was commissioned to paint a picture of the animal using the skin for reference for exhibition to the scientific community. Stubbs was a well-known painter of racing horses, stud bulls and even Indian tigers. His paintings provided meticulous detail of the selected animals, highlighting their individual traits and characteristics. His portrait of a Spanish Pointer hunting dog, for instance, records how it crouches, flattening its back, pointing its head and raising one paw to show that it has located the prey. In the case of the kangaroo, it is upright—as he intuited from the difference between the front and back

① John Simons, *Kangaroo*, Reaktion Books, London, 2013, p. 69.

legs—but there is no indication of how it might move or respond to its environment. The stylised background draws on Stubbs' familiarity with English landed estates and Scottish moors. The skies pile up clouds and pour sunshine on the figure in the foreground for dramatic effect. The portrait provides perspective, but not explanation or understanding. It is not possible to judge even the size of the kangaroo, let alone capture its relationship to other animals or its habitat. If anything, it looks vulnerable and inhabits an empty landscape ripe for exploitation, the *terra nullius* of the British explorers. (See Fig. 2 below.)

Fig. 2 George Stubbs, *The Kongouro from New Holland* (1772)

The name "kangaroo" was first recorded by botanist Joseph Banks in 1770. Banks accompanied Cook on his voyage up the east coast of Australia and collected this name when the HMS Endeavour stopped at Cooktown in North Queensland. He wrote the word as *Kangaru*, derived from the local Yuugu Yimithirr language word *ganguru*. [①]Actually this

① Wendy Moore, *The knife man: Blood, body-snatching and the birth of modern surgery*, Random House, 2010, pp. 318 - 320.

word refers to the Grey Kangaroo only and not to any other type of the genus Macropus but "Kangaroo" is now applied to all four main types including Red, Eastern Grey, Western Grey and the tropical Antilopine. (Tree-kangaroos and rat-kangaroos belong to a different species of marsupials, as do wallabies and wallaroos.)

In 2018 there are probably twice as many kangaroos as people across Australia, and the numbers have undoubtedly grown during the past 200 years because forest was cleared for pasture under European settlement and this benefited kangaroos, who are primarily grass-eaters not forest creatures. Australian farmers have a love/hate relationship with kangaroos, since they compete with sheep and cattle on the pasturelands, but generally speaking Australians value kangaroos highly, and since the latter half of the 19th century they have come to be an icon of the nation.

After Federation in 1901, the kangaroo featured in the new national Coat of Arms along with the emu. It is commonly said that these two creatures were chosen because neither animal can move backwards, so they symbolise a nation bound to move forward. It is also said that the kangaroo must always be shown as a male, reflecting the sexism of the time. This is why the kangaroo in the Australian Coat of Arms has no pouch. The kangaroo's symbolic significance grew during the 20th century as the new nation became more engaged internationally. Over the decades the icon acquired personality traits such as feistiness and swagger and these were also regarded as typical Australian characteristics. In 1950 a Warner Bros cartoon short movie titled *Pop 'Im Pop!* featured Sylvester the Cat and Gracie, a "fightin' kangaroo". The global appeal of Hollywood movies helped to cement this iconic image. The trope of the boxing kangaroo derives from the ritualised fighting of male kangaroos, which looks like a boxing match. In the 19th century outback travelling shows in Australia sometimes featured a fight between a boxer and a red kangaroo wearing boxing gloves. Later, this image of the boxing kangaroo was used when Australia won the "America's Cup" yachting race in 1983, a notable international sporting victory. The same symbol is used by the Australian national rugby league team, who are called "The Kangaroos".

China and the kangaroo

According to Gao Yongwei 高永伟, the first reference to the word "kangaroo" in a Chinese dictionary is in William Lobschied's *English and Chinese Dictionary with the Punti and Mandarin Pronunciation* (1866-1869).① Clearly, before that time, Chinese returning from the goldfields of Victoria and New South Wales had brought some knowledge of Australia back with them, including tales of kangaroos. However, the term used in the Lobschied dictionary was *chang-wei lü* 长尾驴 or "long-tailed donkey", not *daishu* 袋鼠 or "pocket rat", which has been the standard Chinese term since the early 20th century. It is possible that the Cantonese used *lü* (Cantonese *lou*) because this sounds like "roo", a common abbreviation of "kangaroo," widely used even today, or because deer are auspicious animals in the cultural imagination, unlike rats, which are vermin.

When did the first kangaroo reach China? Although Zheng He 郑和 sailed west through the Malacca Straits in the 14th century, it is most unlikely that his fleet reached Australia, and he is also unlikely to have brought kangaroos back for the Imperial Zoo in Beijing as was suggested by Gavin Menzies in his 2002 best-seller *1421: The Year China*

① See https://www.mq.edu.au/about_us/faculties_and_departments/faculty_of_human_sciences/linguistics/linguistics_research/az_research_list/australian_style_blog/australian_style_archive/volume_19_no_1/australian_english_in_english-chinese_dictionaries/.

Discovered the World. [①]However, this fanciful idea inspired a mythical landscape painting by Sydney-based artist Guan Wei 关伟, exhibited by OCAT (*Dangdai yishu zhongxin* 当代艺术中心), Shenzhen, in 2011. Guan Wei's work explores explorer, immigrant and refugee experiences and the strange birds and animals in this landscape are modern interpretations of medieval mythical beasts like the heraldic animals in de Jode's map of the world. This particular landscape is not totally fantastic, however, since the silhouetted kangaroos places it firmly in Australia, but it is a concocted back story for kangaroos and their place in cultural exchanges with China. [②]

Kangaroos, zoos and museums

It is possible that a kangaroo could have been brought to China in the 19th or early 20th centuries, after early Chinese migrants travelled to the "New Gold Mountain" of Australia. If this did happen, the animal would probably would have been placed in a zoo, as zoological gardens proliferated around the world from the late 19th century on, providing modern scientific education facilities for the general public. China's oldest zoo, the Peking Zoo, certainly acquired an Australian emu some time before the Japanese War, the emu being the other animal featured on the national Coat of Arms—so is quite likely also to have had a kangaroo. The emu was recorded later as one of the few animals to have survived the War; most of the others died of starvation and neglect.

I was posted to Beijing in 1975 as the first Cultural Attaché in the new Australian Embassy, with the diplomatic rank of Counsellor. My duties including the encouragement and supervision of scientific,

---

① http://www.gavinmenzies.net/Evidence/10 - annex - 10 - evidence - of - chinese - fleets - visit - to - australia - - - west - coast/.

② http://www.leapleapleap.com/2011/10/guan - wei - spellbound/.

educational and cultural exchanges and one of my first duties was to visit the Beijing Zoo. Meeting the Zoo Director, I learned that they were keen to add Australian animals to their collection and had already commenced discussions with counterpart zoos in Australia. The time was ripe to encourage zoological exchanges. (Of course, we hoped that Australia might secure a panda in those years of "panda diplomacy," but that did not eventuate until many years later.) This was the earliest stage of cultural exchanges, of "getting to know you" and of focussing on the exotic and the "otherness" of the two cultures. An agreement was reached for red pandas to be given to the Taronga Zoo in Sydney in exchange for a pair of kangaroos for Beijing. In preparation for the new arrivals, I briefed the zoo on their requirements for accommodation and food.

When the kangaroos arrived, I made a "consular visit" to check on their welfare. It was depressing to see them housed in a rather small enclosure with little room for exercise. I remember I made some comments to the officials who accompanied me. Of course, this was still a time of economic hardship and living conditions were hard for everyone, not just for zoo animals. Perhaps my expectations were a little unrealistic. It was also a time when both countries were getting to know each other, and not long after the 1972 Communique that set out Australia's "One China Policy".

As a complement to the zoo exchange under the terms of the cultural agreement between the two countries, an exhibition of museum specimens of native fauna, the "Australian Fauna Specimens Exhibition" (澳大利亚动物标本展览), visited China in 1976. The exhibition travelled to Beijing, Shanghai and Guangzhou and was in China for six months in total. It was curated by the eminent zoologist Peter Stanbury. He flew to Beijing for the official opening and gave lectures in all three centres as well as in Hangzhou. Besides displays of specimens, the exhibition included audio-visual material showing, for instance, colourful Australian birds and the extraordinary reproductive system of the kangaroo. I accompanied Dr Stanbury to Shanghai for the opening of the exhibition and have two kangaroo tales arising from that visit.

The first story illustrates how the socialist management structures of that time were not fully conducive to the development of cultural relations with the Western world. Dr Stanbury and I were staying in the elegant Jinjiang Hotel in Shanghai, which was almost empty. There were few overseas business visitors and no tourists. Meals were served in the dining room on the ninth floor. Hotel guests could not choose where they sat (or when or what they ate) and were assigned to a particular table. Our table was reserved for us by a sign that read 澳大利亚动物标本二人（Australian fauna specimens: two persons）. This made us both laugh and I had to explain our laughter to the restaurant staff. They did not take it as a joke. The manager immediately gave instructions for the sign to be changed and apologised in person for any offence caused. I remember this story now with some affection because it illustrates the ridiculous inflexibilities that we all had to cope with under the antiquated management systems of the time.

The second story relates to the technical staff member sent from Australia to ensure that the audio-visual displays were in good working condition for the whole duration of the exhibition's time in China and illustrates the fact that cultural exchanges can have unexpected consequences. One should not rush to evaluate their success or failure but look at them later and see how they have contributed to the long-term development of cultural relations and mutual understanding.

This Australian technician was a typical rough diamond, a very competent guy from the Northern Territory, self-reliant and unflappable. His one weakness was a fondness for beer. He was accommodated in the Jinjiang Hotel in Shanghai for several months while he was looking after the exhibition. As there were no public venues in the hotel apart from the restaurant, and the restaurant itself was only open between specified hours in the evening (from memory, from 6 to 7.30pm), and as there were very few international visitors staying in the hotel with whom he might have chatted in English and no nightlife outside the hotel, he used to order three bottles of beer before the restaurant closed and take them to his room to drink at his leisure.

His interpreter/minder was concerned about the effect on his health of drinking so much beer and probably thought it might affect his ability to look after the exhibition. When the Aussie commented that he was forced to drink alone because there was no public bar in the hotel, the hotel management said they used to have a bar before the Cultural Revolution but they had packed all the equipment away when the political troubles started. Now they had forgotten how to set up the bar but they were willing to try re-opening it. They asked our man to help identify what was needed and advise them. So, for the remainder of his time in Shanghai, he helped set out the stools, the beer mugs and coasters, and when everything was ready he spent his evenings in the bar. This was the first bar to re-open after the Cultural Revolution in Shanghai, and possibly in the whole of China. Other hotels across town sent their staff to learn how it should be done. I am happy to claim that this was a by-product of the Australia-China cultural exchange program and of the arrival of kangaroo specimens in Shanghai.

Kangaroos and currency

In the 1970s, there were few tourist groups visiting China and no outbound tourism at all. Unsurprisingly, the general public knew little about Australia and had only a hazy image of our icons such as kangaroos. The Australian Government established the Australia China

Council in 1979 with the aim of expanding understanding and exchanges beyond official visits by government representatives and delegations, thus underwriting our two countries' long-term future relationship. As the first Executive Director of the Council, I accompanied Council Chairman Professor Geoffrey Blainey and Deputy Chairman Stephen FitzGerald on several visits to China in the early 1980s. In 1980, we learned of the establishment of the first Australian Studies Centre in China at Anhui University, headed by Professor Ma Zuyi 马祖毅, and we paid him a visit.

Professor Ma presented the delegation with a poem he had composed and wrote himself. It was later reproduced in the Council newsletter. It reads:

> A poem
>
> To the tune of *Wanxixia*, dedicated to our friends from Australia.
>
> True is the saying, "A distant land can be brought nigh,"
>
> Though separated by mountains and seas, genial friendship is forging its links
>
> And we feel our hearts warm to each other even before we meet.
>
> There is no barrier in the sphere of cultural exchanges
>
> And the colourfulness of literature is appreciated by all,
>
> So you remember our Li Bai and we admire your Lawson.
>
> Ma Zuyi, Head, Oceanic Literature Research Unit, Anhui University
>
> Presented to the delegation from the Australia China Council on their visit to the Research Unit on 3 June 1980.

We were warmly received by Professor Ma and university leaders but taken by surprise when they informed us that the entire student body had assembled in their largest auditorium and were waiting for us to give a lecture about Australian history and culture. Geoffrey Blainey is a well-known author and an experienced teacher but he had never been given such short notice to speak. I was fully prepared for him to decline the invitation but he thought that would be discourteous. He asked for a few minutes to prepare, and turned to Dr FitzGerald and myself, asking us to turn out our pockets and see what Australian money we might have. He then used our collection of notes and coins to give an introduction to Australian history and culture. This was the second stage of cultural exchange, of providing context and commentary on the exotic, to promote understanding.

The six kangaroos that now feature on the Australian dollar coin were not part of Professor Blainey's talk because that coin was only released in 1988 to mark the bicentenary of European settlement. In 1981 Australian decimal currency (introduced in 1966) included one, two, five and ten cent coins that depicted various native animals and birds. The fifty-cent coin was a twelve-sided design featuring the national coat of arms with the kangaroo and emu. Blainey used these to show that Australia had a unique natural environment and a distinct evolutionary path where marsupials had developed in a way not found anywhere else in the world. He also pointed out that the reverse side of each coin featured the Queen's head, since she was the head of state, and followed by describing how Australia had a British-style parliamentary system with an upper and lower house both being elected (not like the British system where membership of the Upper House is by appointment or hereditary title).

Then Blainey showed the students a one-dollar note that featured contemporary Aboriginal art with a kangaroo design. The design, by David Malangi, an Aboriginal artist from Arnhem Land in the Northern Territory, showed the local Manharrngu people's traditional funeral feast, where kangaroos were the most important element. The note paid respect in this way to traditional Aboriginal culture, which predates European arrival by tens of thousands of years, although it also had a watermark of James Cook, the British explorer who arrived in Australia in 1770. Geoffrey Blainey has always paid great respect to the cultural traditions and history of the first inhabitants of Australia. In his lecture in Hefei, he pointed out that the Royal Australian Mint had never paid David Malangi for his design and that the government clearly believed at that time that copyright did not apply to traditional Aboriginal art. It was H. C. (Nugget) Coombs, the first Governor of the Australian Reserve Bank, who, believing that this was unjust, had rectified the situation in 1967 and authorised payment to David Malangi of $1, 000, a medallion and some fishing gear. In this way, the lecture at Anhui University introduced Aboriginal culture into our cultural exchanges through the role of the kangaroo.

Incidentally, the two-dollar note in circulation at that time featured two important figures in Australian economic history and their stories provided the final part of Professor Blainey's lecture. These people were John Macarthur, a pioneer of agricultural settlement, and William Farrer, a respected agricultural scientist. Macarthur, a pioneer settler, bought merino sheep in South Africa in 1796, brought them to Australia and started Australia's fine wool industry. William Farrer developed the disease-resistant, high-yielding "Federation" variety of wheat that was distributed to farmers from 1903, that is, two years after Federation. In the 1980s primary commodities such as wool and wheat were pillars of the Australian economy and constituted the bulk of our exports to China. That would change over the next decade.

In 2017 there was an art exhibition in the Whitlam Gallery at Western Sydney University by Chinese Australian artist Tianli Zu 祖天丽. Dr Zu, a graduate of the Central Academy of Fine Arts, Beijing, has been resident in

Australia for thirty years and is an Adjunct Professor of WSU. The exhibition, titled *Missing*, was a multi-media installation exploring shadows, memory, time, space and all aspects of the concept of "missing." One large-scale work in the exhibition, called *Not For Sale*, featured semi-abstract landscapes with inserts of the kangaroo one-dollar coin. It is a sad reflection on the wilful destruction of the forest habitat of kangaroos and other native animals for commercial development. Absence, or "missing" is also a significant element of cross-cultural understanding. ①

Celebrities meet kangaroos

In the second half of the 1980s, I returned to Beijing as Commercial Counsellor, in charge of trade and investment. It was an exciting time of reform and opening up. The Australian presence in China grew rapidly. Australian banks, trading companies and manufacturers all opened representative offices. It was a constant whirl of activity. I travelled north and south, east and west across China, following up commercial opportunities. Prime Minister Bob Hawke came to Beijing on an official visit. Just before I arrived, General Secretary of the Chinese Communist Party had visited Australia. Unlike previous state leaders, his visit was not confined to Canberra, Sydney and Melbourne. Instead he flew to the remote Pilbara region of West Australia, where red kangaroos are more plentiful than people. The Pilbara has the world's richest deposits of high-quality iron ore, typically reefs rising from surrounding plains. Here the Chinese government planned its first major overseas investment. This was truly a kangaroo leap, a signal to the world that China was engaging with the world economy and that its relationship with Australia had entered a new phase. Minerals and energy would dominate the trading relationship for

① http://www.tianlizu.com/2017_ Missing.html.

the next two decades, although they have now given way to services such as education and tourism. In this stage of cultural understanding the emphasis was on adaptation, complementarity and cooperation.

President Xi Jinping has visited every state and territory of Australia, including Tasmania, the smallest and least-populated state. He has met national and state leaders and is acquainted with our indigenous animals. From the first years of diplomatic relations onwards, photo opportunities with kangaroos have featured in the programs of most visiting Chinese dignitaries. Mme Peng Liyuan met a kangaroo when she accompanied President Xi Jinping to a meeting of ASEAN Heads of State in Brisbane in 2017.

Kangaroos that are introduced to visiting dignitaries are carefully selected for their friendly and placid nature. This is not always the case. In 1982 I and my family stopped for lunch at a pub in the Monaro high country south of Canberra and met a kangaroo in the paddock at the back of the pub building. This kangaroo was used to visitors and seemed to be friendly, but when he discovered that we had not brought any offerings of food, he became very aggressive. He pinned me between his strong front legs and started kicking with his back legs. My husband had to rescue me. I was left with deep scratches on my arms, and a lasting aversion to kangaroos.

These days kangaroo encounters are no longer reserved for senior officials and government representatives. People-to-people contacts are increasing every year, with growing business contacts, student exchanges and tourism. Consequently, more people in China are familiar with kangaroos and, indeed, they do not need to leave the country if they wish to see them as many zoos in China have acquired kangaroos. In Australia, Chinese tourists are also more adventurous, not confining their trips to major cities but venturing also into rural and remote areas in the hope of seeing kangaroos, emus and other wildlife. Of course, they bring home kangaroo souvenirs, even though these are mostly made in China! Increasingly they do not see kangaroos as quaint exotica but understand how they relate to their environment and their world, and they begin to incorporate their own cultural references.

Chinese Australians meet kangaroos

After the establishment of diplomatic relations in 1972, many Russian people who had been long-term residents in China left to settle in Australia. One such person is Sergei Ivanov, also known as Yao Dixiong, who grew up in Yili, Xinjiang Province. As a child he was fascinated with horses, which are famous in that region, and learned to paint them. After moving to Australia, he continued to work as an artist and in the 1980s he was given a grant by the Australia China Council to create a giant scroll painting of two hundred kangaroos in landscapes taken from various parts of the Australian continent. He completed this mammoth project in time for the celebration of two hundred years of European settlement in Australia. The scroll was later exhibited in Australia and China. Yao Dixiong's work represents a new stage in cross-cultural understanding, using traditional style to frame the work, he placed the animals in their natural environment and in various poses illustrating their habits, although still with a superficial understanding of the complexities of kangaroo typology. ①

The Australia-China Council recognises the significant role that Chinese Australians can play as a bridge between two cultures. In the 2016 national census, 1, 213, 903 people identified themselves as having some Chinese ancestry. Since the 1980s, and particularly in the

① A short documentary recording Yao's two great murals titled "Australian spirit, Chinese heart" is available at https://www.youtube.com/watch?v=bkFuXyAhBhk.

last two decades, the number of Chinese Australians has been growing steadily. The community is now a significant part of Australian society and includes many leaders in business, finance, education, science and the arts who have made outstanding contributions to Australian society and culture. The art scene has been greatly enriched by artists who have settled here. I have mentioned Guan Wei, Tianli Zu and Yao Dixiong. There are many others, including Yixi Ruan, a CAFA graduate who lives in North Queensland. Seeing Australia through Chinese sensibilities and with a strong dose of humour, she paints kangaroos and other native fauna and flora that convey the relaxed, laid-back lifestyle of her new home. A new level of cross-cultural communication is evident where the kangaroo is effortlessly incorporated into a multicultural lifestyle incorporating elements of East and West. ①

Kangaroos and cross-cultural understanding

I have kangaroo-hopped swiftly through 45 years of cultural exchange, illustrating the development of cross-cultural understanding with a series of kangaroo tales. I began with an introduction to my collection of "Chinese Kangaroos." Their "wonkiness" represented a first stage in cross-cultural understanding. They were created by artists and craftsmen who, like George Stubbs when he painted the "Kongorou," had never seen the animals in their natural habitat. They had to rely on imagination and their own experience to create something that made sense in their own terms. That is why they focused on the exotic aspects of the animal, and when they supplied context to this, they simply made assumptions.

① Examples of Ruan's work may be found on her agency website, https://bluethumb.com.au/yixy.

When newcomers to Australia learn more about kangaroos they come to understand how they relate to their habitat and how they interact with other animals and with humans. They come to distinguish kangaroos from wallabies. They learn from farmers why they need to keep kangaroo numbers in check. They appreciate the cultural importance of the kangaroo in Aboriginal culture. The simple icon of the kangaroo acquires multi-layered significance. So, the tale of the kangaroo reflects and encourages cross-cultural creativity. The process of cross-cultural understanding reminds me of what Umberto Eco wrote about reading a book:

> Literary works encourage freedom of interpretation, because they offer us a discourse that has many layers of reading and place before us the ambiguities of language and of real life. ①

Understanding the kangaroo is an essay in cross-cultural communication. The Orientalist representational venture must be replaced by one that is "participatory and collaborative, non-coercive, rather than imposed" as Edward Said said. ②

George Stubbs was handicapped by a gap in geographic space between the object and its representation, and a gap in understanding between the artist and the subject. He was also handicapped by distance and life experience. He worked in the medium he knew and, where he had no experience, he filled in the blank space and moulded the image to fit his conventional understanding of how things ought to be. (Those of us who have engaged in translation will immediately understand this intellectual process.)

Contemporary Australian artist Imants Tillers' work attempts to

---

① Umberto Eco, *On Literature*, London, Vintage, 2006, p. 4.

② Edward Said, quoted in Gauri Viswanathan, ed., *Power, Politics, and Culture: Interviews with Edward W. Said*, New York, Vintage, 2005, p. 12.

understand and interpret the land and the spiritual environment of Australia. He lives in Cooma on the northern side of the Australian Snowy Mountains. His art, like those bleak upland hills, is bare and unforgiving. He has made this regional sensibility his hallmark. What was marginal and peripheral is central in his work.

In his 1988 painting "Kangaroo Blank," Tillers starts with Stubbs' "Kongourou," using the same landscape and cloudscape but removing the central subject, the kangaroo. In its place there is a black rectangle-a void. This does not mean that the background becomes the foreground. The kangaroo remains central but it is both present and absent, in the Buddhist sense of self-annihilation and enlightenment. This is shown by the rays of light emanating from the "Blank" . The viewer is led to engage with the kangaroo at a deep spiritual level, not just to understand it but to experience it intimately and to consider it in perspectives created by the panels of light and shade that break up the background (See Fig. 3 below.).

Fig3. Imants Tillers, *Kangaroo Blank*, 1988

Tillers' work is deeply influenced by Asian religion and philosophy and particularly by the contemporary Japanese artist/architect Shusaku Arakawa 荒川 修作 (1836 – 2010) . New York-based Arakawa and his partner Madeline Ginns wrestled with the "mechanism of meaning", that is, with how new thought is produced by a collision of types. In artistic terms, the process of understanding and interpreting something new and strange, leading to the re-assessment of existing assumptions, results in an explosion of creative energy. ①

All of us are engaged in the process of understanding, interpreting and recreating the world around us, not only to make sense of it and to correct errors, but, hopefully, like Tillers, to create a new and better world, new inspirations and "Kangaroo Blank" .

摘要： 袋鼠为澳大利亚独有，同时也是澳大利亚的国家象征。我个人收藏了一些 1970 ~ 1980 年中国制造的袋鼠小雕像，它们促使我思考中澳间文化相互理解的最初阶段。同样，英国艺术家乔治·史塔布斯（George Stubbs）于 18 世纪 80 年代创作的袋鼠画显示，人类对袋鼠习性及其所处的自然环境认识有限。一些与袋鼠相关的故事展示出中澳文化交流发展的初级阶段。近年来，艺术家们对此问题获得了更深刻的文化理解。现阶段的文化交流能用澳大利亚艺术家提勒斯（Imants Tillers）的作品《袋鼠空白》（*Kangaroo Blank*）加以阐释。

关键词： 袋鼠　提勒斯　文化交流　文化理解

① Shusaku Arakawa and Madeline Ginns, *The Mechanism of Meaning*, Harry N Abrams, New York, 1978.

澳大利亚工党派系之争对澳大利亚外交政策的影响

——以鲍勃·卡尔外长与吉拉德总理在巴勒斯坦“入联”问题上的交锋为例

戴　宁*

摘要：2012 年 11 月 29 日，第 67 届联合国大会对巴勒斯坦申请成为联合国观察员国议案进行了表决。澳大利亚在巴勒斯坦“入联”问题上，一直保持着与美国和以色列一致的立场，投反对票。而此次，作为刚刚成为联合国安理会非常任理事国的澳大利亚出人意料地投了弃权票。这是澳大利亚外长鲍勃·卡尔（Bob Carr）与吉拉德总理进行了激烈交锋，成功地迫使掌握外交决定权的总理吉拉德改变了决策的结果，使澳大利亚顺应了国际大趋势，维护了澳大利亚作为“中等强国”在国际社会的声誉。本文通过分析外长与总理在提升巴勒斯坦地位问题上的交锋，探讨了澳大利亚工党内部派系之争与澳大利亚对外政策的关系。本文认为，鲍勃·卡尔和吉拉德尽管都在不同层次上、从不同角度考虑了国家利益，但更重要的是双方都深受国内选举政治因素和党派利益的影响。鲍勃·卡尔主要对其所在的新南威尔士州工党席位存有担忧，希

* 戴宁，北京外国语大学英语学院副教授，研究方向为澳大利亚政治体制。

望通过在外交上谋求平衡公正的巴以关系，支持巴勒斯坦提升联合国地位来换取阿拉伯人和穆斯林选民在联邦大选中对新南威尔士州工党议员的支持，而吉拉德及其总理办公室幕僚在考虑到争取全国选民，保住工党的竞选优势的同时，又重点以维多利亚州的犹太人选民作为其主要的政治根基，加上犹太人院外集团的强大制约作用，导致外长与总理在巴以政策上发生了严重分歧。从这一事件可以看出，在吉拉德工党政府的外交决策中，投票背后往往牵扯着选票，党派利益常常被置于国家利益之上。

关键词： 澳大利亚工党　鲍勃·卡尔　朱莉娅·吉拉德　外交政策

2012 年 11 月 29 日，第 67 届联合国大会经过两个多月的辩论，对其中一个重要议案——巴勒斯坦申请成为联合国观察员国进行了表决。中国、土耳其、埃及、巴西、阿尔及利亚、阿根廷等近 70 个国家是该决议草案的共同提案国。巴勒斯坦在 2011 年 9 月开始寻求成为联合国的正式会员国，但这一努力遭到美国和以色列等国的反对，而最终未能获得安理会批准。此次巴勒斯坦改变方式，退而求其次，争取获得联合国的“观察员国”地位。联合国 188 个成员国参加了投票，结果是 138 票赞成，9 票反对，41 票弃权，以超过 2/3 票数通过了将巴勒斯坦现有联合国“观察员实体”地位升格为“观察员国”（non-member observer）的决议（《联合国大会第 67/19 号决议》）。换言之，巴勒斯坦被国际社会承认为“事实上的主权国”（De Facto Sovereign State），而不仅仅是一个政治实体，因此有资格申请加入国际刑事法院（ICC），并通过国际刑事法庭提出自己的诉求。中国、俄罗斯、法国和印度等大国都投了赞成票，但美国、以色列和加拿大等国坚持反对立场。英国、德国和澳大利亚则投了弃权票。

澳大利亚在巴勒斯坦“入联”问题上，一直保持与美国和以色列立场一致，认为巴勒斯坦应当与以色列直接谈判，在此基础上获得国际社会对其主权国家地位的承认，巴勒斯坦强行“入联”对于巴以和平进程有害无益。但这次澳大利亚作为联合国安理会非常任理事国，出人意料地投了弃权票，而并未一如既往地支持以色列和美国的立场。此举令澳大利亚国内外舆论一片哗然。政府反对派对吉拉德（Julia Eileen Gillard）工党政府更是大肆抨击。其实，吉拉德政府原本打算按既定方针投反对票，但在最后关头却微妙地改变了立场。

为什么会出现这一结果？一个关键人物——澳大利亚外长鲍勃·卡尔发挥了举足轻重的作用，在很大程度上，是他成功地迫使掌握外交决定权的总理吉拉德改变了决策。通常来讲，外长的职责是贯彻和执行联邦政府的外交政策，维护国家最高利益，代表国家处理外交事务，但为什么鲍勃·卡尔外长能够超越权限，迫使吉拉德政府在巴勒斯坦入联问题上改变立场？他又是出于什么动机而坚决要求吉拉德政府投弃权票呢？本文将通过分析澳大利亚鲍勃·卡尔外长与吉拉德总理在提升巴勒斯坦地位问题上的交锋，来回答以上问题，同时探讨澳大利亚工党内部独特的派系之争是如何影响澳大利亚的对外政策的。

一　鲍勃·卡尔与吉拉德在巴以政策上的严重分歧

鲍勃·卡尔是澳大利亚工党资深政治家，被认为是一个与时俱进、能言善辩的现代工党领袖楷模。鲍勃·卡尔 1947 年 9 月出生于悉尼郊区，1964 年以优异成绩高中毕业，是他家族中第一个高中毕业生。中学期间，他就加入了澳大利亚工党的地方支部，投身政治，1970 年成为新南威尔士州的支部书记，两年后当选为全澳青年工党书记，可见其出色的政治天赋和工作能力。1984 年，37 岁的鲍勃·卡尔在赖恩（Neville Wran）领导的新南威尔士州工党政府内出任规划与环境部部长。1988 年，工党败选后，鲍勃·卡尔被推举为反对党领导人，肩负工党改革的重任，其间他对国际事务和美国历史与政治发展产生浓厚兴趣，立志进入联邦政府从政，理想是担任澳大利亚的外交部部长或驻美大使。1995 年他竞选新南威尔士州州长成功，之后在民生、经济和地方立法方面进行了多项改革，并投入大笔资金改善基础设施，成绩斐然，赢得民心，显示了其雷厉风行的领导才能和风格，故 1999 年和 2003 年两次连任，直到 2005 年 7 月辞职隐退，前后任职十年，是新南威尔士州历史上任职时间最长的州长。

2012 年 2 月，时任澳大利亚外长的陆克文（Kevin Michael Rudd）因与工党领袖、政府总理吉拉德及多位内阁同僚矛盾激化，在访美期间突然宣布辞去外长一职，随即提出挑战现任工党领袖的职位。工党 27 日就领导权问题举行议会党团票决。总理吉拉德以 71 比 31 票战胜挑战者陆克文，继续担任工党领袖，并宣布改组内阁，包括任命新外长。在工党新南威尔士州支部极力推荐下，吉拉德邀请了一直对国际外交事务颇有兴趣、已隐退六年的老政治家鲍勃·卡尔重新出山，接任外交部部长一职。吉拉德对外交政策并无多大兴趣，但又希望她的政府在外交事务上能够与前任政府有所不同并有所创新，显示中等强国风范，因此她需要一个像鲍勃·卡尔这样的人物，既有丰富的从政经验，精明能干又雄心十足，勇于改革。而鲍勃·卡尔本人也欣然接受了吉拉德的邀请，虽然任职从 2012 年 3 月至 2013 年 9 月，仅有 18 个月时间，但也算实现了他在联邦政府从政的心愿。

鲍勃·卡尔担任外长后摩拳擦掌，期待在短暂任期内建功立业。作为澳大利亚外长，他的首要责任和使命毫无疑问是维护和提升澳大利亚在国际社会的形象和地位，在此意义上，他所取得的最突出成绩是帮助澳大利亚获得了国际社会的信任和支持，顺利当选为 2013 ~ 2014 年安理会非常任理事国。同时，他还协助吉拉德政府与中国建立起战略伙伴关系，加快澳大利亚融入“亚洲世纪”的步伐，并且积极促进中东地区的和平，尤其是巴以和平，以提高澳大利亚作为中等强国在国际社会中的作用和声誉。他力图改变澳大利亚政府亲美、亲以“一边倒”的传统立场，而促成澳政府对提升巴勒斯坦在联合国地位的决议投弃权票正是他所取得的最大成果。

鲍勃·卡尔深受其导师、前工党外长加雷斯·埃文斯（Gareth Evans）思想的影响，一直认为澳大利亚作为中等强国对于巴以问题应持公平、积极态度，而对于政府表现出太过软弱、有所偏向的立场十分不满，尤其认为以往联合国有关巴勒斯坦决议表决时，澳大利亚始终站在美国、以色列以及几个太平洋小国之列，成为不折不扣的“一小撮”反对国，这一立场是与整个世界对抗，逆历史潮流而动。这种做法对期望在新世纪跻身世界有影响国家之列，推动历史发展的澳大利亚是个不光彩的记录。他认为，“我们居然与利库德集团亦步亦趋，这助长了以色列最恶劣的本能，纵容他们一步步走向自我毁灭，同时也把我们摆在马绍尔群岛和加拿大之流的地位上。我们在与整个阿拉伯世界和巴勒斯坦人唱对台戏。”①

不仅如此，鲍勃·卡尔就任外长后很快发现，任何关于以色列定居点的事情，哪怕是用“我们表示关切”这样的表述都会被总理和总理办公室否决，任何与以色列相关的中东事务，澳大利亚政府都以犹太人关切为重，这使得鲍勃·卡尔对政府的中东政策更为不满，对以色列产生反感：

> 由于我对定居点问题表示了担忧，招来以色列院外集团的抱怨。按照此理，我们简直不能“表示担忧”了，否则就会遭抱怨。这些游说团锱铢必较，分毫不让，一贯如此霸道。他们到底打算怎样？想让澳大利亚宣布完全支持以色列，支持他们将巴勒斯坦领土统统变成自己的殖民地？想让我们敦促其扩大定居点数量，增加到50万以上？增加一倍？总理的幕僚布鲁斯·沃尔普出主意，让我跟“那个社区”进行一次电视会议。我回答道：没门儿。②

---

① Bob Carr, *Diary of a Foreign Minister*, New South Publishing, 2014, p. 212.

② Bob Carr, *Diary of a Foreign Minister*, New South Publishing, 2014, p. 5.

澳大利亚涉足巴勒斯坦在联合国地位的投票问题也与它争取获得联合国安理会非常任理事国密切相关。上任伊始，鲍勃·卡尔就马不停蹄，长途奔波，出访世界各国，在各种场合施展浑身解数，为澳大利亚在2012年10月联合国表决时争取足够票数进入安理会。澳大利亚政府为拉选票花费了2400万澳元用于游说活动，并承诺向国际社会提供30亿澳元对外援助。

阿拉伯国家对澳大利亚的支持无疑颇为重要，但澳大利亚亲美、亲以的中东政策一直遭阿拉伯国家诟病。2011年，联合国教科文组织曾讨论和表决了接纳巴勒斯坦为正式成员国的问题，澳大利亚一如既往地投了“反对”票，而173个国家压倒性地投了“赞成”票，另有52个国家投了弃权票，这使澳大利亚处于一个只有14个国家的少数派地位，这一小撮国家中包括美国、加拿大和马绍尔群岛等。因此，鲍勃·卡尔出任外长后一心想改革和调整澳大利亚对巴以的政策，尽量平衡与以色列和阿拉伯国家的关系。他深感，如果澳大利亚想要赢得阿拉伯国家的好感和支持，澳大利亚政府不能如此这般地继续充当少数派。“我希望我们能说：我们投弃权票，至少可以说我们不会反对你们的决议。”因为，“支持他们提升地位是一种政治利益。如果我们投‘反对’票，我们会丢掉所有阿拉伯国家的票，一共有二十多票呢，那我们也就别想成功了。”①

为了使澳大利亚政府在巴以问题上实施平衡政策，争取阿拉伯国家支持澳大利亚“入常”，鲍勃·卡尔可谓煞费苦心。一方面，他必须说服吉拉德总理接受对巴以政策的微调，从反对变为中立。他以各种方式劝说吉拉德，希望让她明白，巴勒斯坦成为联合国“观察员国”的决议不会影响以色列的利益，或者影响它在巴勒斯坦地位最终谈判上的位置。外长还希望让她相信，此次表决如果澳大利亚连弃权票都不能投，那将极大地影响澳大利亚的国际地位，阻碍澳大利亚将来在安理会有所作为。但吉拉德不为所动，坚持认

① Bob Carr, *Diary of a Foreign Minister*, New South Publishing, 2014, p. 180.

为“在巴勒斯坦决议问题上缺乏明确立场是我们由来已久的问题，这个问题还会继续存在下去。所以说，在这个问题上没有什么灵活性可言。”[①]

另一方面，鲍勃·卡尔试图在中东问题上向阿拉伯国家和北非国家表示同情，释放善意。例如，2012 年 9 月，外长在联合国大会解决以色列与黎巴嫩燃油污染纠纷事宜期间，专门飞赴开罗，会见黎巴嫩外长，对他明确表示：“这次联大提出动议时，澳大利亚的表现会不同于以往，我们会有更多同情心。”[②] 此事起因是 2006 年以色列发动空袭，炸毁黎巴嫩吉耶发电厂储油罐，万吨重质燃油泄漏，造成黎巴嫩和叙利亚沿岸一百多公里海域被污染，为此，联大提出动议，要求以色列向黎巴嫩赔偿污染治理费，但以色列在美国的支持下拒绝赔偿，因此联大每年都提出此动议。[③] 澳大利亚一直都是投反对票，理由是澳大利亚认为在这个问题上，联合国大会不是一个恰当的讨论场合。而此时，鲍勃·卡尔希望通过某些承诺，改善同阿拉伯国家的关系，从而拉拢阿拉伯国家联盟和非洲国家支持澳大利亚“入常”。

鲍勃·卡尔在游说活动中对中东国家许下的承诺，实际上基本得不到吉拉德政府内阁的支持。因此，外长一干人马在中东外交上提心吊胆，如履薄冰，生怕会得罪他们煞费苦心拉拢到的阿拉伯人和非洲人，致使他们争取澳大利亚“入常”的努力付诸东流。

2012 年 10 月，在联合国安理会非常任理事国的选举中，澳大利亚获得了 193 个成员国中的 140 票，其中包括阿拉伯和非洲国家的支持，这使澳大利亚如愿以偿，历史上第 5 次担任联合国安理会非常任理事国。

鲍勃·卡尔为自己付出外交努力取得成功感到异常兴奋。但由

---

① Bob Carr, *Diary of a Foreign Minister*, New South Publishing, 2014, p. 189.

② Bob Carr, *Diary of a Foreign Minister*, New South Publishing, 2014, p. 223.

③ 2014 年 12 月 19 日，联合国大会最终以 170 票赞成、3 票弃权、6 票反对的投票结果，通过了要求以色列向黎巴嫩赔偿高达 8.5 亿美元的污染治理费的决议。投反对票的国家分别是以色列、美国、加拿大、澳大利亚、密克罗尼西亚和马绍尔群岛。

于其承诺屡遭吉拉德政府内阁的否决，以至承诺往往都最终变成空头支票，从而使鲍勃·卡尔背负不仁不义之名，这让他颇为恼火。外长还曾承诺支持由埃及提出的在中东地区实现核不扩散、建立无核区的议案，并说服澳大利亚政府予以支持。但 2012 年 11 月初，当外长向吉拉德政府提出让澳大利亚驻联合国代表投票赞成埃及议案时，这个提议再次被吉拉德政府内阁枪毙。与此同时，鲍勃·卡尔还欲温和地谴责以色列在东耶路撒冷兴建 1500 幢住宅是明目张胆的扩建定居点行径，但他的“谴责”表述也被吉拉德总理办公室驳回。他认为，就连英国保守党政府尚且可以使用“谴责”一词来发表针对以色列的声明，为什么澳大利亚工党政府不可以。但他却得到吉拉德这样的回复：“一，我们不使用‘谴责’一词；二，发表声明必须经过她的幕僚布鲁斯·沃尔普（Bruce Wolpe）和内阁部长马克·德雷弗斯（Mark Dreyfus）同意；三，不管我们采取什么行动，都要首先告知以色列大使。”[①] 这样一来，当初投票支持澳大利亚入常的中东国家都纷纷在私下里指责澳大利亚翻脸不认人。

在这种情况下，2012 年 11 月 29 日，澳大利亚对联大关于巴勒斯坦申请成为“观察员国”的决议投什么票成了一个关键的考验。如果澳大利亚继续投反对票，那么鲍勃·卡尔的中东平衡外交努力将再次受挫，而且将再度失信于中东国家，那么他日后的外交努力将会遭遇重重困难，澳大利亚在国际社会的声誉和影响力也将受到削弱。因此，外长此时的想法就是必须促使吉拉德政府在巴勒斯坦“观察员国”投票问题上有所改变。

二 投票与选票：国家利益还是党派利益优先

澳大利亚政府对巴以问题的立场和政策，无疑是由澳大利亚的国家利益及其基本外交战略决定的，即无论是自由党还是工党，都

① Bob Carr, *Diary of a Foreign Minister*, New South Publishing, 2014, p. 213.

以澳美同盟为基石，并把保持与美国的密切合作关系作为澳大利亚对外政策的核心，故此在巴以问题上，亲美、亲以是吉拉德政府坚定不移的立场和政策。但吉拉德政府的外交政策还在很大程度上受制于国内政治因素。鲍勃·卡尔外长试图调整澳大利亚对巴以和中东的政策，而吉拉德政府则坚持僵化死板的亲以色列政策，国内选举政治和工党派系利益之争是一个根本的原因。

吉拉德工党政府非常重视跟以色列和犹太人的关系，除了追随美国政策的因素之外，主要有三大内部原因。首先，吉拉德的政治生涯起源于维多利亚州墨尔本选区，以墨尔本为核心的维多利亚州是她的政治大本营，因而她严重依赖该地区选民的支持，其中墨尔本的犹太选民对于吉拉德和工党颇为关键。根据 2011 年人口普查，澳大利亚有近 10 万犹太人，其中三分之二聚集在墨尔本。在这座城市里，有许多活跃于政治圈的犹太人领袖和众多犹太社团，分别代表商界、学术界、文化艺术界等各种不同的利益诉求，但他们共同组成了一个统一的“澳洲/以色列犹太人理事会”［Australia/Israel & Jewish Affairs Council（AIJAC）］，各个不同的犹太社团都是该理事会的成员，而理事会领导层则在一个所有成员认同的机制下，公开公平地选举产生。

澳洲犹太人理事会多年来在澳洲社会积极反映犹太社区对联邦及各州有关政策的意见和建议，并通过其各成员的社会影响力，为犹太社区争取各项合法权益，包括建立犹太教堂、犹太学校等。这个组织明确提出，要通过澳大利亚政府、媒体和其他团体机构，促进澳大利亚犹太人社区的利益和福祉，致力于研究分析亚洲中东等地的发展机遇，并且致力于通过游说政府相关部门，资助媒体和政界人士到以色列游学，出版月刊等，消除人们对以色列的偏见和媒体的不良信息，揭露种族主义和反犹太人的行为和宣传，促进澳大利亚建立繁荣和谐的多元文化社会。[①] 澳洲犹太人理事会在澳大利亚的内外政策制定上，扮演着重要的压力集团角色。由于它积极维

① 见 AIJAC 官网，http：//www. aijac. org. au/about - aijac/。

护少数族裔在澳大利亚主流文化中的做法收效显著，其他族裔群体纷纷效仿。澳大利亚的华人政党领袖在谈及华人参政时常常提及犹太人院外集团的坚持不懈和保护犹太人权益的成功经验，包括运作方式。[①] 有鉴于此，吉拉德以及工党政治家都无法忽视犹太人社区，尤其是维多利亚州犹太人选民的能量和利益，从而深受犹太人社团的影响。

第二，吉拉德能够取代陆克文成为工党领袖，完全是工党内部为获得联邦大选的胜利而做出的布局和选择。2010 年 6 月，在工党占主导地位的右翼议员们认为陆克文民意大降，可能危及工党在 2010 年 8 月的联邦大选，于是维州和新州的右翼大佬们联起手来，扶持吉拉德而将陆克文拉下马。虽然工党最终击败自由党取得胜利，但也只是一次险胜，而且出现了战后第一次悬峙议会（无多数议会"Hung Parliament"）和弱势工党政府。2012 年 2 月吉拉德连任工党领袖，此时所面临的最大任务，就是要带领工党在 2013 年 8 月新一轮大选中再度赢得胜利。因此选票优先，党派利益优先和保住工党执政权，无疑是她推行内外政策的首要原则。改变和调整澳大利亚的中东政策，就有可能动摇她和工党的选民根基，吉拉德显然不会冒这样的政治风险。

第三，工党为了与时俱进，争取选民，自 20 世纪 80 年代后开始转型，从群众型政党向全方位政党转型，一方面淡化了社会主义意识形态，出现了工联主义左翼和自由主义右派的分歧，而且是右派占据主导地位，另一方面扩大了政党的基础，广泛吸收中间阶层选民，打造"全民党"形象。工党的资金来源也发生了深刻变化，工会资金只占少数份额，大部分资金来源于工商企业捐助、党费和社会捐助。[②] 澳大利亚犹太人大多属于中上阶层，而且积极参政干政，因此工党与犹太人社区的关系非同一般。吉拉德身边两个最重要的人物都与犹太人关系密切。1991 年才从美国移居澳大利亚、

① 王国忠、黄兆强等人关于华人的参政访谈。

② 赵婷：《澳大利亚工党政党转型过程分析》，《中国社会科学报》2012 年 7 月 18 日。

曾为澳洲传媒巨头“费发斯传媒”（Fairfax Media）行政总裁的布鲁斯·沃尔普，作为吉拉德的高级顾问、发言人及商界联络人，事事以犹太人关切为重，吉拉德的内阁部长马克·德雷弗斯则被认为是“一位精明的以色列和犹太人支持者”。

工党向来以派系斗争激烈而著称，即便同属右派，新南威尔士州工党右派与维多利亚州右派之间亦存在巨大分歧，这个分歧也体现在如何对待阿拉伯和穆斯林选民问题上。鲍勃·卡尔外长试图迫使吉拉德政府改变和调整对巴以的政策，从深层上分析，有着争取新南威尔士州选民对工党议员支持的重要考虑。至 2011 年，大约有 48 万穆斯林移民居住在澳大利亚，其中差不多有一半来自黎巴嫩、埃及、伊拉克和伊朗等中东地区。澳大利亚还有近 10 万的科普特人（来自埃及的基督教徒）。在鲍勃·卡尔看来，这些科普特人在澳大利亚建立起良好的社区，是值得争取的选民。以外长所在的悉尼为中心的新南威尔士州选区中，阿拉伯人和穆斯林移民数量不断增加，尤其集中在悉尼西南部，此外悉尼的科普特人高达 7 万人。鲍勃·卡尔及一批新南威尔士州议员认为，新南威尔士州是多元文化大熔炉，多元文化和种族在这里有很大势力，反对党自由党正在赢得这一选民群体的支持，而工党在这里的支持率则堪忧，因此争夺阿拉伯人和穆斯林选民，保住新南威尔士州工党席位是当务之急。而争夺阿拉伯人和穆斯林选民最有效的办法，就是在中东问题和巴以问题上调整澳大利亚亲美、亲以的政策，以此向这部分选民表达工党的善意。

鲍勃·卡尔在推动吉拉德总理调整中东政策屡遭失败后，决心在巴勒斯坦“观察员国”投票问题上全力一搏，况且他要实现的调整仅仅是从投反对票变为投弃权票而已。由于工党内部派系利益对立，从总理和外长角度看各有当务之急，各不相让，而且由于总理在拥有决定权的内阁里不顾多数阁员反对，一意孤行，坚持己见，因此鲍勃·卡尔决定将争论议题拿到自己更具影响力的议会党团，利用议会党团各派大佬，迫使代表维州右派的总理改变在联合国巴勒斯坦地位问题上一贯投反对票的做法。这一决定更符合新南威尔士州和澳大利亚工党主流的利益。

外长紧锣密鼓地游说各重要内阁成员和议会党团成员支持自己的主张，赢得了不少议员包括内阁成员的支持。新南威尔士州有些右派议员，如克里斯·鲍文（Chris Bowen）［他在麦克马洪选区（Division of McMahon）的席位岌岌可危］，托尼·伯克（Tony Burke），约翰·墨菲（John Murphy），都急于做出一些积极成绩，以便对他们选区里越来越多的阿拉伯人和穆斯林民众有所交代。悉尼奇夫利选区（Division of Chifley）的艾德·胡西奇（Ed Husic）是有波斯尼亚穆斯林背景的议员，他无疑也站在外长一边，甚至直接跟以色列大使通电话，谴责以色列不要对加沙的哈马斯进行狂轰滥炸。在外长与总理摊牌之前，工党曾经进行过一场党内重要代表参加的讨论，讨论的核心内容就是澳大利亚的各种立场在国内是意味着赢得选民，还是失去选民。“在彬彬有礼地交换意见之后，讨论变得唇枪舌剑，针锋相对，成为代表新州的托尼·伯克与来自维州的史蒂芬·康罗伊（Stephen Conroy）和德雷弗斯之间的激烈交锋。伯克质问他们，悉尼的阿拉伯人社区是否应该与墨尔本的犹太人社区一样，享有同等的照顾和待遇。”① 外长的紧密支持者，新南威尔士州工党书记山姆·达斯亚瑞（Sam Dastyari）更是明确告诫工党党首吉拉德，她应该为新州右派工党议员明年是否还能保住议席感到担忧。

2012 年 11 月 26 日，在需要表决立场的内阁会议上，22 位内阁部长中，已有 10 位部长明确支持鲍勃·卡尔，大部分内阁成员不管是来自哪个派系，也不管是陆克文支持者还是吉拉德支持者，都一致恳求总理吉拉德转变立场，只有两人表态支持总理。即便如此，吉拉德依然固执地坚持议会制度赋予总理在内阁中的特权，坚持投反对票的立场。鉴于工党对内阁决定必须统一口径的纪律规则，以及总理在内阁享有决定权的决策惯例，外长把扭转局面的希望寄托在第二天的议会党团会议上，在那里他已经争取了不少人的

① Bob Carr, *Diary of a Foreign Minister*, New South Publishing, 2014, p. 234.

支持。11 月 27 日可以说是疯狂的一天。

鲍勃·卡尔回忆说：工党高层“在关于巴勒斯坦地位投票问题上的争论越来越激烈，渐趋白热化，压倒所有议题。在参议院会议上，坐在我旁边的维多利亚州右派，极端亲以色列议员史蒂芬·康罗伊激烈批评我，说我的立场是荒谬的，是背叛，是欺骗，并警告说，右派将联合所有这个派系的成员投票反对巴勒斯坦的请求，也就是说，他要逼迫工党右派所有成员进行表决，支持澳大利亚投‘反对’票”①。外长随即打电话给新州工党两个重量级人物达斯亚瑞和菲兹吉本（Joel Fitzgibbon），建议做好准备，阻止维州派系企图以其立场强行捆绑全国工党右派的疯狂举动。

一整晚，双方都在准备秘密武器和破解之道。第二天早上，在议会党团会议召开几分钟之前，总理吉拉德在权衡利弊之后终于妥协，同意了澳大利亚在联合国大会关于巴勒斯坦地位问题上投弃权票。

2012 年 11 月 28 日，《悉尼先驱晨报》头版文章以“后座议员造反，迫使总理放弃支持以色列”为标题，对工党的内部派系斗争进行了评论：

> 茱莉亚·吉拉德遭到绝大多数内阁成员反对，并被议会党团警告可能被赶下台，于是被迫撤回在即将进行的联合国表决上支持以色列的决定。这样一来，在联合国大会给予巴勒斯坦观察国地位表决时，澳大利亚将弃权，而不是像吉拉德希望的那样，跟美国和以色列站在一起反对通过这个决议。周一晚上进行的讨论会紧张激烈，除两位部长——比尔·肖顿和史蒂芬·康罗伊，两人均为维多利亚州工党右派——所有内阁部长都明确反对吉拉德的决定，拒绝她的领导。……派系大佬们警告她，在周二早上召开的议会党团会议上，她将被自己的后座议员拉下马。……外交部长鲍勃·卡尔在内阁会议前见了吉拉

① Bob Carr, *Diary of a Foreign Minister*, New South Publishing, 2014, p. 231.

> 德女士。是他推动了这次反对总理的行动。[①]

《澳大利亚人报》的一则头版报道，更能让人想象出当时的紧张气氛：

> 她到达议会党团会议时，小喽啰告诉她，她的支持者可能凑不够人数。为了避免出现自己在议会党团中被打败的尴尬局面，她终于做出了让步。我可以告诉你，那真是惊心动魄的十二小时。今天早上，她差一点点就丢掉工党领导人的帽子。[②]

这样戏剧性的结局既在情理之中，也令工党上下喜出望外。鲍勃·卡尔外长在国际社会上挽回了颜面。他当即致电驻澳大利亚的巴勒斯坦外交使节，开玩笑地说："这下我可以在阿拉伯人面前露面了。"[③] 但更重要的是，他在争取新南威尔士州的阿拉伯人和穆斯林选民方面做出了巨大的努力。

2013 年 9 月 7 日是澳大利亚大选的日子，正在莫斯科参加 G20 峰会的鲍勃·卡尔接到了新南威尔士州工党总书记詹米·克莱门斯（Jamie Clements）的电话，告知他所有为保住议席的奔波和努力，所有在少数族裔社区的宣讲活动都得到了回报，他帮助工党获得了三个席位。

鲍勃·卡尔对巴勒斯坦的支持是非常有限的。在成功挑战总理之后，他致电拉马拉的巴勒斯坦外长，阐明澳大利亚的观点，一方面祝贺巴勒斯坦在联合国"观察员国"地位问题上取得胜利，但另一方面他认为巴勒斯坦不应该再试图参加其他任何联合国组织，特别是国际刑事法院；巴勒斯坦当务之急是巩固成果，而不是继续

---

① Phillip Coorey, "Backbench Revolt Forces PM to Drop Israel Support", *Sydney Morning Herald*, November 28, 2012.

② David Crow & Dennis Shanahan, "Julia Gillard Facing Rebellion in the Ranks Over Foreign Policy and Media", *The Australian*, November 28, 2012.

③ Bob Carr, *Diary of a Foreign Minister*, New South Publishing, 2014, p. 240.

高歌猛进，不应该刺激以色列，而应通过与以色列人直接谈判来解决问题。[①]

结 语

综上所述，在 2012 年 11 月底联大关于巴勒斯坦成为联合国观察员国投票问题上，鲍勃·卡尔外长与吉拉德总理发生了严重的分歧。从国家利益来看，鲍勃·卡尔一直认为澳大利亚作为中等强国对于巴以问题应持公平、积极态度，同时为了争取阿拉伯和穆斯林国家对澳大利亚竞选联合国安理会非常任理事国的支持，希望吉拉德总理在巴勒斯坦政策上有所调整，而吉拉德总理及其总理办公室幕僚坚持以澳美同盟为基石，对巴以问题坚定不移地采取亲美、亲以的既定立场和政策，反对鲍勃·卡尔为调整巴以政策的一切努力。但更重要的是，两人都十分关注工党在国内大选的选票问题。鲍勃·卡尔作为执政党工党内部资深领袖人物和曾经执掌新南威尔士州时间最长、最受欢迎的州长，他必须考虑到帮助本州议员争取阿拉伯人和穆斯林选民的支持，保住所在工党派系在重要选区的席位，进而保住工党在联邦大选中的整体利益。而吉拉德作为工党的领袖同样为赢得联邦大选而感到焦虑，但她更看重维多利亚州犹太人选民的政策，维护维多利亚派系的利益，加上墨尔本亲以色列院外集团的强大制约作用，因此吉拉德并不愿意在巴以问题上做任何变动。由此，外长与总理发生了严重分歧，以致在巴勒斯坦的联合国“观察员国”地位问题上激烈交锋。最终，鲍勃·卡尔利用议会党团各派大佬，迫使代表维州右派的总理改变在联合国巴勒斯坦地位问题上一贯投反对票的做法，投了弃权票，从而在很大程度上帮助新南威尔士州工党赢得了阿拉伯人和穆斯林选民的支持。从这一事件可以看出，在吉拉德工党政府的外交决策中，投票背后往往牵扯着选票，关键时候，党派利益常常被置于国家利益之上。

---

① Bob Carr, *Diary of a Foreign Minister*, New South Publishing, 2014, p. 263.

The Impact of ALP's Internal Struggle on Australian Foreign Policy

—A Study of the Struggle between Australia Foreign Minister Bob Carr and Prime Minister Julia Gillard over Palestine Status in the UN

Dai Ning

Abstract: In November 29 2012, Australia abstained from the 67th UN General Assembly vote on the resolution to give Palestine observer status in the UN. This is quite unusual considering the fact that Australia has always joined the US, Israel and a handful of other nations in voting against UN resolutions concerning Palestine status. As a matter of fact, Prime Minister Julia Gillard, who was responsible for the decision-making, persisted in voting No to an enhanced Palestine status, but was forced to withdraw Australia's support for Israel after being opposed by her own cabinet and the Labor caucus. All the move was actually pushed by Foreign Minister Bob Carr. The abstention eventually steered Australia, a newly elected UNSC member, away from getting on the wrong side of history by being in lockstep with the US and Israel and antagonizing Arab world hence helped Australia maintain a positive image of Australia as a ' middle power ' in the international community. Why did Mr. Bob Carr, a senior cabinet minister and a veteran Labor leader, stage this revolt against his Prime Minister and force her to change her position in UN voting? The paper analyzes the struggle over the Palestine-Israel issue between the foreign minister and the prime minister and explores the impact of Labor's internal fight on Australian foreign policies.

The author believes that both Bob Carr's and Julia Gillard's primary concern were domestic elections and their factional party interests, more than the Australian national interest in the larger world, even though the concerns for the latter are from different prospective and at different levels. Worried about the labor seats in New South Wales which were greatly challenged by the Liberal party, Bob Carr who had been opted to a more balanced and fair Palestine-Israel policy sought to secure more support from voters of Middle East and Arab background in NSW electorates by taking the diplomatic action of supporting an improved status of Palestine in the UN. Meanwhile, taking a more comprehensive view of Labor strength in the election campaign nationwide, particularly in Victoria, and being much affected by the influential Jewish lobby, Julia Gillard and her Prime Minister Department insisted in sticking to the pro-Israel policy and voting ' no ' to UN resolution on Palestinian status. Hence the fundamental differences in domestic and international policy concerns led to the fight between the foreign minister and the prime minister that reveals the connection between UN voting and domestic election and further the truth that the foreign policy making by Gillard's Labor government is more determined by party interest than national interest.

Keywords: Australia Labor Party; Bob Carr; Julia Gillard; Foreign Policy

为了忘却的纪念

——巴赫金狂欢诗学理论视域下的《上海舞》

颜静兰　刘晓宇*

摘要： 澳大利亚华裔作家布赖恩·卡斯特罗笔下的《上海舞》是一部虚构性自传作品。作者通过蒙太奇般的跳跃式描写，讲述了他的家族在上海的跌宕起伏。这让人醉生梦死的上海舞是人们忘却过去的一种方式，如同一场巴赫金式的狂欢。本文在巴赫金狂欢诗学理论视域下，从人物塑造、语言文化以及时空转换三个方面，探讨《上海舞》中的狂欢化特征。结果表明：纷繁复杂的人物世界以及多样化的人物塑造，构成了一种狂欢式的孤独；言语交际和非言语交际的写作方法使各国文化相互交融，呈现自由平等的狂欢世界；时间和空间的跳跃式叙述带领读者打破时空的界限，在一定程度上也体现了巴赫金式的狂欢。

关键词：《上海舞》　巴赫金　狂欢诗学　多元文化　时空转换

* 颜静兰，华东理工大学外国语学院教授，博士生导师，研究方向为跨文化交际学、文化研究、英美文学。刘晓宇，华东理工大学外国语学院研究生，研究方向为跨文化交际学。

一 引言

澳大利亚华裔作家布赖恩·卡斯特罗（Brian Castro）与中国结下了不解之缘。父亲是葡萄牙人，早年在中国创业。母亲是中英混血儿，外公是广东人。卡斯特罗出生于从澳门到香港的乘船上，出生后其母将他取名为“高博文”[①]。由于家庭环境和多元文化教育的影响，卡斯特罗语言水平极高，会说葡萄牙语、英语、法语、广东话等多种语言。卡斯特罗是一位多产的作家，先后出版《候鸟》（*Birds of Passage*，1983）、《波莫罗伊》（*Pomeroy*，1990）、《双狼》（*Double Wolf*，1991）、《萦系中国》（*After China*，1992）等九部小说和一部论文集《寻找艾斯特利塔》（*Looking for Estrellita*，1999）。

《上海舞》（*Shanghai Dancing*，2003）[②] 是卡斯特罗的第七部小说。作品一经发表，便受到全世界的广泛关注，斩获多个奖项，被评为新南威尔士州（New South Wales）2004 年度最佳小说。国外学者戴维·布鲁克肖（David Brookshaw）将《上海舞》戏剧性地看成是“流散者的流散”[③]；艾莉森·吉本斯（Alison Gibbons）认为作品结合了个人语言特征和全球化过程，充分展现了全球化和个人主体性的双重视角[④]；凯瑟琳·哈勒迈尔（Katherine Hallemeier）认为主人公的边缘文化身份恰恰是小说杂糅主题的最好印证。[⑤] 国内学者王光林在福柯（Foucault）异位移植理论的基

① 王光林：《文化翻译与多元视角：澳大利亚华裔作家布赖恩·卡斯特罗（高博文）访谈》，《当代外国文学》2008 年第 1 期，第 163 ~ 167 页。

② Brian Castro, *Shanghai Dancing* (Australia: Giramondo Publishing Company, 2003).

③ David Brookshaw, "Diasporas of Diasporas: Brian Castro's Shanghai Dancing," *Future Medicinal Chemistry*, Vol. 5, No. 8 (2011), pp. 947 – 959.

④ Alison Gibbsons, "'I Haven't Seen you since (a specific date, time, the weather)': Global Identity and the Reinscription of Subjectivity in Brian Castro's Shanghai Dancing," *Ariel A Review of International English Literature*, Vol. 47, No. 1 (2016), pp. 223 – 251.

⑤ Katherine Hallemeier, "Writing Hybridity: The Theory and Practice of Autobiography in Rey Chow's 'The Secrets of Ethnic Abjection' and Brian Castro's 'Shanghai Dancing'", *Antipodes*, Vol. 25, No. 2 (2011), pp. 125 – 130.

础上，探讨华裔散居作家如何摆脱文化身份的苦恼[①]，他还从雅各布森（Jokobson）符际翻译的视角，展现作者卡斯特罗通过照片、地图等意象来传达东西文化间意符的现代性[②]；施云波、朱江则在后殖民主义视域下，将卡斯特罗塑造成一名“脱域的游牧舞者”[③]；马丽莉认为作者卡斯特罗心理上的“无根”状态，使他一直以“混杂”的文化身份，书写着类似自己人生经历的故事。[④]

《上海舞》的伟大之处在于其丰富的肌理，作为一部虚构性自传作品，主人公安东尼奥·卡斯特罗（Antonio Castro）身上或多或少有作者的影子。小说主要采用第一人称叙述手法，通过蒙太奇般的跳跃式描写，将记忆和回忆穿插其间，展现了主人公家族在上海的跌宕起伏。在时空的交错变换中，小说呈现出多元的主题。全书共 59 节，包括“开往中国的慢船”“突然冒出的尼日利亚人”“溯河北上”“世界屋脊”等，这些看似毫无联系的标题却展现了一个家族难以忘却的纪念。在这个错综复杂的多元环境中，作者运用碎片式非线性结构，将沉默寡言的母亲、放浪不羁的父亲、精明能干的姐姐、小偷、传教士、赌徒、醉汉等多种人物形象展现在读者面前。亚马逊书评给予这本书很高的评价，认为这部作品“给人留下深刻印象，它既是历史，又是小说，还是一本跨越了各种文学形式的书籍，讲述的是具有普遍意义的人类经验”。

二　巴赫金狂欢诗学理论

苏联著名文艺学家、思想家、理论家米哈伊尔·巴赫金

① 王光林：《“异位移植”——论华裔澳大利亚作家布赖恩·卡斯特罗的思想与创作》，《当代外国文学》2005 年第 2 期，第 56～63 页。

② Wang Guanglin, “Translating Intersemiotically: Photographing West and East in Brian Castro's Shanghai Dancing,” *Asia Pacific Translation and Intercultural Studies*, Vol. 3, No. 3 (2016), pp. 201～222.

③ 施云波、朱江：《布赖恩·卡斯特罗：脱域的游牧舞者》，《南京师范大学文学院学报》2015 年第 3 期，第 145～149 页。

④ 马丽莉：《身份与创造力：解读布来恩·卡斯特的〈中国之后〉》，《外国文学研究》2006 年第 4 期，第 97～102 页。

（Mikhail Bakhtin，1895～1975）是一位多产的学术研究者，被世人誉为文学批评的奇才。曾经默默无闻的巴赫金得以誉满全球，多亏了法国学者朱莉娅·克里斯蒂娃（Julia Kristeva）[①]。克里斯蒂娃向西方世界引介巴赫金的学术思想[②]，不仅造就了巴赫金的世界名誉，也很好地宣传了自己的“互文性”理论。[③]

巴赫金在其著作《陀思妥耶夫斯基诗学问题》[④]和《弗朗索瓦·拉伯雷的创作和中世纪与文艺复兴时期的民间文化中》阐述了狂欢化理论。狂欢化理论基于欧洲狂欢节文化和长篇小说话语研究，有其深厚的思想渊源。它吸收了古希腊神话中颠覆传统、及时行乐的“酒神精神”和古罗马“农神节”中打破等级限制、强调奴隶和主人之间自由平等的精神。巴赫金的狂欢化理论所提倡的对抗权威和颠覆官方力量，在一定程度上体现了后现代主义的学术思想。

巴赫金将世界一分为二，认为“似乎在整个官方世界的彼岸建立了第二个世界和第二种生活，这是所有中世纪的人都在或大或小的程度上参与，都在一定的时间内生活过的世界和生活”[⑤]。第一个世界是常规性的、具有严格等级秩序的官方世界；第二个世界是颠覆性的、自由自在不受拘束的狂欢世界，在这个世界中“充满了两重性的笑，充满了不敬和猥亵，充满了同一切人、一切事的随意不拘的交往”[⑥]。巴赫金认为，欧洲 14～16 世纪文艺复兴时期的作家最能体现民间的狂欢文化，他们冲破中世纪的思想束缚，不断用民间文化来对抗所谓的官方文化。狂欢世界颠覆了传统的官方

① 赵雪梅：《克里斯蒂娃与后现代文论之发生》，《文艺理论研究》2018 年第 1 期，第 69～79 页。

② 曾军：《克里斯蒂娃在“词语、对话和小说”一文中对巴赫金理论的借鉴和改造》，《外国文学研究》2014 年第 1 期，第 133～139 页。

③ 祝克懿：《互文性理论的多声构成：〈武士〉、张东荪、巴赫金与本维尼斯特、弗洛伊德》，《当代修辞学》2003 年第 5 期，第 12～27 页。

④ Mikhail Bakhtin, *Problems of Dostoevsky's Poetics* (London: University of Minnesota Press, 1894).

⑤〔俄〕巴赫金：《巴赫金全集》第六卷，石家庄：河北教育出版社，1998，第 6 页。

⑥ 夏忠宪：《巴赫金狂欢化诗学研究》，北京：北京师范大学出版社，2000，第 83 页。

生活，超越了现实的局限，强调全民参与和自由平等。在这个世界中，人没有高低贵贱之分，没有社会等级差异，人与人之间的关系也越来越亲昵，实现了理想中的“乌托邦”。

文学中的狂欢遵循“狂欢节-狂欢式-狂欢化”的发展规律。

（一）狂欢节

狂欢节是充满节日氛围的庆典活动，在某种程度上体现了人民生活的世界观。狂欢节是一种全民参与的活动，不论是古希腊罗马时期的“酒神祭祀”、农神节，还是中世纪文艺复兴时期的广场文化，都体现了民间文化与大众文化相结合的特点。在这种节日中，奴隶与奴隶主共度节日，一起狂欢，没有等级之分。在现代社会中，这种狂欢节日依然存在，例如西方的万圣节、中国少数民族的泼水节等，都是民间文化的深刻体现。

狂欢节上的笑文化是民间文化的代表，具有蓬勃的生命力。“狂欢节上的笑涉及了交替的双方，笑针对交替的过程，针对危机本身。在狂欢节的笑声里，有死亡与再生的结合，否定（讥笑）与肯定（欢呼之笑）的结合。这是深刻反映着世界观的笑，是无所不包的笑。”① 狂欢节用“笑声”的力量来消解官方世界的观念，代表了非官方的民间立场。在狂欢节中，自由和平等的愿景容易实现，人与人之间相互尊重，相亲相爱，实现了理想中的世界。

（二）狂欢式

巴赫金认为狂欢式是“一切狂欢节式的庆贺、礼仪、形式的总和”②，包括外在特征和内在特征两部分。外在特征指的是全民参与和仪式感，狂欢节是全民参与的活动，有一定的礼仪和仪式。人与人之间不存在等级的限制，自由而平等。内在特征强调世界感受的核心是“交替与变更的精神、死亡与新生的精神”③，强调

① 〔俄〕巴赫金：《巴赫金全集》第五卷，石家庄：河北教育出版社，1998，第167页。

② 〔俄〕巴赫金：《巴赫金全集》第五卷，第175页。

③ 〔俄〕巴赫金：《巴赫金全集》第五卷，第175页。

形象的双重性，“狂欢式所有的形象都是合二为一的，他们身上结合了嬗变和危机两个极端：诞生与死亡、祝福与诅咒、夸奖与责骂”。[①] 狂欢式的生活主张颠覆了传统的秩序和法令，打破了之前相互对立的关系。狂欢式的世界感受是狂欢节诸多形式背后潜在的文化意蕴，因此狂欢式的思想总是要转移到具体的形式中去感受。

告别死亡、迎接新生这种除旧迎新式的变更精神象征了狂欢式思想的双重性和相对性。巴赫金认为，任何事物的存在都不是单一的，而是双重的、相互的。正如狂欢节上的加冕仪式：顺利“加冕”的同时也注定了未来将要“脱冕”的结局。加冕和脱冕在一定程度上代表了事物的两个方面，体现了二者互相依存、交替进行的内在含义。双重性和相对性是一致的，“人民大众就是用这种精神向僵化的制度、秩序和思想发出挑战”。[②]

（三）狂欢化

“狂欢式转化为文学的语言就是狂欢化”。[③] 狂欢化的显著特征主要包括直接描写狂欢节式的庆典活动；突出节庆上的礼仪形式以及扩大狂欢广场的内在含义，“文学作品中情节上一切可能出现的场所，只要能够成为形形色色的人们相聚和交际的地方，诸如大街、小酒馆、澡堂、船上甲板，甚至客厅……都会增添一种狂欢广场的意味”。[④] 除了狂欢场景外，狂欢化更注重越出常规的生活世界和传统的时空定义。“狂欢化的时间是超越了传记体的时间，它仿佛是从历史时间中剔除的时间，它的进程遵循着狂欢体特殊的规律，包含着无数彻底的更替和根本的变化”。[⑤]

狂欢化是更为宽泛的精神文化现象，狂欢化的氛围使人们暂时

① 〔俄〕巴赫金：《巴赫金全集》第五卷，第 175 页。

② 程正民：《巴赫金的文化诗学研究》，北京：中国社会科学出版社，2017，第 64 页。

③ 〔俄〕巴赫金：《巴赫金全集》第五卷，第 175 页。

④ 〔俄〕巴赫金：《巴赫金全集》第五卷，第 419 页。

⑤ 夏忠宪：《巴赫金狂欢化诗学研究》，第 78 页。

忘却官方世界严格的等级秩序。文学作品中体裁结构的狂欢化是文学思潮的创新所在，创造了一种别具一格的生活样式。

三 《上海舞》中的狂欢化特征

《上海舞》作为一部具有多元主题的作品，展现了卡斯特罗家族难以忘却的纪念。通过蒙太奇般的跳跃式描写，主人公讲述了他的家族在上海的跌宕起伏。“跳舞是人们忘记过去的一种方式，但是记忆一直在那儿”。[①] 这让人醉生梦死的上海舞，如同一场巴赫金式的狂欢。本文从人物塑造、语言文化、时空转换三个方面，探讨《上海舞》中的狂欢化特征。

（一）狂欢化的人物塑造

卡斯特罗笔下的《上海舞》呈现了一个纷繁复杂的人物世界[②]，“一代又一代，秘密、鸦片、小妾、无言的母亲、狂妄不羁的父亲、精明的姐姐、说谎者、传教士、赌徒、天地会成员、情人、裂唇的侏儒、英雄般的孤儿”等。[③] 小说中的人物似乎都没有单一的身份，正是多样化的人物形象，才使得所有这些元素融合在一起，构成一种狂欢式的孤独。

1. 安东尼奥·卡斯特罗的狂欢

主人公安东尼奥·卡斯特罗在澳大利亚生活 40 年之后，抛却当前的婚姻和生活，毅然决然踏上重返中国的路，找寻祖先忘却的纪念，“好似一名圣徒在进行朝觐”。[④]

“我在澳大利亚生活了 40 年。我的头脑一直不正常。时光流逝。然后我产生了回到中国的欲望，回到那些沉沉浮浮的城市，任

① 〔澳〕布赖恩·卡斯特罗：《上海舞》，王光林、邹囡囡译，上海：上海译文出版社，2010，第 419 页。

② 王晓丹：《论〈上海舞〉中的身份建构》，《当代外国文学》2011 年第 3 期，第 151 ~ 156 页。

③ 〔澳〕布赖恩·卡斯特罗：《上海舞》，第 418 页。

④ 〔澳〕布赖恩·卡斯特罗：《上海舞》，第 2 页。

由记忆的潮汐不时将其展现”。[1]

在中国这片陌生又熟悉的土地上，他迷失了自己，“中国，一朵开放的鲜花，在其心中则躺着令人灰心而痛苦的衰败”。[2] 在交错变换的时空中，安东尼奥寻觅着自己家族的历史，实际上也是在追寻自己的身份。

安东尼奥漂泊不定的人生之旅造成了他身份的模糊，让他一直处于“无根”的生活状态。混血的安东尼奥虽然说着流利的英语，却被社会抛弃和隔离，排除在主流生活之外。当遭遇意外，被别人趁火打劫丢失护照后，安东尼奥没有了活下去的欲望。他一次次地寻觅，一次次地失败，孤独与落寞让他寄希望于酒和女人。似乎只有在莺歌燕舞和酒醉金迷中，他才能感受到生活的意义。

“在绝望之下，我开始跳舞，我歌唱台风了不起的强度，歌唱自然的伟大荣耀和恐怖，歌唱两者交融在超自然的吼叫和全能的力量，沿着上帝的手而下”。[3]

此时此刻的上海舞是安东尼奥向世界宣泄的一种工具，是反抗秩序、突破身份限制、呼吁自由的最佳方式，“一旦跳舞，乱伦和禁忌就都给消除掉了”。[4] 在所谓的官方世界中，安东尼奥受到禁锢和限制，内心的痛苦和烦闷无处发泄。而舞蹈作为雅俗共赏的大众型娱乐方式，是与官方世界相对应的狂欢世界的典型代表。只有在这个狂欢世界中，安东尼奥才能通过跳舞暂时忘却身份的模糊和不确定，享受内心片刻的欢愉，这犹如一场巴赫金式的狂欢，安东尼奥在狂欢中忘却过去，消除记忆。

2. 阿纳尔多·何塞·卡斯特罗的狂欢

主人公的父亲阿纳尔多·何塞·卡斯特罗（Arnaldo José Castro）拥有戏剧性的人生，是个典型的享乐主义者。他不屑于读

① 〔澳〕布赖恩·卡斯特罗：《上海舞》，第2页。
② 〔澳〕布赖恩·卡斯特罗：《上海舞》，第40页。
③ 〔澳〕布赖恩·卡斯特罗：《上海舞》，第156页。
④ 〔澳〕布赖恩·卡斯特罗：《上海舞》，第193页。

书，人生中读过的唯一一本书就是《铁面人》，他认为“过去的唯一用处就是能从中找到未来”。[①] 在小说最前面的族谱图中，我们可以看出阿纳尔多有过三次婚姻，而主人公安东尼奥正是第三次婚姻的产物。婚姻和家庭象征着幸福的港湾和避风塘，阿纳尔多对待婚姻的儿戏态度，也反映了他生性风流的一面。

“他开始沉溺于酗酒，到湾仔去跳舞。在湾仔，他跳得浑身是汗，从中找到了某种共鸣，行将死去的堂兄记忆出现了偏差，而他们还把这些当作是自己的记忆，封在时间的蜡中，形成了痴呆蜂窝”。[②]

阿纳尔多擅长跳舞，每天辗转于各大舞厅，喝酒、跳舞和女人成了他生活中不可或缺的东西。他对跳舞的痴迷程度使他曾在 1924 年上海一家舞厅里举行的斗牛舞比赛中和搭档卡维塔·嘉道理（Kavita Kadoorie）获得了冠军。

阿纳尔多及时行乐的人生态度让他看淡生死问题，在小说“新闻大战”这一节中，阿纳尔多充分表现了他享乐主义的人生态度——“生活就是为了吃，生活就是为了爱”[③]，要抓住当下的乐趣，忘却过去，“现实就是狂欢”。[④]

“如果没有过去和未来，也就没有害怕……阿纳尔多·卡斯特罗手上拿着报纸，对他的堂弟说道……所以干嘛要担心呢，如果你担心你死，如果你不担心你还是死”。[⑤]

阿纳尔多这种狂欢化的生活方式，深刻体现了他思想中的双重性。“生”的背后是“死”，而“死”也意味着未来的重生。生死更替的自然规律，让他有机会逃避现实，在纸醉金迷的上海舞中获得心灵上的愉悦，忘却现实的残酷。人固有一死，何不积极乐观地看淡人生，享受生活的乐趣？在舞蹈比赛这种类似于“狂欢节”

① 〔澳〕布赖恩·卡斯特罗：《上海舞》，第 60 页。
② 〔澳〕布赖恩·卡斯特罗：《上海舞》，第 161 页。
③ 〔澳〕布赖恩·卡斯特罗：《上海舞》，第 212 页。
④ 〔澳〕布赖恩·卡斯特罗：《上海舞》，第 221 页。
⑤ 〔澳〕布赖恩·卡斯特罗：《上海舞》，第 212 页。

文化的活动中，阿纳尔多体会到人与人之间的自由和平等，从而获得前所未有的快乐。

（二）狂欢化的语言文化

作者布赖恩·卡斯特罗精通各国语言，重视文字的力量，“文字可以一样有效地阻击抱负”[①]，这一语言优势也体现在《上海舞》的创作过程中。《上海舞》运用后现代主义写作手法，将语言和图片相结合，采用碎片化叙述和非线性结构，打破了传统体裁的限制，使作品在语言文化上呈现出狂欢化的特征。语言是文化的载体，不管是言语交际还是非言语交际，《上海舞》的写作特色也在一定程度上体现了作者的文化意图。

1. 言语交际的狂欢化

小说主体虽然用英语写成，但其中不乏汉语、西班牙语、葡萄牙语等语种的任意切换，语言文字的背后是各国文化的交流碰撞，体现了多元文化的大狂欢。“整个大陆失去平衡，多元文化碰撞了起来”。[②]

“因为一旦赋予了声音，婴儿就会咳嗽、叫骂、尖叫，扑嗒（Puta）！扑嗒！扑嗒！伴随着锅炉的呼哧声”。[③]

在小说一开始，“Puta”这个词就一语双关，将其在西班牙语和葡萄牙语中的深层含义隐射出来：“Puta”在葡萄牙语和西班牙语中含有妓女的意思，因此“Puta”也象征着主人公后续的“召妓”行为。显然，在等级森严的官方世界中，“召妓”是被禁止和唾弃的。只有在自由平等的第二世界（也就是这里所说的狂欢世界），这个行为才被允许。作者在小说一开始便挑战权威，用一语双关的形式抗议官方世界，为狂欢世界呐喊。

“中国有句说法：各人吃饭各人饱，各人生死各人了”。[④]

---

① 〔澳〕布赖恩·卡斯特罗：《上海舞》，第 210 页。

② 〔澳〕布赖恩·卡斯特罗：《上海舞》，第 153 页。

③ 〔澳〕布赖恩·卡斯特罗：《上海舞》，第 1 页。

④ 〔澳〕布赖恩·卡斯特罗：《上海舞》，第 58 页。

“时间就是金钱。一英寸时间就是一盎司黄金”。[①]

在“节奏自由”这一节中，作者提到了中国谚语“各人吃饭各人饱，各人生死各人了”[②]，还有英国谚语“时间就是金钱。一英寸时间就是一盎司黄金”[③]，体现了作者精湛的多语言功力。谚语是一个国家民俗文化的典型代表，作者在这里选取的中式和英式谚语都强调时间易流逝，珍惜时间，及时行乐。享乐主义的人生观也体现了狂欢文化的精神世界。

“我在吃着免治，这是一道澳门人吃的杂烩，由碎肉、洋葱、大蒜、切成方块的卷心菜和松脆的土豆片一起放到橄榄油里煎炸，再配上酱油、干藏红花粉和咖喱”。[④]

在“葡式免治”这一节中，作者介绍了“免治”这种澳门式杂烩。一个国家的饮食特征也体现出这个国家特定的文化。还有代表各国文化的不同节日和习俗：逾越节、清明节、三合会、教会和日式枕边书。这一道文化杂糅的语言盛宴，对作者而言，“代表了难以忘怀的混乱和安全，并象征着我自己的混杂，生活的混乱，世界的混合，昏厥”[⑤]，在一定程度上也体现出作者不愿意被“定义化”，不想被贴上固有的标签，想要呈现自由平等的狂欢世界。

2. 非言语交际的狂欢化

小说中语言文化的狂欢化还体现在非言语交际的过程中。非言语交际指的是除语言符号以外的其他符号系统，包括肢体语言、面部表情、副语言和周边环境等。克里斯蒂娃在阐述其解析符号学思想时，指出语言不是一个静态的符号系统，而是一个动态的意指过程。[⑥] 她认为“符号系统是一个具有否定自身的异质性和僭越性的

---

① 〔澳〕布赖恩·卡斯特罗：《上海舞》，第59页。
② 〔澳〕布赖恩·卡斯特罗：《上海舞》，第58页。
③ 〔澳〕布赖恩·卡斯特罗：《上海舞》，第59页。
④ 〔澳〕布赖恩·卡斯特罗：《上海舞》，第176页。
⑤ 〔澳〕布赖恩·卡斯特罗：《上海舞》，第176页。
⑥ 孙秀丽：《解析符号学批判——克里斯蒂娃研究之一》，《外语学刊》2006年第5期，第25~28页。

语言实践系统”。[①]《上海舞》中具有丰富的非言语交际，在动态的意指过程中，无声地传达潜在的狂欢思想。

其中最典型的代表是外公维吉尔·容（Virgil Wing）的非言语交际。外公是军阀的儿子，但却对外科和整形移植手术感兴趣。他偷了父亲的钱，前往西方学习外科和整形技术。在主人公眼中，外公十分腼腆，像个学者。

“我一生当中只见过外公维吉尔两到三次，但是我可以清楚地回忆起这些时刻。他在他的书房里，不喜欢孩子打扰，他微笑着向我挥挥手，让我离开，然后轻轻地把门关上”。[②]

外公一系列非言语交际的动作，表明他喜欢安静，想要拥有自己的空间，不喜欢世俗的纷扰。在狂欢世界中，每个人都拥有自己的一片“净土”，人们可以随心所欲地相互交流或躲在自己的空间里独自思考。外公在面对孩子时非常和蔼可亲，但同时他也渴望保护隐私，享受一个人的宁静。

在“模拟”这一节中，作者这样描述外公的笑——“在他的眼镜背后，他笑得会像魔鬼一样。据说他对什么都笑，仿佛通过这一微笑，生与死都可以愉快地摆正位置，消除过错和痛苦，但对那些敏感的人来说这种无情也可能产生恐怖”。[③] 巴赫金狂欢诗学理论认为笑文化是民间文化的代表，具有蓬勃的生命力。外公的笑，这种看似表达情感的方式，也是一种狂欢式的呐喊，对现实不满的强烈控诉。

“我记录了上百个我在利物浦医院修补的外国面孔，将没有脸形的哭号和烧焦的骨头改造成一种特殊的风度，脱离了公众视野的恐怖，每一张被烧过的脸，每一块芥子气伤疤后面，都有一张亚洲面孔”。[④]

---

① 刘文：《异质性：克里斯蒂娃的符号系统和言说主体》，《哲学动态》2005 年第 7 期，第 35 页。

② 〔澳〕布赖恩·卡斯特罗：《上海舞》，第 120 页。

③ 〔澳〕布赖恩·卡斯特罗：《上海舞》，第 120 页。

④ 〔澳〕布赖恩·卡斯特罗：《上海舞》，第 131 页。

外公维吉尔·容虽然跨越两个世纪和两种文化，但他一直处于中西文化的矛盾之中。他将烧伤的面孔整容成亚洲面孔，虽然拯救了被烧伤者的面部，却无法拯救其注定悲惨的命运。外公不满现实的残酷，却又无法通过自己的力量改变战争的无情与恐怖。因此他只能通过“笑”来排遣内心的无奈与失落。

（三）狂欢化的时空转换

《上海舞》作为一部虚构性的自传，打破了小说与自传的界限，将“理论包含在叙述之中，刻意地对传统的文化身份提出挑战”。[①] 作者通过蒙太奇般的跳跃式叙述，将不同的时间和空间并置于读者面前，带领读者穿越时空，感受一场时空转换的花样狂欢。

1. 狂欢化的时间

时间上，《上海舞》打破了传统的线性时间规律，使得过去与现在交替上演，在时间变换的过程中，将家族祖先的故事娓娓道来。17 世纪西班牙宗教裁判的年代，祖先艾萨克·德·卡斯特罗（Isaac de Castro）因坚持自己的宗教信仰而被活活烧死，伊斯雷尔·德·卡斯特罗（Israel de Castro）成功拯救一艘船，成为一名黑人英雄，受到人民爱戴；19 世纪，祖先何塞·马纳利赛·奥索里奥·德·卡斯特罗（José Manalisay Osorio de Castro）来到中国创业；20 世纪祖母多拉·西德尔（Dora Siddle）作为传教士，从利物浦乘船来中国；20 世纪 30 年代父亲阿纳尔多·何塞·卡斯特罗（Arnaldo José Castro）在纸醉金迷的上海夜夜笙歌。小说采用现在时描述几个世纪的故事，仿佛一切都发生在现在，让读者有种身临其境的感觉。读者在阅读家族故事时，不免会有困惑，时间上的跳来跳去，缺少清晰的脉络结构。作者打破传统的线性时间叙述，将“过去”与“现在”杂糅在一起，体现了时间上的狂欢特征。

---

① 〔澳〕布赖恩·卡斯特罗：《上海舞》，第 416 页。

“他的母亲说，他们家的人说话时总是唱歌。这个家族特点可以回溯到他的曾曾祖父，本雅明·奥索里奥·德·卡斯特罗（Benjamin Osorio de Castro）……工作很辛苦，但是他们有的是时间，在这个城市的语言中，没有时态，因此时间中也就没有过去，现在和未来，而是一种持续的梦幻和历史的融合，这就是现在，而且永远是……”。[①]

“此外，这个地方沉迷药物，记忆缺失，但也十分可爱。由于与世隔绝，并为此感到骄傲，这儿的居民患上了一种嗜睡症，只有在狂欢节的时候他们才会醒来”。[②]

“我们可以用慢镜头来再现往事，她说，这样事情可以倒退到一个不同的时间……模模糊糊的汽车和人在一条几乎空旷的大街上闪烁；有轨电车公然反抗起了普通时间，仿佛光年疯狂停滞”。[③]

《上海舞》展现给读者的不仅仅是一个家族的起起落落，穿插其间的历史史实，例如日本侵华、澳门回归等也一并展现给读者。真实与虚构的模糊性给读者造成困惑，让读者难以理解这59个小故事之间的内在联系。时间穿梭的跳跃，也让读者感受到狂欢式的氛围。作者不再强调普通意义上的时间，而是将各种时间杂糅在一起，构成多样化的狂欢艺术。

2. 狂欢化的空间

巴赫金狂欢诗学理论认为，狂欢化的世界不同于强调等级秩序的官方世界，人与人之间的自由平等以及包容才是狂欢世界的中心。“正如万物的开始总是被当作礼物或片刻的癫狂送给我们”[④]，读者在来回跳舞的过程中感受着作者的“记忆和忘却”。“跳舞是人们忘却过去的一种方式，但是记忆一直在那儿”。[⑤]

---

① 〔澳〕布赖恩·卡斯特罗：《上海舞》，第107页。

② 〔澳〕布赖恩·卡斯特罗：《上海舞》，第364页。

③ 〔澳〕布赖恩·卡斯特罗：《上海舞》，第18页。

④ 〔澳〕布赖恩·卡斯特罗：《上海舞》，第6页。

⑤ 〔澳〕布赖恩·卡斯特罗：《上海舞》，第419页。

空间上，以主人公安东尼奥的回忆为起点，作者带领我们在上海、伦敦、悉尼、澳门等地来回跳舞，感受着碎片化的混乱世界。不同地方的交错上演像一个个舞台，“打破了单一的文化身份，再现出多元文化的杂糅”。[①] 作者来回变换空间地点，给读者带来不同文化盛宴的同时，也展现了作者自身对于多元文化的包容性。狂欢的上海舞消除了地域和文化的限制，读者在纵情舞蹈的过程中，“得到的是方向的迷失和稳定性的消除”。[②]

“他们把我送到了澳大利亚，漫长的下午，我用祖母绿的水笔在那儿书写着。别的同学在周边踢着足球，我则躲在一股牛粪味的手球场后边，在练习本上拼命地写着。我坐在一根腐烂的枕木上，上面给油弄得黑兮兮的，在阳光晒黑的木头上，有两个苍白的条纹，这就是过去火车车轨铺设的地方，条纹里的两个洞满是蛛丝和新近滚过的泥球。放眼田野，你看到了栅栏和防风林，乌鸦发出沙哑的声音，沿着水流向家飞去”。[③]

空间是符号的载体。年少时期的安东尼奥在澳大利亚这个陌生的城市迷失了自己。他想要融入这个城市，却无奈被排除在主流生活之外。年少的他只能通过写作来排遣内心的落寞与痛苦。由于安东尼奥所处的空间并没有给他带来认同感，他便不断怀疑自身，想要在祖先曾经奋斗的城市获得归属感。一个个城市不断变化，读者在来回穿梭的过程中，不禁感受到狂欢世界的自由与平等。个人有权选择去往的城市，而城市作为空间也不应该排斥个人。人作为独立的空间影响着外部世界，外部世界（空间）反过来也影响着个人。

四　结语

澳大利亚华裔作家布赖恩·卡斯特罗笔下的《上海舞》是一

① 〔澳〕布赖恩·卡斯特罗：《上海舞》，第420页。

② 〔澳〕布赖恩·卡斯特罗：《上海舞》，第4页。

③ 〔澳〕布赖恩·卡斯特罗：《上海舞》，第163～164页。

部具有多元主题的作品。在巴赫金狂欢诗学理论视域下，《上海舞》呈现出较高的研究价值。狂欢诗学理论强调狂欢式的世界感受，遵循“狂欢节－狂欢式－狂欢化”的发展规律，它不仅关注狂欢化的文本呈现方式，更注重狂欢生活背后人们的内心感受和生存状态。本文从人物塑造、语言文化和时空转换三个方面，探讨《上海舞》中的狂欢化特征。结果表明：纷繁复杂的人物世界以及多样化的人物塑造，构成了一种狂欢式的孤独；言语交际和非言语交际的写作方法使各国文化相互交融，呈现自由平等的狂欢世界；时间和空间的跳跃式叙述带领读者打破时空的界限，在一定程度上也体现了巴赫金式的狂欢。这让人醉生梦死的上海舞，是人们忘却过去的一种方式，为的是那些忘却的纪念。

《上海舞》作为一部虚构性自传作品，打破了体裁的限制。“上海舞。从一根古老的线轴上抛一根线：得到的是方向的迷失和稳定性的消除”。[①] 卡斯特罗受到美国华裔作家汤婷婷（Maxine Hong Kingston）作品《女勇士》（*The Woman Warrior*，1976）的启发，他认为，“体裁的交织缓解了真与伪二分法中精神分裂症似的压力”。[②] 因此他在创作的过程中，力图打破传统写作的条条框框，将理论包含在叙述之中，跳脱地讲述主人公的家族历史。小说通过蒙太奇般的跳跃式叙述、碎片化描写、时空交错和非线性结构，展现了卡斯特罗高超的后现代主义写作手法。小说中，上海、伦敦、悉尼、澳门等地只不过是安东尼奥的一个个舞台，让读者感受碎片化的狂欢世界。当音乐响起，“跳舞是人们忘却过去的一种方式，但是记忆一直在那儿”。[③] 巴赫金狂欢诗学理论作为文学与文化融合的产物，为文学文本的批评和解读提供了全新的视角。将《上海舞》与狂欢诗学理论相结合，对研究澳大利亚少数族裔文学作品具有现实意义。

① 〔澳〕布赖恩·卡斯特罗：《上海舞》，第 4 页。
② 〔澳〕布赖恩·卡斯特罗：《上海舞》，第 417 页。
③ 〔澳〕布赖恩·卡斯特罗：《上海舞》，第 419 页。

For the Forgotten Commemoration —*Shanghai Dancing* From the Perspective of Bakhtin's Carnival Poetics

Yan Jinglan, Liu Xiaoyu

Abstract: *Shanghai Dancing*, written by Chinese Australian writer Brian Castro, is a fictional autobiography. The author describes his family's back and forth dancing in Shanghai through the way of montage description. The dream life of Shanghai dancing is an approach for people to forget the past, just like Bakhtin's carnival. This paper, from the perspective of Bakhtin's carnival poetics, explores the carnival characteristics in *Shanghai Dancing* from characterization, language and culture, transformation of time and space. Results indicate that the complex world and diverse characters constitute a carnival style of loneliness; the writing methods of verbal communication and nonverbal communication blend the cultures of various countries, presenting a free and fair carnival world; the jumping descriptions of time and space break the boundaries and to some extent reflect the Bakhtin-style carnival.

Keywords: *Shanghai Dancing*; Bakhtin; Carnival Poetics; Multi-culture; Transformation of Time and Space

中澳在高等教育领域合作办学的发展与前景

苏佳卓*

摘要： 自中澳建交以来，教育及相关服务已然成为两国双边关系的重要内容。澳洲政府教育与培训部于 2018 年 4 月公布的数据[①]显示，中国已连续几年成为澳洲在册国际学生的主要生源地（占总人数的 31%）。中澳两国政府一直积极拓展在教育尤其是高等教育领域的多元合作。自 1994 年首个本科及以上学历中澳合作办学项目（以下简称中澳合作办学项目）由原国家教育委员会（后更名为中国教育部）批准招生以来，两国在高等教育领域的合作办学一直处于方兴未艾之势。但是纵观历史，中澳合作办学活动的开展并非一马平川，而是深受中国教育改革及相关政策的影响，呈现周期性发展的态势。本文以中国教育部就中外合作办学颁发的各个条例及法规政策为导向，分析它们对中澳合作办学的推动及制约作用，梳理中澳合作办学的发展和现状及未来前景。

关键词： 中澳合作办学　合作办学机构　合作办学项目　中外合作办学政策

---

* 苏佳卓，上海大学悉尼工商学院高级讲师，研究方向：跨境教育、中澳合作办学、第二语言习得。

① https：//internationaleducation. gov. au/research/International - Student - Data/Documents/MONTHLY%20SUMMARIES/2018/Apr%202018%20MonthlyInfographic. pdf.

跨境教育广义上指的是一个主权国家在另一个主权国家开展教育教学活动。根据原国家教育委员会（后更名为中国教育部）于1995年颁布的《中外合作办学暂行规定》[①] 和2003年国务院颁布的《中华人民共和国中外合作办学条例》[②]，中外合作办学被定义为中国教育机构同外国教育机构依法在中国境内合作举办以中国公民为主要招生对象的教育教学活动，是公益性事业，是中国教育事业的组成部分。中外合作办学分为合作设立机构和合作举办项目两种形式。

一 中澳合作办学现状概述

首个本科及以上学历中澳合作办学机构成立于1994年，截至2018年7月，根据中国教育部中外合作办学监督工作信息平台（以下简称“合作办学监管平台”）[③] 公示的数据，共有151个本科及以上中澳合作办学项目（以下简称“办学项目”）和6家本科及以上中澳合作办学机构（以下简称“办学机构”）被教育部批准招生。然而，其间共有45个合作办学项目陆陆续续停止招生或退出办学[④]，而目前在办的合作项目数为106个，机构数为6家。其中高达86%的项目是本科学位项目（91个），而硕士项目仅为15个，占总样本的14%（见图1）。相对于项目，办学机构的办学层次普遍较高，6家机构中本科招生的只有2家，既招本科生又招硕士生的也有2家，剩余的2家中有1家仅开设硕士学位课程，另一家则开设硕士及博士学位课程（见图2）。

据统计，全国共有72所高等院校和澳洲学校建立了合作办学

① http：//www. moe. gov. cn/s78/A20/s8359/moe_ 864/tnull_ 4510. html，浏览时间2018年7月27日。

② http：//www. moe. gov. cn/s78/A20/gjs_ left/moe_ 861/tnull_ 8644. html，浏览时间2018年7月27日。

③ 数据于2018年7月27日摘自中国教育部中外合作办学监督工作信息平台，http：//www. crs. jsj. edu. cn。

④ 中华人民共和国教育部，“教育部办公厅关于批准部分中外合作办学机构和项目终止的通知”，http：//www. moe. gov. cn/srcsite/A20/moe_ 862/201807/t20180705_ 342056. html。

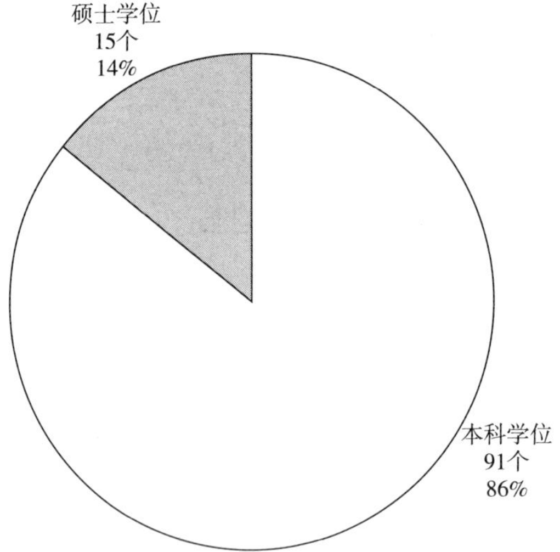

图 1 中澳合作办学项目办学层次

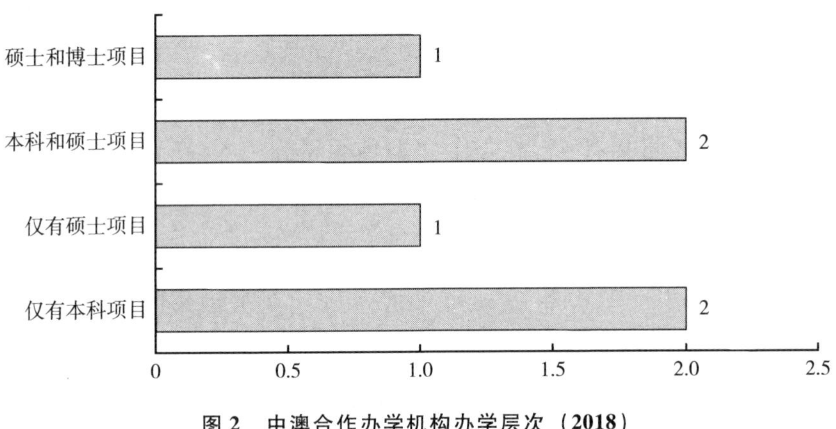

图 2 中澳合作办学机构办学层次（2018）

项目。其中，“985 工程”学校和“211 非 985 工程”学校分别有 7 所和 15 所，而剩余的 50 家“其他”类型高校则是合作办学的主力军，占整体样本的69%。考虑到中国目前只有 39 所“985 工程”院校，其中已有 7 所和澳洲院校建立合作关系，说明澳洲高校还是比较受中国重点高校青睐的。而且从图 3 中可见，与其他类型的学校相比，“985 工程”高校更倾向于和澳洲高校建立高层次的合作项目，以达到强强联手培养高水平国际人才的目的。

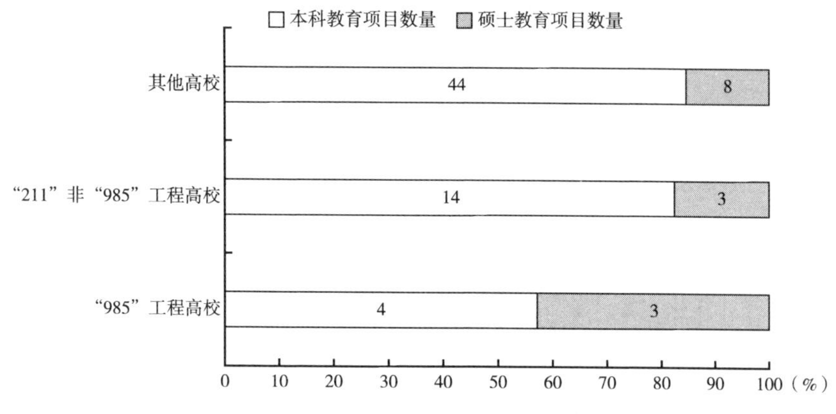

图 3 中方高校分布和开设项目层次（2018）

就澳方学校而言，目前已有 32 所高校参与中澳合作办学（详见图 4）。参与合作办学项目的学校有 31 所，其中只开展本科教育项目的有 21 所，只开展研究生教育项目的有 2 所，另有 8 所院校既开发了本科又开发了硕士合作办学项目。参与中澳合作办学机构的澳洲高校共 7 所（因为东南大学西塔学院是由东南大学和两所澳洲大学一起建立的，所以虽然目前只有 6 家中澳合作办学机构，但是有 7 所澳洲高校涉及）。由图 5 所见，40% 的合作院校属于 4 星或 5 星高校，学校整体质量较好，符合教育部"引进国外优质教育资源"的要求。

总体来说，中澳合作办学专业分布均衡，覆盖哲学、经济学、法学、教育学、文学、理学、工学、农学、医学、管理学和艺术学。数据统计显示（见图 6），工科专业占所有统计样本的 39%，经济学占 13%，管理学占 29%。这三个专业类别总计占所有中澳合作办学专业的 80% 以上。据图 7 和图 8 所示，中澳合作办学热门专业也呈阶段性变化。2011 年之前，商科诸如会计、工商管理、国际经济与贸易等专业，是中澳合作办学的大热方向。而 2011 年后，工程类专业取而代之，合作办学较集中在电气工程、土木工程、机械工程、环境工程、计算机科学与技术等专业。这一转变也正响应了 2015 年中央《关于做好新时期教育对外开放工作的若干意见》中提出的“重点围绕国家急需的自然科学与工程科学类专业建设，引进国外优质资源”的倡议。

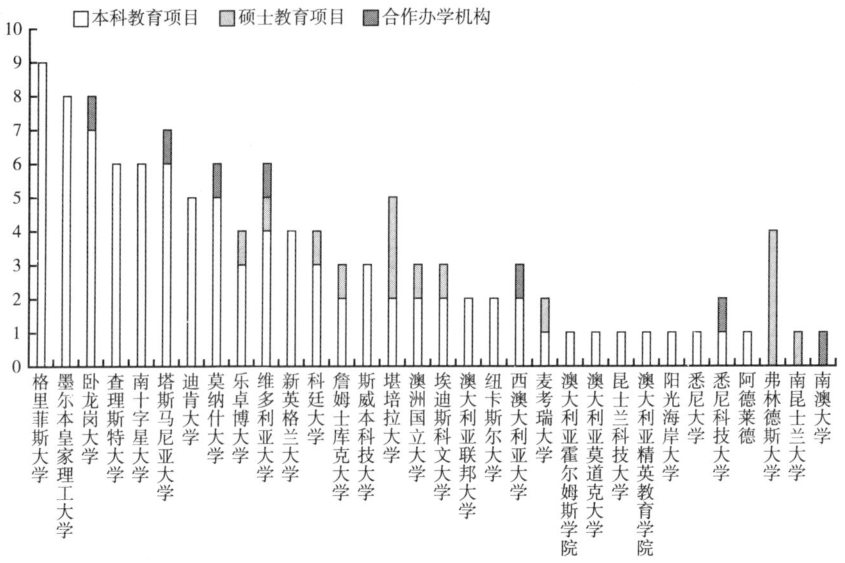

图 4　中澳合作办学澳方学校分布

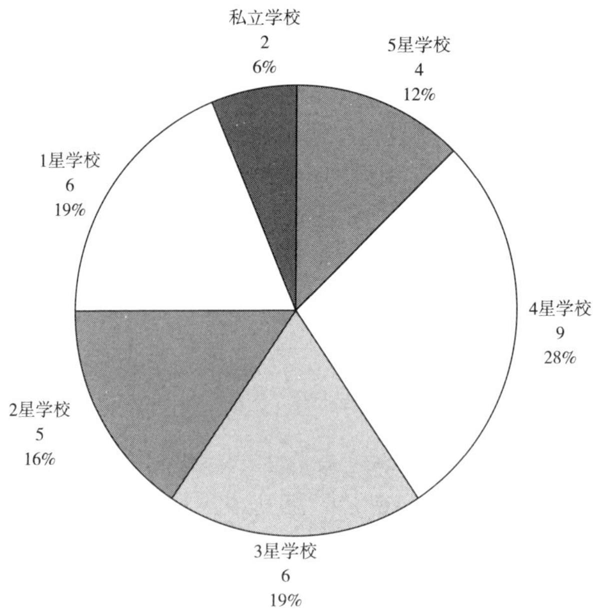

图 5　中澳合作办学澳方学校类型

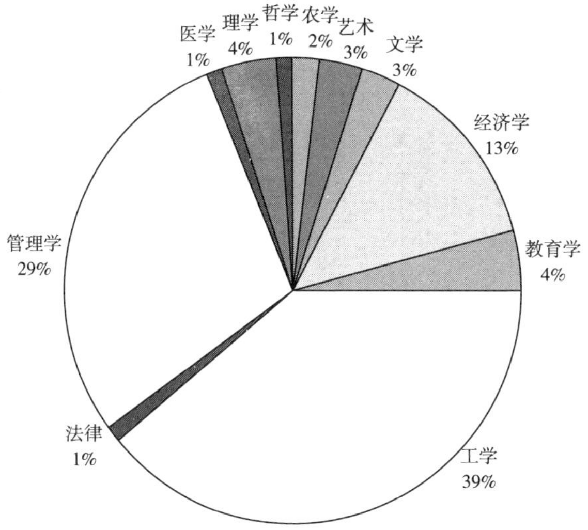

图 6 中澳合作办学专业分布

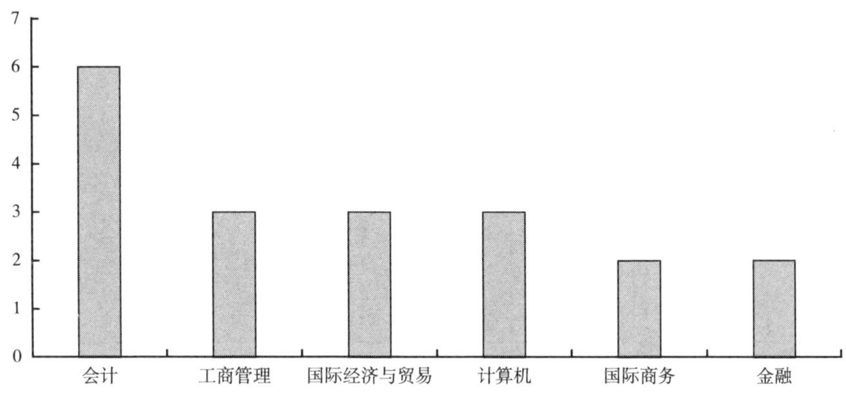

图 7 1994～2010 年中澳合作办学最热门专业

就地域分布而言（见图 9），山东和江苏是中澳合作办学的大省，各有 13 个在办项目及机构。这种格局的分布反映了地区教育国际化的发展与该地区的经济发展水平及开放程度呈现正向关联。相对于内陆经济欠发达地区，沿海地区尤其是东部地区的高等教育国际化意识较强，也更注重吸引境外优质教育资源来提升本地区的教育竞争力。

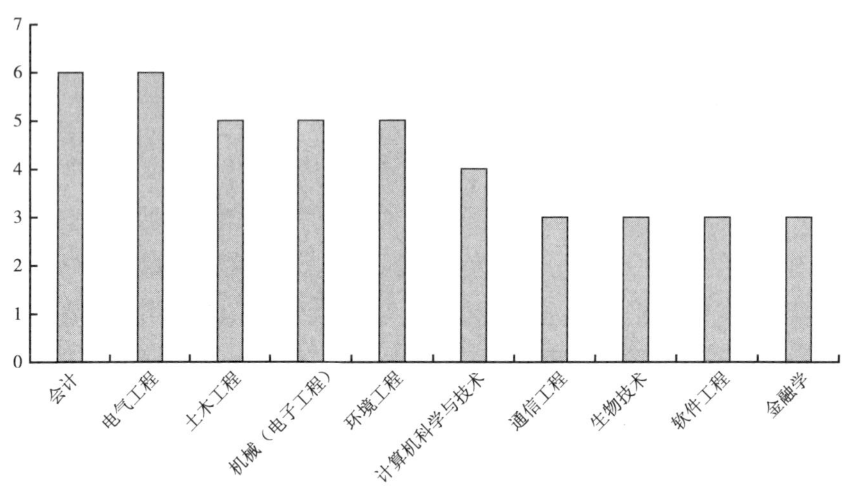

图 8　2011 年至今中澳合作办学热门专业

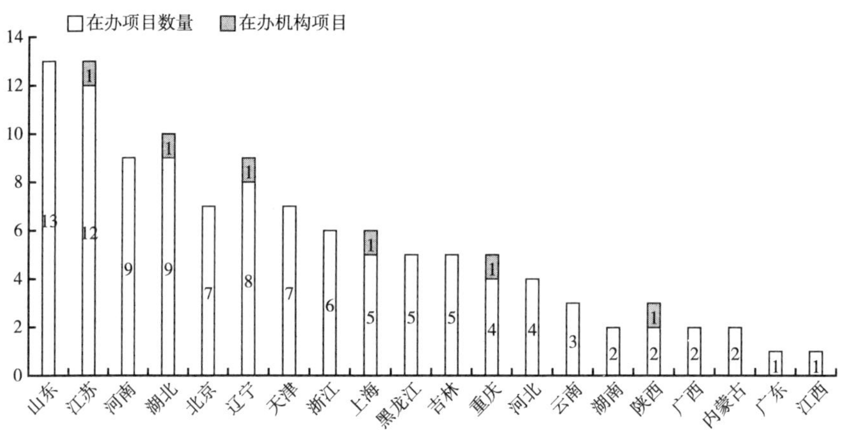

图 9　中澳合作办学项目与机构地区分布

二　中澳合作办学发展

根据中澳合作办学机构与项目在我国发展的概况和政策演变，可将其划分为探索发展期、规范发展期、优质快速发展期、提质增效发展期四个阶段。

（一）探索发展期（1994 年～2003 年）

促使中澳跨境合作办学的因素可以追溯到 20 世纪 80 年代。随着改革开放浪潮的推进，国家需要一大批了解西方文化、操作能力强、适应市场能力强的复合应用型人才，然而当时国内高等教育师资力量严重不足。1985 年，《中共中央关于教育体制改革的决定》[①]指出："要通过各种可能的途径，加强对外交流，使我们的教育事业建立在当代世界文明成果的基础上"，从而从政策上赋予了高校开展国际教育和学术交流的权利，并扩大了学校办学的自主权。1992 年邓小平同志发表南方谈话，推动各行各业包括教育行业对外开放的力度。1993 年 2 月，《中国教育改革和发展纲要》颁布，指出要进一步扩大教育对外开放，加强国家相互交流与合作，允许在国家有关法律和法规范围内进行国际合作办学。同年 6 月，原国家教委颁布了《关于境外机构个人来华合作办学问题的通知》，进一步明确了中外合作办学的定义、办学原则和地位，对合作办学进行了初步规定。

与此同时，位于南半球的澳大利亚政府正在通过缩减高等教育经费来缓解经济压力，并且试图将高等教育输出作为国家的一项重要出口产业。杰克逊（R. G. Jackson）委员会于 1984 年向联邦政府提交了一份关于澳大利亚海外援助项目的考察报告，明确指出教育应当是一种出口产业，并建议在高校间引入良性的竞争机制。1992 年，澳大利亚政府重新规划和定位教育国际化政策，主张以教育质量和教育价值观为重点，向亚太地区推广澳大利亚的高等教育。[②]面对国内教育资源供大于求的现状，并在经济压力和政策导向的双重影响下，澳大利亚高校纷纷以创业姿态，主动到海外寻求市场，以合作的形式向境外高校提供付费课程以维持学校的正常运营和发展。

---

① 《中共中央关于教育体制改革的决定》，教育部网站，1985 年 5 月 27 日发布。

② 王留栓、褚丽：《澳大利亚高等教育国际化概述——从发展教育出口业谈起》，《复旦教育》1999 年 2 月 25 日。

在国家政策和国际环境的影响及上海市教育委员会的大力支持下，第一家中澳合作办学机构——上海大学悉尼工商学院于 1994 年正式批准成立。该机构属于非独立法人机构，是第一所高校与高校间进行合作办学的机构，中澳双方办学主体分别为上海大学与悉尼科技大学，可以同时招收国家计划内学历生和自主招收计划外学生。

为了规范中外合作办学机构和项目的发展，国家教育委员会于 1995 年颁布了《中外合作办学暂行规定》，详细规定了中外合作办学的意义、性质、必要性、应遵循的原则、审批标准和程序、办学主体及领导体制、证书发放及文凭学位授予、监督体制等各个方面[①]，从而标志着中外合作办学走上了依法办学、依法管理的规范道路。然而这段时间，中澳合作办学的步子迈得比较小，1999 年首批 3 个合作办学本科项目诞生，而首个硕士项目和第二家办学机构（辽宁大学亚澳商学院）于次年（2000 年）获批招生。

2001 年，我国正式加入世界贸易组织（WTO）。入世意味着我国对跨国界、跨文化、跨学科的涉外型复合人才存在迫切需求，这无疑为中澳合作办学打开了更广阔的市场，从而导致国内高校纷纷与境外高校开展交流合作，试图通过引进境外优质教育资源以提高自身的教育质量和标准。[②] 中澳合作办学在 2002 ~ 2004 年间经历了第一个快速发展期，其间共有 17 个本科学位项目和 6 个硕士学位项目获批成立。然而该时期开发的项目参差不齐，鲜有澳洲一流大学来华合作办学。而且无论在开设专业上还是地域分布上，都呈现了不均衡性。就地域而言，办学主要集中在经济发达的东部沿海省市和大城市。而专业设置也比较狭窄，主要以工商管理类为主，其次为外语类、信息技术类、经济类和教育类。

① 《中外合作办学暂行规定》，中华人民共和国教育部，1995。

② F. T. Huang, *Transnational Higher Education in Asia and the Pacific Region*, RIHE International Publication Series, 2006 (10): 9 - 10.

（二）规范发展期（2004～2010年）

为了更好促进中外合作办学从无序到有序的发展、规范中外合作办学活动、促进监管的法制化和制度化建设，我国第一部有关中外合作办学的行政法规《中华人民共和国中外合作办学条例》于2003年3月正式出台，标志着中外合作办学的监管步入了法制化的轨道。为了配合该条例的实施，教育部于2004年6月颁发了《中华人民共和国中外合作办学条例实施办法》，进一步明确了中外合作办学中的审批和管理办法，细化了有关中外合作办学的管理和规范方面的制度与措施。2006年6月、2007年4月和2009年7月，教育部又分别发布了《中外合作办学若干问题的意见》《关于进一步规范中外合作办学秩序的通知》和《关于开展中外合作办学评估工作的通知》，并且重点推进"两个平台"和"两个机制"建设，即：依托教育涉外监管信息网开通中外合作办学监管工作信息平台；开发中外合作办学颁发证书认证工作平台；有选择地在部分省市按学科大类开展中外合作办学质量评估，建立中外合作办学质量评估机制；根据法规的要求强化办学单位和各级管理部门的责任，建立中外合作办学执法和处罚机制。受一系列规范性条约的影响，此6年间，通过审批的项目寥寥无几。根据合作办学监管平台数据统计，目前仍然在办的中澳合作办学机构和项目中，仅有2个本科项目和1个硕士项目在此期间受批首次招生。

（三）优质快速发展期（2011～2016年）

2010年，教育部颁布《国家中长期教育改革和发展规范纲要（2010～2020年）》，明确提出"扩大教育开放"，"办好若干所示范性中外合作学校和一批中外合作办学项目"的战略部署。自2011年起，中外合作办学的复核和审批从一年一次增加到一年两次。审批进程的明显加快导致中澳合作办学进入了第二个蓬勃发展期。合作办学监管平台数据显示，2011～2016年，中澳高校跨境合作新增了3所中澳合作办学机构，分别为：东南大学-蒙纳士大学苏州联合研究生院（2012年）；西南大学西塔学院（2016年）和华中师范大学伍伦贡联合研究院（2016年）。在此期间，获批的项目数量也呈现井喷状态。根据合作办学监管平台数据统计，目前仍然在办项目中有11个本科项目和1个硕士项目于2011年获批；2012年，获批的数量到达峰值，包括20个本科项目和3个硕士项目；2013年和2014年，通过审批的项目数量有小幅回落，但是连续两年本科的项目数量均高达13个，2014年还有2个硕士项目获批。2015年全年获批的项目有7个，其中6个为本科项目，1个为硕士项目。2016年被批准的本科项目有2个。

同时，随着近20年中外合作办学发展经验的积累，教育部对中外合作办学的监管力度也有所增强。教育部于2013年发布《关于近期高等学校中外合作办学相关情况的通报》①，通报了有关高等学校中外合作办学存在的突出问题，包括外国高校“连锁店”办学和中介机构②参与包办中外合作办学等。又于2014年下发《教育部关于进一步加强高等学校中外合作办学质量保障工作的意见》，强调要引进名校和强校，从而全面推进了中外合作办学的质量工程建设。因而这一阶段所成立的中澳合作办学机构及项目整体质量较高。

就办学主体而言，三家机构的中方办学机构均为国内985/211高校，而澳大利亚合作方也均为澳洲5星和4星高校。就办学层次而言，除了西塔学院是本科招生，其他两家机构开设的均为硕士及以上高等学位课程，开展前沿科研活动，旨在打造培养具有创新能力和创业才能的高水平国际人才的培养基地。三所机构开设的课程专业也比较均衡，既有文科（翻译专业）、商科（工商管理专业；经济学专业），又有工科［计算机科学（技术）专业，电子与通讯专业；电子信息工程专业；交通工程专业；工业设计专业；生物技术；食品质量与安全专业］。因此三家办学机构都体现出较高的办

① http：//www.cfce.cn/a/zcfg/zcwj/2013/1121/2176.html，浏览时间：2018年9月6日。

② 中介机构指的是留学中介，合伙经纪人和其他第三方机构。

学水准，属于优质办学机构。就 72 个合作办学项目而言，绝大多数为学历教育，即招生纳入国家普通高等教育招生计划或全国研究生招生计划。且专业分布也很均衡，覆盖哲学、经济学、法学、教育学、文学、理学、工学、农学、医学、管理学和艺术学各个领域。

（四）提质增效发展期（2016 年至今）

我国发展中外合作办学的初衷是通过引进国外优质教育资源来有效补足国内高等教育资源紧缺的短板。[①] 这种“拾遗补缺”作用的定位，导致中外合作办学整体水平不高，学科建设得不到重视，专业辐射带动作用不明显。2016 年 2 月，中央下发《关于做好新时期教育对外开放工作的若干意见》[②]，明确指出，“要完善准入制度，改革审批制度，开展评估认证，强化退出机制，加强信息公开，建立成功经验共享机制，重点围绕国家急需的自然科学与工程科学类专业建设，引进国外优质资源，全面提升办学质量”，标志着中外合作办学迈入了更加注重内涵建设及创新引领的新阶段。在这一阶段，中澳合作办学也顺应新趋势，从追求数量转变为追求质量的发展。合作办学监管平台数据显示，截至 2018 年 7 月，仅有 9 个中澳合作办学项目通过审批。

三　中澳合作办学的未来发展

2018 年 6 月 19 日，教育部印发了《关于批准部分中外合作办学机构和项目终止的通知》[③]，45 个中澳合作办学项目榜上有名。其实早在 2016 年，中共中央办公厅和国务院办公厅就已联合下发

---

① 朱兴德：《中外合作办学新阶段更应注重内涵建设》，《中国高等教育》2017 年 8 月。

② 中华人民共和国教育部，《关于做好新时期教育对外开放工作的若干建议》，http：//www. moe. gov. cn/jyb_ xwfb/s6052/moe_ 838/201605/t20160503_ 241658. html。

③ 中华人民共和国教育部，《教育部办公厅关于批准部分中外合作办学机构和项目终止的通知》，http：//www. moe. gov. cn/srcsite/A20/moe_ 862/201807/t20180705_ 342056. html。

《关于新时期做好教育对外开放工作的若干意见》，明确指出要强化中外合作办学的退出机制。数量上的暂缓发展并不意味着中外合作办学政策“收紧”了，中外合作办学被“叫停”了。相反，只有淘汰那些教育资源引进不足、教学质量不高、学科能力不强、合作模式项目不具明显竞争力的项目，才能筛选出更符合时代发展、满足学生和家长高质量教育需求、保障学生权益的优质中澳合作办学教育资源。强化退出机制对中澳合作办学而言，无疑是一件好事并鞭策在办机构和项目自检自省，从原本一味追求规模扩展的量化发展并轨到提质增效内涵发展的新方向努力。在此新趋势下，中澳合作办学可以说有着很大的发展潜力。

2018 年 9 月 10 日召开的全国教育大会上，习近平总书记指出“要扩大教育开放，同世界一流资源开展高水平合作办学”。[①] 同月召开的第九届全国中外合作办学年会，也传递了中外合作办学应当“坚持党的领导”“加强思想政治教育”和“提升中外合作办学水平”的新动向，及“强化中外合作办学对国内教育改革和‘双一流’建设促进”的新办学政策目标。[②] 因而，当前在办的中澳合作办学机构和项目应当把握新的历史机遇，顺应中外合作办学发展的新趋势，结合“双一流”战略，不断探索自身的办学特色，从教学、师资和管理三方面入手，通过融合创新教育模式、科学安排教学内容、完善教师团队结构、建立外教监管制度，发展内涵建设。同时聚焦学科建设，充分发挥自身在提升学校教学实力和国际化水平等方面的作用，努力培养出具有国际竞争力的高素质人才。此外，还应当建立内部评估机制，从内部进行不定期自审自查，规范办学秩序。对有意向申请中澳合作办学机构或项目的高校，应当仔细甄选合作伙伴，引入强校名校，在理工农医等自然科学领域及先进制造现代农业和新兴产业等领域开展合作，优化学科专业结构，为增创“双一流”添砖加瓦。

① 中国人民共和国教育部，http：//www. moe. gov. cn/jyb_ xwfb/s6052/moe_ 838/201809/t20180910_ 348145. html。

② 中国教育新闻网，http：//www. jyb. cn/zgjyb/201809/t20180919_ 1226988. html。

再者，在2018年年会期间召开的“教育部中外合作办学评估研讨会”上，教育部学位中心副主任林梦泉强调“中国要制定一套引领国际跨境教育质量保障评价的中国模式和中国标准，增强国际影响力”。[①] 在此倡议下，中澳合作办学的中方办学主体在今后引进优质资源时，不能再一味地照搬引进，而应积极思考与创新，对引入的资源进行改造嫁接，使其符合中国地气，促使更多的成功中国案例的产生。同时也应有意识输出自己的优质资源，反哺澳方合作院校，并且把办学成功的经验输送到世界教育大平台，以增强我国在全球教育治理和教育规则制定中的话语权。

Development and Prospect of China – Australia Joint Programs for Higher Education

Su Jiazhuo

Abstract: Education has always been a vital component of bilateral relationship between China and Australia since their establishment of formal diplomatic relations in 1972. According to the data released by Australian Department of Education and Training n April 2018, as high as 31% of international students registered in Australia schools and universities come from China, and Australia has been the second most popular destination for oversea study among Chinese students. The governments of both countries have always been eager to expand their multi-dimensional cooperation in education, especially in higher education. Since the first Chinese-Australian joint program in China approved by the State Education Commission of China (the predecessor to the Ministry of Education) in 1994, Chinese-Australian Transnational

① 中华人民共和国教育部中国涉外监管信息网，http://www.jsj.edu.cn/news/2/1184.shtml。

Higher Education in China has undergone over two decades, which, however, is developing in fluctuation and greatly influenced by Chinese educational reform and related policy guidelines. This report will examine a series of policy guidelines related to transnational education issued by China's Ministry of Education and evaluate their impetus and restriction on the development of Chinese-Australian transnational education delivery in China.

Keywords: Chinese-Australian Transnational Higher Education in China; Chinese-Australian Joint Ventures; Chinese-Australian Joint Programs; Chinese Transnational Education Policy

澳研历史回顾专栏

Special Column: History of Australian Studies

编者按

1979 年 1 月，九名优秀学者经过严格遴选，成为“文革”后中国派遣的首批赴澳留学生。从悉尼大学学成归国后，他们在各自所在的大学陆续建立了澳大利亚研究中心，并推动了 1988 年中国澳大利亚研究会的建立和国内澳大利亚研究界与英语学科的发展。这九名学者即如今熟知的澳研前辈“九人帮”成员，包括（依年龄分别为）北京大学胡壮麟教授、对外经贸大学杨潮光教授、北京外国语大学胡文仲教授、上海对外经贸大学黄源深教授、南京大学钱佼汝教授、苏州大学王国富教授、西安外国语大学杜瑞清教授以及已经逝世的侯维瑞先生和龙日金先生。

2018 年 6 月第十六届中国澳大利亚研究国际学术研讨会正值中国澳大利亚研究会成立 30 周年，我们有幸请到七位健在的先生出席或以文字的形式分享这段重要历史，这里面不仅有他们在澳学术上不断求索的经历，还包括与澳大利亚缔结的长达数十年的深厚情谊。

为此，本栏目专门收录了各位先生的演讲与回忆，并保留了英文原稿以飨读者。澳研前辈们的亲身经历以及澳研发展初期的故事将鼓舞更多的学者为澳大利亚研究事业做出贡献，推动国内澳研专业继续向前发展。

第一张："九人帮"在悉尼大学的合影
（前排左起：龙日金、侯维瑞、黄源深；
后排左起：钱佼汝、胡壮麟、杨潮光、胡文仲、王国富、杜瑞清）

第二张：中国澳大利亚研究会成立合照（1988 年）

Our Story: the Story of the Group of Nine

Hu Wenzhong

In 1978 China started opening to the outside world and one of the strategic moves was to send teachers overseas for further studies. Nine were selected through a national examination from among young and middle aged teachers across the country and their destination was Australia. This is what is later known as the Group of Nine. The group includes Du Ruiqing (from Xi'an), Hou Weirui (Shanghai), Hu Wenzhong (Beijing), Hu Zhuanglin (Beijing), Huang Yuanshen (Shanghai), Long Rijin (Chongqing), Qian Jiaoru (Nanjing), Wang Guofu (Suzhou) and Yang Chaoguang (Beijing). The oldest in the group was forty-five and the youngest thirty-five.

It was an exchange program signed with the Australian government. At the time there was no direct flight from Beijing to Sydney and we had to change planes first in Guangzhou and then in Hong Kong. Upon arrival we were met by two officials from the NSW Department of Education and taken directly to the International House close to Sydney University. Not knowing our level of English, Sydney University prepared for us a program of newspaper reading and spoken English. We negotiated with the university administration and insisted that we take degree courses and be enrolled as MA students. With support from

Professor Leonie Kramer, Head of the Department of English, and Professor M. A. K. Halliday, Head of the Department of Linguistics, the university registrar finally agreed. Six of us were enrolled in the English Department and the rest in the Linguistics Department. Hoping to learn as much as we could while abroad, we took a lot more courses than required and frequently worked late into the night.

At the weekend friends from the Australia-China Friendship Association and China Education Society would come to pick us up and take us to their homes or arrange outings for us. This happened week after week and we became the envy of the whole International House. We were the only foreign students given such special treatment. Sometimes our Australian friends would arrange visits and meetings outside of Sydney for us, which helped us understand Australian society and culture better. In August 1980 the China Education Society arranged for us a visit to Gandagai, a typical Australian country town whose history is interwoven with many ballads and folk songs. It was a 400 mile trip from Sydney and we had to break our trip at several points. Each time our friends would stop at a nearby pub for a beer. By the time we arrived we were half filled with beer and not a few were tipsy. But we found to our surprise that our Gandagai hosts had prepared more beer for us. It was on this trip that I realized what beer meant to Australians.

By the end of two years we graduated from Sydney University with MA degrees and two of us with MA Honours. We returned to our home universities and resumed teaching. With fresh input we were able to offer new courses in English and American literature, Australian literature, linguistics, and stylistics. In time we all attained full professorship and five of us became doctoral supervisors. We also took up administrative posts: eight of us became heads of English departments and one was appointed editor-in-chief of a university publishing house. Later three of us were made vice president or president of their universities. Several became leading figures of professional organizations. The Group of Nine helped establish six Australian studies centres in the country and in 1988 the national association for Australian studies was set up with Hu Wenzhong and Huang Yuanshen as its president and vice president. Richard McGregor, an Australian journalist, once said, "Some have developed a taste for Lawson, others Patrick White. But all have become Australia's champions in the People's Republic. "[①] Several of the group were given national awards and awards from Australia-China Council and two were granted awards for their life-long achievement in China's foreign language education. Professor Hu Zhuanglin is acknowledged as the leading academic in systemic linguistics in China and senior professor of Peking University with numerous publications. Professor Huang Yuanshen's *A History of Australian Literature* and Professor Hou Weirui's *A History of Modern English Fiction* are classic works in their own field. Professor Wang Guofu translated and edited *Macquarie English-Chinese Bilingual Dictionary*, which has become an indispensable work in translating and studying Australian English. Professor Du Ruiqing is editor-in-chief of the *New Century Chinese-English Dictionary* (revised edition), which is one of the most influential Chinese-English dictionaries. The list of publications authored by the group is too long to enumerate. When the Group of Nine have made their mark and won recognition in the academic field, the late Professor Wang Zuoliang said, "Judging by what the group have achieved academically, I believe Sydney University must be a top-notch institution of higher learning. "

2009 was the 30th anniversary of the Group of Nine's arrival in Australia. Professor Dame Leonie Kramer and Professor John Cleverley, founder of the China Education Centre, came to Beijing to join our reunion. By this time there were only the seven of us in the group with Professor Hou and Professor Long having passed away more than ten years ago. Now on the eve of the 40th anniversary of our trip to Australia we wish to thank Sydney University and its staff, especially Professor Kramer, Professor Halliday and Professor Cleverley, for their guidance and mentoring. We are grateful to the Australia-China Council and our other friends in Australia for their enduring help over the years.

---

① *The Weekend Review*, May 31, 1997.

How We Learned to Read and Think Critically

—A Glimpse of the Life at Sydney University

Huang Yuanshen

"…our universities are both conservative and radical: conservative in that they preserve and teach knowledge of the past, and radical in that they encourage an informed critique of the past, and discussion by students of the merits and defects of their reading."

Dame Leonie Kramer

In February 1979, we nine of us were sent to Sydney University for two years' professional training, with indeed a feeling of being catapulted onto a new planet. Everything was novel to us, far more in academic than in physical sense, though the unique style of the university architecture left us dumb-founded at the very first sight. An Australian class seemed altogether different from what we could recall its Chinese counterpart of our schooldays. Back in China, a language teacher acted in class most likely as a scholarly model for students to imitate and follow, very often blindly. Students accepted what they had read and had been taught hardly with a doubt. Criticism in its cultural implication was a word never heard of. As both students and teachers for more than two decades, we had been quite used to this educational pattern of practice and things had come out well until one day we were accidently transplanted into the Australian academic soil.

We belonged to a tiny group of the lucky few chosen, through a competitive national examination, from thousands of qualified teachers representing various universities and colleges in China. With the confidence possibly intrinsic to all winners we held that nothing could stop us from scoring further triumph. We believed that the immediate future at Sydney University would be days of all sunshine. But this turned out to be untrue for soon we nearly met our Waterloo. In our new class students were brought to the centre of attention and required to present their views on a set topic based on the extensive reading of reference books. Teachers only played the role of a guide or, so to speak, a chair-person, making sure that the discussion got going on the right track. To quote Professor Dame Leonie Kramer, "they encourage an informed critique of the past, and discussions by students of the merits and defects of their reading." We were taken by surprise, for we never thought that in class we would be chief speakers, discussing the merits and defects of our reading, which used to be accomplished by teachers. We took it for granted what we had to do was just to listen and take notes of lectures as being the case with our language courses before. We were thus forced into a situation where we had to be the audience, not speakers in a seminar because for one thing, we were unable to fulfill the reading assignments as an outcome of habitual slow perusal of anything we came by and for another, we could hardly form our own judgment of our reading as we had never been urged to read critically and think independently. This lack of critical capacity as a consequence became a stumbling-block to the post-seminar writing of papers, which later had bedeviled us for quite some time.

So we approached our supervisors Professor Leonie Kramer, Dr

Catherine Runcie and their colleagues for advice. We were then enlightened that, of the past knowledge, we should distinguish between right and wrong, the appropriate and the inappropriate to decide what to preserve and what to abandon. To achieve this purpose, a critical attitude should be adopted towards whatever had been read and taught. So we were encouraged to think critically in reading, discussion and writing, which, in our Australian days of "apprenticeship", increased accordingly in great proportions.

We realized that three problems were crying out to be settled: reading speed, critical power and writing capacity. Our later training was more or less a wrestle with these thorny issues.

Never did we consider reading a problem until the first days of cultural immersion at Sydney University, because our understanding used to be thought fairly good and our vocabulary big enough to cope with the reading of diversified subject matter. However, we read too slowly to catch up with the assignments of the courses we had now selected. Reading speed became a major hindrance necessarily to be removed in no time. Measures which sounded ingenious and feasible were soon taken, with each of us having our own knacks. I compelled myself to read faster by setting a limit on the time to be consumed for each page. A chopstick was then invested, as expediency, with a new function of guiding the eyesight by pointing at and moving along each sentence at a reasonably fast speed. It really worked, for by and by I was used to reading faster. I also made it a must to read more than 300 pages of novels per day and had stuck to the practice all through the period at Sydney University. At first I found that it was almost an impossible task and had to reduce the time for sleep to achieve the aim. But gradually I grew accustomed to it and in those two years my reading speed was fast enough to cover all the representative works of the major Australian writers in history.

Our critical faculty was weak for the chronic lack of practice in critique. Language learning to us had all along been a process of linguistic appreciation without slightest effort of criticism involved. We were taught and later taught our students to savor the beauty of the language, often at the expense of the meaning implied. We stopped in reading from time to time to enjoy and jot down "useful phrases and beautiful sentences", which had become our major concern of reading. Now we determined to change the reading habit by shifting our focus from "language points" to the evaluation of the contents expressed through the language. We made a critical note of what had been read, specifically an episode, a chapter or the whole book. Short comments, fragmentary yet in a way original, were accumulating in written form from day to day. Eventually we learned to read in a critical mode. Discussions with our changed role in them of active participants helped to sharpen our critical faculty. Writing further enhanced our skill of criticism.

Writing was however always the weakest of our three major language skills: reading, speaking and writing. Our writing skill at its best in school days deteriorated almost with each passing year. Meanwhile, in the academic system of Sydney University writing seemed overwhelmingly important as each course was evaluated by paper writing. I believed I need to write more in order to write better. For that reason, I chose to do my MA degree by both course work and thesis writing, although one of them was adequate as specified by the university rules. In course paper writing I decided on a demanding topic: "Matthew Arnold's 'Disinterestedness' Reconsidered" in spite of my supervisor's dissuasion for my sake from doing it. I searched for reference books on the topic and read carefully what I could lay my hand on with a critical eye as we had been learning to do so. In my paper while identifying the value of "disinterestedness" applied in criticism by Arnold, I did not spare its initiator by revealing the underlying flaws of his theory. My endeavor came out fruitful as was noted in Professor Kramer's memoir (BROOMSTICK, Personal Reflections of Leonie Kramer): "Huang came to me to say that he would write on Matthew Arnold's concept of disinterestedness. He brooked no suggestion that it was too difficult, and earned an 'A' for his efforts." However to concoct an MA thesis was a much more arduous task than writing a course paper, not just for scale but for complication. Also Henry Lawson, the topic of my thesis, had been nearly exhausted. The attempt to find something new was no more than the effort to dig in a dried well to retrieve water. Unless further depth was reached the labor would end up futile. So I resorted to close reading with a critical mind of the complete works by Lawson and found to my satisfaction enough to say which was worthwhile but unsaid. The thesis writing, a hard battle in a sense, incurred more work and less sleep in the last few months before graduation. But the toil proved most rewarding, as Professor Kramer marked the thesis with an "A" and "Distinction". Anyway our writing skill improved immensely in the two years' training at Sydney University.

The strengthened capacity for reading, criticism and writing brought us on to the right path of the academic pursuit and made it easier for us to adapt to the educational system there, leading up to the successful completion of our MA study. What seemed most valuable, when I recall the days at Sydney University now, is perhaps not the MA degree we attained, but the ability we acquired to read and think critically. We owe it all to the staff of Sydney University, particularly Professor Dame Leonie Kramer, Dr Catherine Runcie and their responsible colleagues. We thank them all.

Stories of Our Study and Life in Australia Forty Years Ago

*Yang Chaoguang**

Respectable Chairman,

Dear Friends, Australian and Chinese:

Hello, everyone!

First of all, I'd like to thank the hosts for inviting me to this great event. I'm very happy to meet so many friends here, old and new, Australian and Chinese.

I did not realize that a significant change in my life would take place when we, the Group of Nine, landed at Sydney Airport in early February 1979 after a long and exhausting flight of more than 16 hours via Hong Kong from Beijing. There we were warmly met by Mr. DeVogue and Ms. Horniman, two officials from the Department of Education of the government of New South Wales. After briefing their schedule to us, they drove us directly to an International House attached to the University for accommodations during our stay in Australia. The International House was a sort of hostel, one room for each. There that night, we all slept so soundly that when they took us to a city tour the

* A Speech at the 16th International Conference of Australian Studies in China.

next morning, we were all ready to see the new world. We visited the town House and the city museum, the harbor bridge and the worldly famous Sydney Opera House. We were deeply impressed by the beauty of the city. I still remember how much I enjoyed the chocolate ice-cream they treated us to. It was so big, so sweet, so tasty and so very cheap! Just half an Australian Dollar I remember. I had never eaten any ice-scream before, not to say, chocolate ice-scream! Please do not forget it happened forty years ago, and not long after the ten-year long great national havoc, followed by the ultimate down-fall of the Gang of Four. Only tiny hawthorn ice-candies were available to people like us then in China.

On the third day, the Chancellor of Sydney University interviewed us in his office, and expressed his kind concern by asking us about our long journey from China, and about our accommodation in Sydney. Then he introduced us to the heads of the graduate program of the Art Faculty: Prof. Krammar and Prof. Halliday, who were to be our supervisors during our two-year study there. The same Chancellor met us again a year later and inquired after our life and study and the progress we had made. Both Prof. Krammar and Prof. Halliday were worldly known scholars, one in literature and the other in linguistics. It was our pure luck to have come under their guidance. They were very strict and highly responsible academically, but very kind and considerate towards our life. They even took pains to host us now and then in their respective home and to have a face to face chat. Therefore, it goes without saying that we should attribute all the achievement we made in those two years to them, and to those relevant professors at the departments of literature and linguistics. It is a great loss to both Australia and China and also to all of us the Group of Nine that both of them have already left this world! At the end of two years of study, the university honored us with a very formal and grand ceremony for the granting of M. A. degree. It was specifically held for the Nine of Us with hundreds of leading academic personnel of the university present. The next morning, leading media of Sydney and the country reported this great event in their front page, with a big picture of us Nine, and with commentaries in favor of the good relation unfolding between China and Australia then. Our two years of experience in Australia proved to be very fruitful and greatly beneficial to us all, that is, including me of course. For, in the following 33 years of teaching linguistics and pragmatics at the University of International Business and Economics and ten years at the University of International Relations in Beijing, what I had learned in Australia was a solid base in my work and became my life-long career.

Our life in Australia was also highly rich and colorful. In the International House where we spent our first year, we soon became the focus of attention of almost one hundred tenants who came from all corners of the world, from countries in Africa, Europe, the Middle East, North and South Americas, and Asia, in addition to New Zealand and different parts of Australia, forming into a really big international family. Many of them were eager to make friends with us and to know things about China, I myself developed quite an intimacy with one American, one Australian aboriginal, one Italian, two Koreans and two Japanese. Now and then in the weekend they would drop in on me for a friendly chat over tea or coffee. Through exchange of ideas, we usually found a lot of common ground. People at large like to develop friendly relations with each other. All wish to live in peace and harmony. All want personal development to improve their living conditions. The one American I got to know was a girl of strong will and great ambition. She wanted to run for chairpersonship of the tenents' union in the International House, and sought our support in the election. As she had been quite friendly to us, we decided to back her up. Eventually with our strong support, she got elected. What surprised me was that she told me confidentially that when she went back to the US, she would run for the Senate, and then for the presidency of the US! I wonder how far she has succeeded in her ambition! One Australian aboriginal female student took me to her home village to meet her old parents during the long break between school terms, and asked me a lot about the life of China's minorities and China's policy toward minorities. What impressed me deeply was her strong determination to learn the science of language well so that she could compose a writing system for her tribal people. I expressed my deep respect of her and wished her the best of all. For I am sure her dream would someday come true. One Israeli also treated me at her home and expressed her wish to develop friendly relations with the Chinese people. I even made a new friend in a swimming pool! He was then a teacher of physics at a senior middle school in Sydney. When he found that I was from Beijing, he invited me to his home with sincerity. So, the following Sunday, we talked over his dinner table for full three and a half hours!

One incident is worth mentioning here. The tenants at the International House made a decision to hold an international night on the New Year's Eve 1980. Each country should contribute home-made food with a performance of dance or songs at the party. We nine of us decided to serve Jiaozi and chorus a song "In Praise of Our Motherland" . It so happened that there was one graduate from Taiwan. He was all alone. He asked to be allowed to join us in the chorus. So with our consent, he spent two nights learning to sing the song. Eventually at that international night, he went onto the stage and sang the song with us. So, there was one China that night. .

During our two-year stay in Australia, it was so arranged that each of us nine had one Australian family. My Australian family was an elderly couple, Mr. and Mrs. Whitson. The husband, Duncan, was a native Australian and his wife, Mary, was an Irish, Both were pious

Christians. They hosted me at their home almost every other weekend. I was almost moved to tears when the old lady told me that she bought a Chinese recipe book and learned to cook Chinese food especially for me. I will never forget their loving-kindness shown to me in those days. They even invited me to their daughter's marriage ceremony at a district church and also to the dinner party that followed. It so happened that in accordance with their national custom, as the family's most distinguished guest that night, I was given the right to hug and kiss the bride at the party. To my great surprise and embarrassment, they took a snap shot of it when I was giving the bride a kiss. Then they threatened that they would mail the photo back to my wife in China, with a note that Mr. Yang had married an Australian girl in Sydney, and that according to Australian law, if a husband stayed away from his wife for over six months, their marriage would become null and void, and so Mr. Yang could be legally married with another female in Australia. I was aghast, but I fought back instantly, saying if they didn't mind I would really take her back to Beijing. Immediately there were shouts and laughter. All the people laughed a hearty laugh, and chorused the folk Australian national anthem "Waltsin' Watilder" at the top of voice. It was really a happy night. Australians love humor and like to crack jokes. They are an optimistic, warm-hearted and merry people!

May our friendship between China and Australia and between the two peoples will continue and develop in the years to come!

Thank you for listening.

My Teacher M. A. K. Halliday's Personality and Academic Attitude

Hu Zhuanglin

When I was asked by my friends or students about my impressions of Australia, I would always talk about my teacher, Prof. M. A. K. Halliday. This morning I would still stick to this point because Prof. M. A. K. Halliday just passed away two months ago, at 8 p. m. , April 15, 2018 at the age of 93. My teacher, my supervisor left me forever. I can't overcome my sorrow at hearing the sad news. Various feelings poured into my mind.

1. Strictness and leniency in supervising students

Prof. Halliday held a positive view of China's university education. In January 1979, a group of 9 Chinese teachers were accepted by Sydney University to receive their advanced education. Me and two other members chose to study in the Department of Linguistics. It was Prof. Halliday, the chairman of the department, encouraged us to do MA degree. In addition to this, we should take two more courses than the local participants in each term or semester. Seeing that we were puzzled, he explained to us patiently: "I know quite well the academic level of university education in China and also know you Chinese students all work very hard." He then pointed out that many Australian postgraduates were learning part-time because they still had to teach in the high schools. As for those young postgraduates, they had also to work part-time in order to pay for their fees or living allowance, especially during the long holidays between the two terms. He further pointed out, "You all receive scholarship from your government. Your tuition and living allowance are paid by your government. Therefore, you have enough time to take courses." Thus, Mr. Long and I did earn all the credits and finished the final paper required for the university's MA (Pass) degree in one year, and moved on to finish MA (Honours) the second year.

Another story is about our performance in his seminar. When we listened to Prof. Halliday's lecture, we tended to ask him a lot of questions, especially those related to the Chinese language. Very often Michael would remind us, "This is seminar. It's better for you not to ask me questions all the time. You should ask and discuss these questions among yourselves. So far as I know, the term 'postgraduate' is 'yanjiusheng' in Chinese, that is to say, you should learn to study and analyse questions by yourselves. You should not just sit on the bench, listening to lectures and taking notes." It goes without saying that I

A photo taken together with Prof. Halliday before leaving the University of Sydney in May 1981, the one at the left being the late Mr. Long of the former Southwest Normal University.

benefited quite a lot from his teaching.

2. Honest, practical and realistic attitude toward achievements

Before I went to Australia, a friend of mine, Prof. Zhao Shikai of the linguistic institute of China Academy of Social Sciences, advised me to know something about the London School as Prof. Halliday got his doctorate degree with Firth as his supervisor. Because of this, the western academic world had always seen him as a successor of the London School and called him a "Firthian". However, Prof. Halliday didn't care much about my question about the London School later.

It was in 1991 when I prepared a paper for celebrating the 90th birthday of Prof. Wang Li (Michael's supervisor in 1950 – 1951), I began to notice many of Michael's ideas were found in Wang Li's publications, so my paper was entitled "Wang Li and Halliday", but I was still not quite sure whether Michael got his ideas from Wang Li directly or not (Hu, 1991).

Until 2013, I found in many of Michael's interviews taken after his retirement (Martin 2013), he always reminded the interviewer (s) that he got his linguistic knowledge and research methods mainly through two Chinese scholars, Wang Li and Luo Changpei. This is "the first input" of his academic thoughts (Hernandez, 1998; in Martin 2011: 147-160). In a 2010 interview, he simply used the passive voice in his reply. "I was called a Firthian by my friends... But it was not just him; I was also influenced by one professor in China in particular. His name was Wang Li" (Rasheed, 2010, in Martin 2011: 208).

Personally, I had the chance to ask him the following question, "If you continued to do research on the Chinese language after graduation, but not English, would it be difficult for you to develop your systemic-functional linguistics? Would you fail to be a world renowned scholar?" There are two points clearly mentioned in his reply. One is that he himself would choose to go on with his study in Chinese, but his university ordered him to focus on English. Another point is more important. He said, although his corpus changed from the Chinese language to English, the basic theoretical framework, the guiding principles and research methods had already been harbored in his mind when he did research on Chinese. This confirmed the enlightening effects of those Chinese supervisors.

In passing, I would also mention one of my encounters with Michael.

Once I had a talk with Michael in his office. He took a book written by a Chinese linguist Gao Mingkai down from his shelf and told me: "Gao Mingkai's book is also worth reading." Shamely, I didn't keep his words in my mind at that time.

Even in 2011 I was invited to deliver a paper to celebrate the 100th Anniversary of Kao Mingkai's birthday. I still didn't care much about the relation between the two scholars. It was 5 years later when I wrote a paper about the Chinese origin of Michael Halliday's academic thoughts, I came to notice that Michael was also influenced by Gao Mingkai on many academic issues, and came to recall the deep meaning expressed by Michael during our talk in 1979.

Thus, I was quite impressed by Michael's good quality to acknowledge the truth. Although he held the Brtish passport, and his PhD's supervisor was Prof. Firth, he did not betray himself, he did not deceive the academic world. His honesty sets a good example to me.

3. Marxist approach to linguistic research

The reason for Prof. Halliday to get wonderful achievements academically, is somewhat related to his experiences in China. He was "liberated" twice when the PLA marched into Beijing in early 1949 and Guangzhou a year later, and consequently influenced by the Chinese revolution and Marxism. This urged him to join the Marxist Linguistics Group of the British Communist Party after he returned to England. When interviewed by Hasan, Kress and Martin, he said, "I always wanted to see what I was going toward as, in the long run, a Marxist linguistics—working on language in the political context." (Hasan, Kress & Martin, 1986; in Martin ed., 2013: 117-8) "What we shared was a Marxist view of language. We were trying to understand and build up a theory of language which would be ... giving value" (Hernandez, 1998, in Martin ed. 2013: 150).

As a result, many of his views about system and function, word and grammar, clause and text, instantiation and realization, theory and practice etc., are actually guided by the Marxist principle of "One divides into two." In addition to this, Halliday should also be highly praised for his views about "Two combines into one". This can be illustrated by his description about "continuum" and "system", as shown in the following graphs.

All this suggests that Michael Halliday had a good command of "the

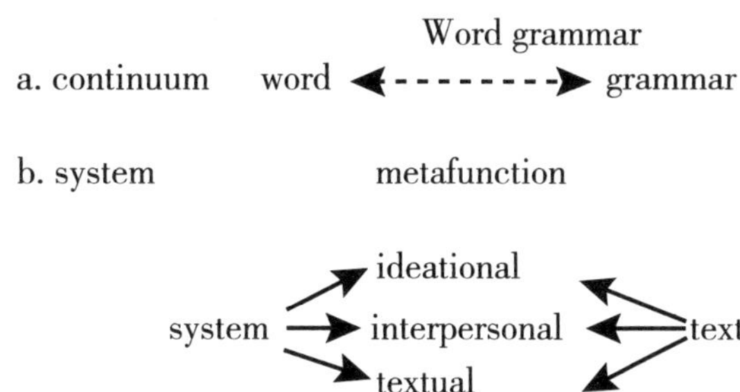

law of the unity of opposites" underlying historical materialism and dialectic materialism. His "probabilistic" approach predicted the arrival of the contemporary notion of "Big Data".

I am glad to mention here that in China, a scholar, He Yuanxiu by name, has published a book in 2016 entitled "*Halliday's New Marxist Approach*".

4. No end to knowledge and appliable linguistics

In my talks with Michael Halliday, he touched upon this view very often, that is, there is no end for theory, no end for academic research. If someday someone declares his theory or academic finding has reached perfection, this suggests he begins to lose his direction to move forward, he will just stop there, and he will disappear finally.

For another thing, with the development of systemic-functional Linguistics home and abroad, we have already witnessed that within SFL there are various approaches, such as Sydney School, Cardiff School, linguistic semiotics, computational linguistics, ecological linguistics, etc.. Even within the Sydney School, there are different views between Martin and Hasan. Once I invited Michael to talk about his critical views toward all these, he refused to say any word. As a matter of fact, he talked about his views already in his theory of appliable linguistics. The chief objective of appliable linguistics is to provide guiding and critical principles to the evaluation of a theory, such as the construction of meaning, the objective and mechanism of an approach, its social account, its practicality, etc. . This is the reason why I hold the view that the objective of appliable linguistics does not merely serve as a guide to different schools or approaches within SFL, it can also be applied to linguistic theories other than SFL (Hu, 2017) . This also shows that Halliday on the one hand acknowledged the right of existence for different theories or schools, and, on the other hand, suggested that we should focus our attention on its objective, theoretical background, methods and value. There is no point for us just to say "yes" or "no" for a theory or school. This also tells us that based on what we did in the past and present, we should always look into the future and explore new breakthrough.

5. Love for China and China dream

As it is known to all, Michael wrote a story about his visit to China when he was just 4 years old, and chose to learn Chinese in the army after leaving school. He received his undergraduate and postgraduate education at Peking University and Linnan University respectively (Hu, 2015, 2016) . Here, I would like to restrict myself to two points.

First, he was the only foreign scholar highly acknowledged and supported by universities in China so far, which can be illustrated as follows:

——He was offered Guest Professorship of Peking University in 1996.

—— "The Halliday Intelligence Research Center of Appliable Linguistics" was established by Hong Kong City University in 2006.

——He was awarded Honorary Doctorate by Beijing Normal University in 2011.

—— "The Halliday Center of Linguistic Publications" was set up by Sun Yat-sen University in 2013.

The second point is the setting up of the International Halliday-Hasan Fund for Linguistics" at Beijing Normal University in April

The Ceremony of Offering PKU Guest Professorship to Prof. M. A. K. Halliday in 1996

2015. Michael donated all his lecture payment (RMB 100, 000) from Beijing Normal University to the fund. His objective of educating the young generation in China is worthy of our appreciation. This should be further stressed the fact that Michael flew alone to Beijing at the old age of 90, to launch the foundation ceremony and attend China's 14th National Conference of Functional Linguistics. The organizer of the conference also held an evening party to celebrate his 90th birthday. All the participants felt ease at that time witnessing his good health and high spirits in attending all these events.

Prof. M. A. K. Halliday at the 2015 Events.

References

Martin, J. R. *Interviews with M. A. K. Halliday—Language Talking Back on Himself*, London/New York: Bloombury, 2013.

He, Yuanxiu（何远秀）, *Halliday's New Marxist Approach to Linguistics*（《韩礼德的新马克思主义语言研究取向》）, China Academy of Social Sciences（中国社会科学院）, 2016。

Hu, Zhuanglin（胡壮麟）, "Wang Li and Halliday"（王力与韩礼德）, *Journal of Peking University*［《北京大学学报（英语语言文学专刊）》］, 1991。

Hu, Zhuanglin（胡壮麟）, "Interpreting Halliday's Appliable Linguistics"（解读韩礼德的 Appliable Linguistics）, *Journal of School of Sichuan Foreign Languages*（《四川外语学院学报》）, 2007（6）。

Hu, Zhuanglin（胡壮麟）, "Developing linguistic Theories with Chinese Features: In Commemoration of 100th Annivresary of Gao Mingkai's Birthday"（发展中国特色的语言理论研究——纪念高名凯先生诞生 100 周年）, *Modern Foreign Language Research*（《当代外语研究》）, 2013（3）: 1-6。

Hu, Zhuanglin（胡壮麟）, "Halliday's China Dream"（韩礼德的中国梦）, *Foreign Languages in China*（《中国外语》）, 2015, 12（6）: 15-19。

Hu, Zhuanglin（胡壮麟）, "The Chinese Origin of Halliday's Academic Thoughts and its Return",（韩礼德学术思想的中国渊源和回归）*Foreign Language Research*（《外语

研究》)，2016 (5)，9 -13。

Hu, Zhuanglin (胡壮麟)，"*The Chinese Origin of Halliday's Academic Thoughts and its Return*" (《韩礼德学术思想的中国渊源和回归》). *Foreign Language Teaching and Research Press* (外语教学与研究出版社)，2018。

The Little Bit I have Done for the Australian Studies

Wang Guofu

Thank you, Mr Chairman,

Good morning, Ladies and Gentlemen,

I feel greatly honored to be here today. First of all, I'd like to express my heartfelt thanks to the organizer of the conference for his kindness of inviting us the 7 old men to join in the celebration of the 30th anniversary of the founding of the Australian Studies Association in China. 30 years ago, a small group met here in Beijing for the First International Conference of Australian Studies in China and the setting up of the Association. Ever since the Australian studies scholars in China would be able to meet regularly every other year to compare notes and exchange ideas. The Second Conference was held in Xiamen University in 1990, at which a decision was made that the Third Conference would be held jointly in Shanghai and Suzhou. This decision gave birth to the Australian Studies Centre of Soochow University. As the founding chairman of the center I thought to myself that we had to do something as our contribution to the Australian studies in China. I suddenly found that it was a good opportunity to realize my long-cherished dream, that is, to compile and publish a dictionary on Australian words and expressions.

This idea has to be traced back to my early days in Australia.

As you all know, forty years ago Australia was little known to us Chinese. I only knew it was a country in the southern hemisphere and known for its merino wool. Therefore, when I was notified that we would be sent to Australia for further study, I immediately rushed to the school library in the hope of finding something to read about the country. But unfortunately, to my great disappointment, I could find nothing at all, either in Chinese or in English. So you can see that I went to Australia with the scantiest knowledge of the country. Yet I thought then probably it would be OK, for I had already studied English for more than 20 years and had passed the national English examination.

But things were not so easy as I had expected. In the first few months I met with quite some difficulty in understanding Australian English.

When we first arrived in Sydney, we were accommodated with board and lodging at the International House close to Sydney University. Mr De Graaf, the director of the house, gave a barbecue party at the weekend in honor of the first group of Chinese students to Australia. In his welcome speech he taught us some Australian expressions, he said: "... I'm not pulling your leg. I'm a fair dinkum Aussie. I'm not kidding ..." . Of course I didn't understand what he had said, for I had never come across these expressions either in reading or in conversation, though I had learned English for many years, and thus looked puzzled until he explained them to us. He said, " 'fair dinkum' means 'genuine, true; really, truly', 'I'm not pulling your leg' and 'I'm not kidding' both mean 'I'm not making fun of or teasing you. " Australian people speak, of course, English but Australian English is not all the same as British English. It is a national variety. It has its own characteristics as Mr Geof Whitlam says in his foreword to our dictionary, "from the first days of British settlement in 1788 Australians have developed many words and expressions which are today identifiably Australian. ” No wonder I had met so much difficulty in language in my first days in Australia.

What is more, many Australians speak English with a strong broad accent, which also caused a lot of trouble to me. When a man said “I'm going today”, it really sounded to me , like “I'm going to die”. I was surprised at it and looked at him in bewilderment. I'm not kidding, fair dinkum. I said to myself that if there had been some books on Australian English so that I could have worked on them before I came here, life would have been a bit easier.

Since then I did my best to collect such books wherever and whenever I could. At that time I had a vague idea to compile and publish some books on Australian words and expressions in future after I returned home when chances presented themselves. I was sure that latecomers would be able to benefit from them and would have less difficulty in language than we had when they set foot on this piece of lucky land.

Chances had not come until ten years after I came back home. In 1990 Mr. Neil Courtney, a foreign expert from Monarch University, and I worked together to compile *the English-Chinese Dictionary of Australianisms* which was published in 1992 shortly before the 3rd International Conference of Australian Studies in China and the book was launched at the conference. The publication of the book led to my working as a visiting scholar at the Macquarie Dictionary Research Centre for 6 months in Macquarie University. At the end of my stay there I was given the copyright of *the Macquarie Concise Dictionary* to take back to China and have it translated into Chinese and published there.

Back to Suzhou in May 1993, I organized a team of 40 odd translators from 5 colleges in Suzhou area to work on it day and night for two long years. *The Macquarie English-Chinese Bilingual Dictionary* was published by Soochow University Press in April 1999, for which I was awarded the

Australia-China Council's Translation Prize. Two book launches were organized for the dictionary by the Australian side, one in Beijing and the other in Shanghai. Mr Alexander Downer, the Foreign Minister of Australia, gave a speech at the Beijing book launch while Dr David Kemp, the Minister of Education of Australia, gave a speech at the Shanghai one. Mr Downer says in his preface to the dictionary, "The dictionary is itself an excellent example of what can be achieved through cooperation."

At the turn of the century I handed over the Australian Studies Centre of Soochow University to Professor Wang Labao. I was pretty sure that the young scholars would do a better job in Australian studies in the days to come.

My last project in Australian studies was *the English-Chinese Dictionary of Australian Education* which was published by Wuhan University Press in 2003. In that year I retired from Soochow University to the last phase of my life. But in 2008 I was given a medallion of Australia-China Council Award for the little bit I had done for the Australian studies.

That's all for my story. Thank you for your attention!

Home Away From Home

—The Host Family Scheme

Qian Jiaoru

In the early days of government-sponsored student exchange programs between China and Australia long before self-funding Chinese students began to swarm Australian campuses, Chinese faces from the mainland were a rare sight at that time much as foreign faces were likely to be stared at in China in the 1970s. For some historical reasons the Chinese people had been estranged for many years from people in other countries and this made their later efforts to understand each other more or less strenuous.

Soon after we settled down to our studies at the University of Sydney, we were introduced to the Host Family Scheme, which had already been in existence in Australia to help foreign students overcome initial culture shocks upon their arrival in a new land and to facilitate their understanding of the local culture. With the arrangements made by Mr. Jan de Voogd and Miss Val Horniman of the Sydney Office of the Commonwealth Department of Education at 59 Goulburn Street in downtown Sydney, each of us was assigned to an Australian host family to begin a relationship that continued to develop after we returned to our respective institutions in China.

My host family was the Christmas's in North Sydney, a devout

Christian family of four members: Gerald, a successful lawyer, his wife Rosemary and their children Paul and Sally. Our first few contacts were polite but somewhat strained. Each side took care not to say or to do anything that might be considered inappropriate in a culture they did not know much about. One of the things I remember clearly was about formality at meals. As Christians, the Christmas family followed the routine of saying grace before meals. Although I knew about this practice, I was not sure whether I should join in the ritual or just sit still and wait till they finished. When I asked them what I should properly do in this situation, I was very kindly told that I could do what I thought best. They did not say yes or no, leaving the decision to my own discretion with due respect for my individual judgment.

Later on, as we saw more of each other and came to know each other better, the psychological barrier that inhibited open and free communication in the beginning began to break down. We could now discuss family matters and personal hobbies and interests. When they learned that I was a classical music lover of sorts, they most generously put me on their family season ticket at the Sydney Opera House. I was thus perhaps a more frequent visitor than the rest of the Group to that renowned concert hall, where I had the rare pleasure of listening to live symphonic concerts for the first time in my life. I remember enjoying the Sydney Symphony Orchestra under Louis Fremaux playing masters of classical music as well as contemporary Australian composers. One special occasion that stuck in my memory was a concert featuring the visiting Chinese violinist Sheng Zhongguo, who played the beautiful Chinese piece The Butterfly Lovers followed by Tchaikovsky's Violin Concerto in D Major. It was a thrilling performance that received an ovation from the enthusiastic audience not only because of the soloist's technical virtuosity but also because he was the first musician from China to visit and perform in Australia shortly after the unusual period in which Western music was denounced in his country as bourgeois and mind corrupting.

After I returned to China in 1981 my contact with my host family went on for a number of years in the form of exchanging greeting cards and pictures of our children in their different stages of growth. In 2002, I met Gerald and Rosemary again in Sydney when I was attending a symposium there commemorating the 30th anniversary of the establishment of formal diplomatic relations between China and Australia. The lapse of twenty years between our two meetings did not seem to have weakened the bond that had brought us together. And of course I did not forget to tell them again how thankful and appreciative I was of their hospitality in giving me a home when I was away from home.

第16届澳大利亚研究国际学术研讨会（2018年6月21~23日）

16th *International Conference of Australian Studies in China Group of Nine—My story*

Du Ruiqing（杜瑞清）

Good morning, fellow conference participants, friends old and new, ladies and gentlemen,

It's an immense pleasure to be invited by the conference and to share my story in Sydney, Australia, as a member of the Group of Nine. First of all, I must say that I had two most memorable years in Australia and I owe much to the University of Sydney for what I was. The two years in Sydney was my first extensive experience overseas and the exchange program I was fortunate to take with eight other members of the group put a new dimension on me. Upon returning to Xi'an with the knowledge I had gained, I initiated courses in American/British literature (with some Australian literature thrown in) to address the pressing need of my home institution in curricular building. I returned a different and better me in the eyes of my colleagues. Professionally, at the least, I became confident enough to say "I don't know" when I came across things, particularly about the English language, that I really didn't know much about.

The academic program in Sydney was rigorous. In addition to regular, required courses I had, with other members of the literature group, a special course in literary criticism and theory, which Dr. Catherine Runcie drew up and co-taught with Professor Leonie Kramer, who was chairperson of the English Department. Also, I had the privilege to have Dr. Runcie tutor Professor Hou and me Australian, American and British fiction. It was actually a customized course geared to the need for my teaching back in my home institution.

Well, for the Group of Nine, memories of Sydney are indelible. And the stories can be told days and nights on end. As the time allocated to us is limited, I will not repeat what others have told and will move my tale from on-campus to off-campus, focusing on the friendship I made in Sydney and what that friendship entailed and led to in the ensuing years.

Though inundated with classes and papers the group of nine often times went to parties at the invitation of Australian friends. At one of these gatherings I became acquainted with Professor Thomas Stapleton, who was, according to *Times*, a distinguished leader in paediatric medicine. He had served as Secretary General of the International Paediatrics Association and, at the time we were in Sydney, director of the Institute of Child Health with the Royal Alexandra Hospital for Children.

We became pals. Actually he was a friend to all of us. I understand that he was one of those who helped manoeuvere the special ceremony for our graduation and alerted the local media to the occasion for coverage. During the two years in Sydney he used to take me out at weekends for visits to his friends living in different neighborhoods. When we arrived he would ask me to knock at the door while he was parking his car. At first, I gave the gentle, soft knock, hardly loud enough for the host or hostess to hear. To me, a Chinese not yet acculturated with things Western, too loud a knock would sound impolite. Hearing such a knock, the professor would grin and remind me of the need and cultural appropriateness to knock at the door as Australians did. Another time, I learned the lesson and knocked as hard as circumstances would allow, but nobody answered the door after what seemed to be a long while. I then started knocking at very short intervals. An impatient knock which would also displease, even irritate the host or hostess.

These intercultural nuances, though trivial and insignificant, stood me in good stead in the outreach, international programs I had endeavored as an administrator and in my professional career.

The friendship I developed with Professor Stapleton went well beyond weekend excursions and tidbits in intercultural communication. During our conversation at one time, Professor Stapleton told me, with an air of arrogance, a bit of flaunting even, that he had the privilege to visit many military hospitals across the globe, and he lavished praise on them. Then he said that he didn't know of any in China and suspected that most probably there was none in the country. Noting what I sensed a touch of scornfulness, I retorted, stating that China was not lagging behind other countries in this respect. It boasted several military hospitals, all first-class, by Chinese standards. No sooner had I said that than I became regretful. I realized that I might have disclosed a military secret. Mind you, it was 1979, almost 40 years ago when China was closed to the outside world. And when I heard him say that he would twist people's arms and visit the one in Xi'an on his next trip I became very uneasy. I knew that as a social activist he was good at wheeling and dealing and would most likely talk to people and venture the visit. What if my inadvertent remark about the military hospital and the university landed me in trouble? I became even a bit scared.

Well, Professor Stapleton did manage to visit the Fourth Military Medical University with its affiliated hospitals , which is now renamed

Air Force Military Medical University（空军军医大学） and much to my relief, the experience turned out to be a most delightful and fruitful one.

Professor Stapleton impressed his local hosts and, in turn, the hospitality and the ethos of the university and its hospitals opened the door for him and led to a life-long relationship. The visit yielded welcome, almost unexpected fruits, most important among which is the Oxford Research Scholarships on an annual basis for young, up-coming scholars of the military medical university. The program was started in the early 1980s with a total of 40-odd candidates recommended, screened and dispatched over a span of three decades. Professor Stapleton used to come to Xi'an every year, attending screening sessions and giving lectures, even when he developed the hunch back and had to walk with the help of a stick. And every time he was in Xi'an we would meet and have a meal at my place.

During the young scholars' year-long stay for their research projects, Professor Stapleton provided board and lodging for them in his cottage, in exchange for the help in the house and garden. On weekends he would cook a big breakfast for them.

The Air Force Military Medical University cherishes unforgettable memories of the Professor and had a bronze bust made in his honor. And I am happy to report that many of the young recipients of the Oxford Research Scholarship have become top-notch scientists or medical doctors in their field.

Well, this is the end of my story today, one of the numerous stories that each and every one of you in the audience has and eager to share with others, particularly stories in the changing world. I look forward to hearing them.

Thank you.

《李尧译文集》专栏

Special Column: Prof. *Li Yao's Translation Series of Australian Literature*

编者按

为纪念李尧教授从事文学翻译四十周年，本刊特辟出“《李尧译文集》专栏”，发表了胡文仲教授、Robert Dixon 教授为该文集撰写的“总序”。这两篇序言不但是对李尧教授四十年来文学翻译成果的评论，也是对我国澳大利亚文学翻译渊源与现状的检阅，读来有颇多教益。专栏还发表了中国澳大利亚研究会会长、北京外国语大学副校长孙有中教授于 2018 年 4 月 12 日在澳大利亚西悉尼大学举行的“《李尧译文集》新书发布会”上所做的热情洋溢的讲话。这篇讲话是对李尧教授的鼓励，也是对我国从事澳大利亚文学翻译与研究的学者的鞭策。西悉尼大学校长 Barney Glover 的讲话盛赞了李尧教授为中澳文化交流以及两国人民相互理解所做出的贡献，充分表达了他对中国人民美好的感情。张剑教授的讲话，高屋建瓴地从学术的角度，对《李尧译文集》做了极好的评价，我们在此刊出，以飨读者。

《李尧译文集》序　一

胡文仲

德国文学、法国文学、英国文学、俄罗斯文学、美国文学和日本文学介绍到我国已经有了很长一段历史，从 19 世纪末到 20 世纪初出现了大量各国文学译本。特别是日本文学，据查，在明代已经有李言恭、郑杰编纂的日本短歌 39 首被译为中文。澳大利亚文学进入中国则是近期的事。1953 年上海出版公司出版了 James Aldridge 的小说 *The Diplomat* 的中文译本，这是我国出版的第一部澳大利亚小说。1954 年出版了 Frank Hardy 的《幸福的明天》（*Journey into the Future*）和《不光荣的权力》（*Power Without Glory*），此后又陆续出版了一些长篇和短篇小说以及一些诗集和剧本，包括 Katharine Susannah Prichard 的《沸腾的九十年代》（*The Roaring Nineties*），Judah Waten 的《不屈的人们》（*The Unbending*）等。[①] 但是，总的来说，在 20 世纪 50～70 年代，我国的澳洲文学翻译不仅数量很少，而且，由于当时的时代背景，翻译的选题范围狭窄，作品内容单一。

这一局面的改变得益于 1978 年我国开始实行的改革开放政策。在这一年，发生了一些对澳洲文学翻译具有深远意义的事情。安徽大学成立了大洋洲文学研究所，推出《大洋洲文学》期刊，翻译出版了澳大利亚、新西兰的一些文学作品。人民文学出版社出版了

① 陈弘：《20 世纪我国的澳大利亚文学研究述评》，《华东师范大学学报（哲学社会科学版）》2012 年第 6 期。

刘寿康翻译的《劳森短篇小说集》。那一年年底，教育部将全国选拔出的9位中年教师集中于北京，准备派往悉尼大学。这就是日后人们戏称“九人帮”的一批学者。在悉尼大学，他们虽然分属英文系和语言学系攻读硕士学位，但多数都选修了澳大利亚文学课程。这一批学者在学成归国后，在推动国内澳大利亚研究方面发挥了重要的作用。也就是在那一年，李尧先生开始了他的漫长的文学翻译之旅。

20世纪80和90年代是一个热气腾腾的时代。澳大利亚文学翻译呈现出勃勃生机。在这一时期出版的澳大利亚文学作品包括Alan Marshall的《我能跳过水洼》（*I Can Jump Puddles*），Rolf Boldrewood的《空谷蹄踪》（*Robbery Under Arms*），Patrick White的《风暴眼》（*The Eye of the Storm*）、《人树》（*The Tree of Man*）、《探险家沃斯》（*Voss*）、《树叶裙》（*A Fringe of Leaves*）和《镜中瑕疵》（*Flaws in the Glass*），Miles Franklin的《我的光辉生涯》（*My Brilliant Career*），Randolph Stow的《归宿》（*To the Island*），Thomas Keneally的《辛德勒的名单》（*Schindler's List*）和《内海的女人》（*Woman of the Inner Sea*），Peter Carey的《奥斯卡和露辛达》（*Oscar and Lucinda*）以及一批短篇小说集和诗集。Jack Hibberd的剧本《想入非非》（*A Stretch of the Imagination*）不仅翻译出版，而且在京沪两地公演。综前所述，可以看出我国译者不断拓展澳大利亚文学翻译的范围，将不同背景、不同流派的作家纳入自己的视野，使得澳洲文学翻译在我国不仅数量激增，而且内容也发生了实质性的变化。

致力于翻译和介绍澳大利亚文学的中国学者是一个群体，既包括早期的马祖毅、刘寿康等，也包括80年代初从澳大利亚归来的留学学者黄源深、胡文仲等，他们一直处在澳大利亚文学翻译、教学和研究的第一线。译者中还包括朱炯强、叶胜年、曲卫国、欧阳昱、李尧等。这一大批译者在介绍和推广澳大利亚文学方面成绩显赫。其中李尧的贡献尤为突出。除了文学翻译，还应该特别提到黄源深教授撰写的《澳大利亚文学史》以及王国富教授主编翻译的《麦夸里英汉双解词典》，这两部巨著对于澳大利亚文学研究和翻译都起了重要的作用。

李尧先生致力于文学翻译四十年，主要从事澳大利亚文学翻译，也翻译出版了部分英美文学作品，总计 52 部，字数逾千万，在我国翻译界如此多产的译者实属少见。李尧翻译的作品涵盖澳大利亚作家老中青三代，既包括老一代作家 Patrick White，Thomas Keneally，Alex Miller 等，也包括中年作家 Peter Carey，Nicholas Jose 等，还包括一些年轻的儿童文学作家。从文学流派看，现实主义、现代主义和魔幻现实主义都囊括其中。此次出版的《李尧译文集》只占他翻译的澳大利亚文学作品的约三分之一。收入文集的作品大部分获得过文学大奖，在澳洲文学中具有一定的代表性，有些则是考虑到作家在中国的影响或者题材与中国有关。这一译文集集中反映了李尧在澳大利亚文学翻译方面的成就。

李尧先生 1966 年毕业于内蒙古师范大学外语系，从事记者工作和文学创作 20 余年，发表过报告文学、散文、小说等近百万字，1986 年成为中国作家协会会员。正是由于李尧的作家背景，他翻译的文学作品具有一个突出特点：文字优美，行文流畅。阅读他翻译的作品给人以欢畅淋漓的感觉。李尧回忆说："我翻译小说的时候，常常是从一个写小说的人的角度出发，像我自己写小说一样，体会、捕捉作者的思路，创作的技巧，注意人物性格化语言的翻译。不是只从字面上去对应。我看懂原文，就用自己的语言而不是字典上的意思去翻译。这样译出来的东西就比较鲜活，可读性强。"翻译 Alexis Wright 的《卡彭塔利亚湾》（*Carpentaria*）难度很大。作者是澳大利亚当代最有成就的原住民作家。小说涉及澳大利亚原住民的宗教信仰、部族矛盾、生产生活方式、风土人情、历史渊源等，而且写作方法也比较独特。李尧在翻译这部小说前，大量阅读了有关澳大利亚原住民历史文化的著作，同时不断和作者联系，取得她的帮助。悉尼大学在授予李尧荣誉文学博士学位时指出："《卡彭塔里亚湾》是李尧毕生从事文学翻译和自 1972 年至今 40 余年来中澳文化交流的巅峰之作。"有评论指出："《卡彭塔利亚湾》是纯文学性文本，李尧先生翻译策略选择，让译文洋溢着一种梦幻般的抒情色彩，充满文学情调，让读者感受到澳大利亚古老土地的荒芜。”①

翻译从来都不是简单地把一种语言变成另一种语言的过程。王佐良先生对于翻译，特别是文学翻译，曾经发表过许多重要的论述。他指出：“因为有翻译，哪怕是不免出错的翻译，文化交流才成为可能。语言学家、文体学家、文化史家、社会思想家、比较文学家都不能忽视翻译。这不仅是因为翻译者的辛勤劳动才使得一国的文化遗产能为全世界的人所用，还因为译者做的文化比较远比一般细致、深入。他处理的是个别的词，他面对的则是两大片文化。”② 李尧正是通过他的文学翻译将独特的澳洲大陆文化介绍给了拥有悠久历史文化传统的中国人民。

李尧先生几十年来耕耘在澳大利亚文学翻译这片土地上，他的勤奋努力非常人所可比拟，他经常夜以继日地工作，节假日也很少休息。他在澳大利亚文学翻译方面的成就获得了广泛的认可，于1996 年、2008 年、2012 年三次获得澳中理事会颁发的澳大利亚文学翻译奖。2014 年被悉尼大学授予名誉文学博士学位。表彰词指出：李尧“在中国，在文学翻译和澳大利亚研究方面做出了杰出的贡献。他把许多澳大利亚作家介绍给中国读者，包括帕特里克·怀特，汤姆·肯尼里，亚历克西斯·赖特，为中国读者更好地了解澳大利亚和澳大利亚人民提供了丰富的资源。”

澳大利亚文学翻译在中国的成功首先是由于译者的努力和奉献，但与澳大利亚作家们对中国的友好感情也紧密相关。许多译者都与澳大利亚作家有过密切而友好的交流，从他们那里得到了无私的帮助。澳中理事会在推动澳大利亚文学翻译和澳大利亚学术研究方面也起了至关重要的作用。最后，还应该提到中国出版界对于澳大利亚文学翻译的兴趣和关注。没有他们一以贯之的支持就不可能

① 张华：《纽马克文本翻译理论与李尧文学文本翻译策略》，《安徽工业大学学报（社会科学版）》2016 年第 5 期。

② 王佐良：《翻译中的文化比较》，《王佐良全集》第 8 卷 252 页，外语教学与研究出版社，2016 年。

有今天澳大利亚文学翻译在中国的丰收。

2018 年适逢中国澳大利亚研究会成立 30 周年，也恰是李尧先生从事文学翻译 40 周年。北京外国语大学、内蒙古师范大学、西悉尼大学和在华澳大利亚研究基金会共同发起出版的十卷本《李尧译文集》既是对于李尧几十年来从事澳大利亚文学翻译的充分肯定，更是繁茂的中澳文化交流之见证。我们相信，澳大利亚文学翻译事业今后在我国必将取得更长足的进步，在促进中澳文化交流方面也必将起到更大的作用。

胡文仲

2017 年 8 月 27 日

《李尧译文集》序　二

罗伯特·迪克逊

我十分荣幸地应邀为李尧教授这套重要的澳大利亚文学优秀翻译作品写序。这套书为庆祝李尧教授从事澳大利亚文学翻译四十周年，由青岛出版社出版，恰逢我们两国建立外交关系四十五周年。我要指出的是，这两个周年纪念日密切相关。

高夫·惠特拉姆领导的工党早在1955年就承认了中华人民共和国。可是直到十七年之后，1972年12月2日，该党才成为执政党。1972年12月21日，高夫·惠特拉姆就任总理不到三个星期，便与中国政府签订了澳大利亚与中华人民共和国建立外交关系的联合公报。根据《公报》，两国政府同意“在互相尊重……平等互利、和平共处的原则基础之上，发展两国间的外交关系、友谊和合作”。

1973年1月12日，澳大利亚驻华大使馆在北京正式开馆。同年晚些时候，高夫·惠特拉姆成为第一位访华的澳大利亚总理，并且与周恩来、毛泽东进行了历史性的会晤。惠特拉姆创建的澳大利亚与中国的外交关系一直被描绘为20世纪我们两国之间发生的最重要的事件，时至今日，仍然是两国关系的重要基础。

除了贸易和旅游业，文化教育交流对于我们两国关系的发展起到越来越重要的作用。从1970年代起，这种交流便将澳大利亚文学研究囊括其中。建立外交关系之后，1975年，第一批5位中国学生到澳大利亚的大学学习。李尧教授为几代中国读者翻译澳大利亚文学的生涯一直以这种文化交流为中心。

1966年，李尧从内蒙古师范大学毕业之后，作为作家和文学杂志编辑并一直在内蒙古工作，直到 1992 年到中国商务部培训中心任英语教授。他于 1986 年加入中国作家协会，专事文学翻译。从那时起，开始和北京外国语大学胡文仲教授合作翻译澳大利亚文学作品。胡文仲教授是悉尼大学的研究生，所谓“九人帮”之一。“九人帮”是“文化大革命”之后，第一批从中国到澳大利亚攻读硕士学位的学者。1979 年，他们师从我的前辈——悉尼大学澳大利亚文学教授雷欧妮·克雷默爵士。我那时是英语系一个年轻的辅导员，正在做博士论文。时至今日还清楚地记着活跃在系里的这几位中国访问学者。

“九人帮”学成回国之后，对推动中国的澳大利亚研究起到很大的作用。从那时候起，中国各地已经建立起 30 多个澳大利亚研究中心。许多学者把澳大利亚文学翻译介绍给中国读者。不少“中心”开设澳大利亚文学课程。包括北京大学、北京外国语大学——李尧教授在那里教授澳大利亚文学翻译——华东师范大学、人民大学、安徽大学、苏州大学、内蒙古大学、内蒙古师范大学。

最初，是胡文仲教授鼓励李尧从事澳大利亚文学研究与翻译。1980 年代，他们在北京相识。胡教授说，澳大利亚文学在中国还是一块未开垦的处女地。他鼓励李尧作为翻译者致力于这一领域，做出贡献。“文化大革命”前，中国读者对美国、英国、俄罗斯、法国、德国和其他欧洲国家的文学比较熟悉，但是对澳大利亚文学知之甚少。那时候，只有亨利·劳森、弗兰克·哈代和少数几位“社会主义现实主义”作家通过翻译为中国读者所知。1991 年，上海译文出版社出版了胡教授和李尧合作翻译的帕特里克·怀特的《人树》。帕特里克·怀特是澳大利亚最著名的作家，1973 年获得诺贝尔文学奖。他之所以影响深远，是因为和早期现实主义作家不同，他的小说通过国际现代主义文体创新，展示了澳大利亚社会与澳大利亚风土人情。

和胡教授合作之后，李尧坚持翻译澳大利亚文学，把他已经继承的传统传承下去。迄今为止，他已经翻译了多达 35 部的澳大利亚文学作品。其中包括布莱恩· 卡斯特罗、理查德·弗兰纳根、阿尼塔·海斯、考琳·麦卡洛、大卫·马鲁夫、亚历克斯·米勒和金姆·斯科特等。还有历史与非小说译作出版。李尧大多数翻译作品的出版都得到澳中理事会、澳大利亚理事会文学委员会和在华澳大利亚研究基金会的资助。为纪念中澳建交四十五周年重新选择出版的这套译著包括业已在澳大利亚和世界范围内赢得盛誉的作品。这些作品有的获得"迈尔斯·富兰克林文学奖"，有的获得"英联邦作家奖"，有的获得"布克国际文学奖"。他的译著还包括帕特里克·怀特的长篇小说《人树》《树叶裙》、自传《镜中瑕疵》；表现澳中关系最早的两部小说：布莱恩·卡斯特罗的《候鸟》和亚历克斯·米勒的《浪子》；著名学者、前澳大利亚驻华大使馆文化官员尼古拉斯·周思的《长安大街》。还有赢得"布克国际文学奖"的三位作家的作品：彼得·凯里的《凯利帮真史》、托马斯·肯尼利的《内海的女人》、理查德·弗兰纳根的《古尔德鱼书》。除了获得"迈尔斯·富兰克林文学奖"和"英联邦作家奖"的《浪子》之外，李尧还翻译了亚历克斯·米勒的《别了，那道风景》和《煤河》。李尧还翻译了一些重要的非小说类作品，包括大卫·沃克的家族史《光明行》和马拉·穆斯塔芬的《哈尔滨档案》。这两本书都从不同的角度记录了中澳两国普通人之间的关系。

最近几年，李尧紧跟澳大利亚文学的最新发展，继续把澳大利亚作家的新作品介绍给中国读者。他对澳大利亚儿童文学和澳大利亚原住民作家的作品特别关注。这个纪念译文集也收入相关的作品。从2010年起，李尧在澳中理事会的支持下，选择并组织力量翻译了十本澳大利亚儿童文学经典，包括深受几代读者喜爱的埃塞尔·帕德利的《多特和袋鼠》、梅·吉布斯的《小胖壶和小面饼》、埃塞尔·特纳的《七个澳大利亚小孩儿》、多萝西·沃尔的《眨眼睛的比尔》、鲁斯· 帕克的《糊里糊涂的树袋熊》和科林·蒂勒的《暴风雨中的男孩》。这些书由人民文学出版社出版，在中国很受欢迎。《多特和袋鼠》《七个澳大利亚小孩儿》新版将由中国青年出版社出版。李尧决心为推动澳大利亚儿童文学作品在中国的翻译出版做出更大的贡献。他将翻译介绍更多的儿童文学作品，收入他的“考拉丛书”中。

自 2006 年开始，在他的好朋友——学者、作家、前文化参赞尼古拉斯·周思教授的帮助下，李尧一直在研究、翻译澳大利亚原住民文学。已经出版的作品有金姆· 斯科特的《心中的明天》、亚历克西斯· 赖特的《卡彭塔里亚湾》和阿尼塔·海斯的《我是谁》。他目前正在翻译亚历克西斯·赖特的《天鹅书》。鉴于澳大利亚原住民文学到目前为止还没有系统地介绍到中国，对大多数中国读者而言，那还是一个不熟悉的领域，李尧希望这些书能使中国读者对澳大利亚有更多的了解。

除了从事文学翻译以及在北京大学、北京外国语大学教授澳大利亚文学翻译之外，李尧从 1988 年中国澳大利亚学会成立以来，一直担任学会理事。1996 年，他因翻译亚历克斯·米勒的《浪子》获得澳中理事会首次在中国颁发的翻译奖，2008 年因翻译尼克拉斯·周思的《红线》、2012 年因翻译亚历克西斯·赖特的《卡彭塔里亚湾》又连续两次获此殊荣。2008 年因其在澳大利亚文学翻译领域的杰出贡献，获澳中理事会颁发的金奖章。

也许因为怀特作为澳大利亚唯一的诺贝尔文学奖获得者享有盛名，李尧也因其在中国翻译介绍帕特里克·怀特的作品在澳大利亚广为人知。在过去的 25 年里，他和胡文仲教授合作翻译的《人树》先后印刷三次，销售量超过 20000 册。怀特的自传《镜中瑕疵》也被印刷三次，销售量超过 12000 册。他翻译的《人树》《镜中瑕疵》《浪子》《凯利帮真史》和《卡彭塔里亚湾》在中国受到好评和欢迎。不少学生依据李尧第一次介绍到中国的这些世界第一流的澳大利亚文学作品，撰写硕士和博士论文。

李尧的译作《卡彭塔里亚湾》作为他毕生从事文学翻译以及 40 多年来两国文化交流的巅峰之作，也许特别值得一提。这部小说从原住民的视角出发，以一种也许可以称之为原住民魔幻现实主义的独特的风格想象了澳大利亚的生活。在中国的澳大利亚文学翻译者中，也许只有李尧因其具有丰富的经验，可以接受挑战，将这样一部杰作从一种完全不同的文化翻译为中文。2012 年，他克服了重重困难，得到多位中国著名作家的支持，在久负盛名的人民文学出版社出版此书。诺贝尔文学奖获得者莫言在澳大利亚驻华大使馆为《卡彭塔里亚湾》新书发布会揭幕。

今天，李尧依然活跃在澳大利亚文学研究的舞台上。最近，作为在墨尔本召开的“澳大利亚文学研究会 2017 年会”（ASAL）的贵宾，他对兴趣盎然、不无赞赏的澳大利亚学者讲述了自己毕生的工作。李尧总是乐于倾听同事们对新的、有趣的选题的建议。比如说，最近中国读者对托马斯·肯尼利的作品很感兴趣，他就计划翻译《耻辱和俘虏》。他对澳大利亚原住民文学和儿童文学依然表现出浓厚的兴趣，计划翻译他的朋友亚历克斯·米勒的新小说。他与大卫·沃克教授正在合作撰写关于他和他的家族在解放战争前后、新中国成立初期以及“文化大革命”中经历的纪实文学作品。这是一本他的许多澳大利亚朋友热切期待阅读的书。

李尧在中国长期致力于澳大利亚文学翻译，表现出非同寻常的献身精神。在中国，没有人比李尧对澳大利亚文学作品更了解。他在澳大利亚作家和文学工作者中有许多朋友。2014 年，我在悉尼大学历史悠久的大会堂参加了授予李尧荣誉文学博士的典礼。对于这所无论在澳大利亚还是中国，在澳大利亚文学研究领域发挥基础性作用的大学，这是一个骄傲的时刻。“我热爱澳大利亚文学，”李尧说。“它是世界文学的重要支柱。在过去的四十年里，我和许多澳大利亚优秀作家结下深厚的友谊。在翻译他们作品的过程中，我自己的生活也发生了巨大的变化。”回顾往事，我们可以看到，李尧的文学翻译生涯，堪称实现 1972 年《公报》初衷的楷模。今天，我们依然为之努力，那就是“在互相尊重……平等互利、和平共处的原则基础之上，发展两国间的外交关系、友谊和合作”。

罗伯特·迪克逊

澳大利亚人文科学院院士

悉尼大学澳大利亚文学教授

2017 年 7 月

李尧教授新书发布会上的演讲

孙有中

尊敬的校长巴尼·格洛弗教授、副校长蓝易振教授、副校长德博拉·斯威尼教授、李尧教授、副主编刘永贵先生、女士们、先生们：

晚上好！

我和我的同事们离开了北京寒冷的早春，期待来到悉尼可以享受温暖的秋天。我们来了以后发现这里的秋天的确很温暖，而且还有点热。衷心感谢你们热情的接待，感谢新老朋友们能来参加这次聚会，我们感受到了热烈的欢迎。

我代表北京外国语大学和中国澳大利亚研究协会，感谢西悉尼大学为了我的同事和朋友李尧教授的澳大利亚文学翻译系列书籍而举办这个发布会。我还要特别感谢西悉尼大学的澳大利亚——中国艺术和文化研究院，在华澳大利亚研究基金会以及内蒙古师范大学为此项目提供的慷慨资助。同时也感谢青岛出版社的支持。韩静博士在这个项目中发挥了不可替代的重要作用，在此由衷感谢她。

我衷心祝贺李尧教授的新书出版，同时也想表达我个人对他的钦佩。美国 19 世纪诗人朗费罗在他著名的诗篇《人生颂》中写道：“艺术源远流长，而时光稍纵即逝。”我们偶尔会停下来思考一个问题：如何有意义地度过我们短暂的一生？李尧教授的答案很简单：翻译。这样一位学者，把毕生精力都投入到翻译事业中去，并且集中精力翻译澳大利亚文学作品，难道我们不应该向他致以最高的敬意吗？

翻译的意义在于，它是使一个国家的人民理解另一个国家的人民的心灵和思想的最有效的方式，甚至也许是唯一有效的方式。翻译让我们看见一个美好的新世界，它在我们的文化与另一种文化之间建立了桥梁，拓宽了我们的视野。让我们的生活更加丰富多彩，更有意义。

因此，让我们感谢李尧教授为翻译事业作出的不懈努力以及他为中澳两国之间的互相开放、互相联系、互相理解和友好情谊做出的卓越贡献。

谢谢大家。

新书发布会演讲

巴尼·格洛弗教授
西悉尼大学校长

各位亲爱的同事和朋友们，下午好！欢迎大家来到西悉尼大学！

在此，我欢迎李尧教授，欢迎北京外国语大学副校长孙有中教授以及他的同事们，欢迎所有出席此次“澳大利亚文学在中国交流会暨李尧教授新书发布会”的嘉宾们。今天，我们在塔鲁我人民的土地上举办这场活动，我们承认塔鲁我人民的祖先几千年来对这片土地的传统拥有权。西悉尼大学也希望借此良机对所有的塔鲁我人民致以诚挚的敬意。

我非常荣幸，也非常高兴能够在这里帮助李尧教授——一名杰出的中国翻译家，发布他的澳大利亚文学作品译文集。

李尧教授曾是内蒙古师范大学英语专业的学生，1966 年毕业以后，他成了一名记者和作家，同时也是中国作家协会的一员。1979 年初，一本文学杂志的月刊发表了他的首篇译作——一则查尔斯·狄更斯的短篇故事。此后，他逐渐放弃了写作，而专注于成为一位译者。随后，他成了商务部的一名教授。

李尧教授接触到澳大利亚文学的契机是一本亨利·劳森的作品集，这本书是他在西澳大利亚的一位同事艾莉森·翰威特送给他的。他翻译的第一本澳大利亚文学作品是《赶牲口人的妻子》，这篇译作曾在一本中国杂志上发表。此后的 30 年，李尧教授或是独立翻译，或是与别人合作，共翻译了 30 多本书，其中包括很多澳大利亚小说，比如帕特里克·怀特的《树叶裙》、托马斯·肯尼利的《内海的女人》、理查德·弗拉纳根的《古尔德的鱼书》、皮特·凯里的《凯利帮真史》、尼古拉斯·周思的《红线》、亚历克斯·米勒的《浪子》、亚历克西斯·赖特的《卡彭塔利亚湾》、达西·尼兰的《行囊》、布莱恩·卡斯特罗的《候鸟》、金·斯科特的《心中的明天》。李尧教授也翻译一些非小说文学，例如帕特里克·怀特的《镜中瑕疵》、达奇·尼兰的《澳大利亚牛津史》以及玛拉·穆斯塔芬的《间谍和秘密——哈尔滨档案》《为什么是中国》。最近，李尧教授翻译了一些澳大利亚儿童文学以及关于澳大利亚原住民文化的作品。1988 年，李尧教授首次来到澳大利亚，他拜访了帕特里克·怀特，两年后，怀特逝世。他所翻译的怀特的《人树》以及科琳·麦克洛克的《呼唤》再版无数，销售量超过 30000 本。

昔日创造型作家的经历使得李尧教授对澳大利亚文学作品中的一些写作技巧了如指掌，因此他的中文译作十分到位、流畅，可读性非常强。他的译作让许多中国读者认识了澳大利亚作家，激发了他们对澳大利亚文学创作的兴趣，这些读者里就有中国的诺贝尔文学奖得主莫言。莫言是一名作家，同时也是中国作家协会的现任主席。而对于这些译作对澳大利亚的影响，我们还需要拭目以待，但是我认为在中澳文化交流的过程中，这些影响随时都会出现。

李尧教授说他自己深深地为澳洲人民所吸引，但大多数中国人都不太了解澳大利亚文学，所以他认为像他这样的中国译者们有责任翻译更多优秀的澳大利亚文学作品，让中国民众了解澳大利亚这个国家、澳大利亚人民以及澳大利亚文化。作为一名译者，李尧教授经常与原著作者合作，有时他会主动联系甚至亲自拜访他们。正因如此，他结交了很多澳大利亚作家朋友，今天我们也邀请到了他们中的一些。我们希望大家一起加入，庆祝李尧教授终身致力于澳大利亚写作，并祝贺他致力于推广澳大利亚文学和文化所取得的成果。

李尧教授因其对中澳文化交流的贡献而获奖无数。2015 年，他被悉尼大学授予荣誉博士学位。2017 年，他的故事被列为澳中自 1972 年建交以来的 45 个故事之一。

李尧教授参加了 2012 年的澳大利亚文学周，开幕式上举行了由他翻译的亚历克西斯·赖特的《卡彭塔利亚湾》一书的发布会。诺贝尔奖获得者莫言为他的译本撰写了序言，并在仪式上发表了演讲。澳大利亚驻华大使弗朗西斯·亚当森女士和中国作家协会会长铁凝女士也出席了仪式。

李教授表示，随着中澳的经济联系越来越密切，两国之间似乎缺少一些信任。尽管澳方认为中国试图把影响力扩散到澳大利亚，但澳大利亚似乎没有像许多其他西方国家那样在中国投射所谓的软实力。李教授认为自己的作品不是一种软实力投射，而是一个学者为了让自己的同胞更了解澳大利亚所做的努力的一部分。他希望澳大利亚的译者可以做同样的事情。

李尧教授几十年来一直在朝着这个方向努力。李教授为澳中两国的学术和文化联系，以及澳大利亚文学的翻译工作做出了长久的贡献。他的工作得到了西悉尼大学澳大利亚 - 中国艺术与文化研究院的支持。我们还将继续支持中澳两国的艺术和文化交流项目。

西悉尼大学相信澳大利亚的未来和亚洲密不可分，我们希望通过各种艺术和文化项目扩大与中国的联系，因为艺术和文化可以凝聚人心；艺术和文化的交流可以把两国人民的心灵融合在一起。我们对李尧教授在这方面为中澳两国所做的贡献表示敬意。我们将通过澳大利亚 - 中国艺术与文化研究院和西悉尼大学的其他项目为两国的艺术文化交流提供更多支持。我希望李尧教授在他的领域继续保持创作，取得更大的成就，以促进两国的交流和理解。谢谢。

澳大利亚文学与中国读者

张　剑

2018 年 1 月，翻译家李尧教授的《澳大利亚文学经典译文集》（10 卷）由青岛出版社出版，在澳大利亚的大学和文学界引起了广泛的关注。同年 4 月，西悉尼大学和澳大利亚国立大学为这套丛书举行了发布会，邀请了李尧本人、澳大利亚作家尼古拉斯·周思（Nick Jose）、西悉尼大学教授盖尔·琼斯（Gail Jones）、北京外国语大学教授张剑和李建军共同举行了一次“中澳文学对话会”。对话会聚焦李尧教授翻译的澳大利亚文学作品，同时也引起了人们对澳大利亚文学的本质、内容、风格以及相关问题的思考。

一　什么是澳大利亚文学?

与英国文学悠久的历史相比，澳大利亚文学相对年轻。作为英国文学的一个分支，澳大利亚文学经历了一段自我塑造和身份构建的时期。1985 年，当北京外国语大学的胡文仲教授到澳大利亚的巴拉腊特参加澳大利亚文学研究会的年会时，他发现已经没有人谈论“什么是澳大利亚文学”了，这也意味着在当时，这一问题已不再是一个值得讨论的话题。

我认为澳大利亚作家在 20 世纪中后叶所面临的情况，与爱尔兰和加勒比海地区的作家面临的情况类似。大部分澳大利亚作家是英国人的后裔，英国文化深植于他们的成长过程中。莎士比亚、弥尔顿、华兹华斯、迪福、奥斯丁、狄更斯是他们所受教育的一部分。澳大利亚作家和英国作家说同一种语言，他们自然在文学特色和规范上也有许多相同的见解。因此，在 20 世纪 80 年代之前，澳大利亚文学一直被视为英国文学的一部分。

然而，澳大利亚由于在地理位置上与英国相距甚远，越来越意识到自己是一个亚太国家。胡文仲教授提到的有关“什么是澳大利亚文学”的争论，很有可能是澳大利亚人企图从英国分离出来、建立独立的澳大利亚身份的努力的一部分。这也可能是 20 世纪 90 年代关于澳大利亚是否变为共和国的辩论背后的动力。将澳大利亚文学独立出来，与它的母体文学——英国文学区分开，可能是为了在其早已实现的政治独立的基础上，进一步实现其文化独立。

在爱尔兰和加勒比海地区，谢默斯·希尼（Seamus Heaney）、德里克·沃尔科特（Derek Walcott）和类似的作家也在将自己与英国传统区分开来进行着相似的挣扎。他们从英语和英国传统中汲取了太多东西，因此不得不好好思考如何处理他们在成为作家之前与英国文化建立的紧密关系。在解殖民后的环境中，他们无法完全抛弃已经继承的传统，而只能在其中引入改变，从而开辟出一条不同的道路。我认为澳大利亚作家为了形成自己的地方特色和独特风格，也做了同样的努力。

美国在 19 世纪和 20 世纪，在殖民时期结束以后的很长时间里，都仍无法摆脱英国文学对他们的影响，因为那曾经是他们文化传统的一部分。爱默生（Emerson）在 19 世纪 50 年代谈到自力更生和文化独立，但直到 20 世纪 20 年代，美国作家依旧将欧洲视为文明的中心。从《流亡者归来》（*Exile's Return*）和《亨利·亚当斯的教育》（*The Education of Henry Adams*）等书中可以看出，美国的流亡作家如亨利·詹姆斯（Henry James）、埃兹拉·庞德（Ezra Pound）、欧内斯特·海明威（Ernest Hemingway）等，都去了欧洲以寻求文化的踪迹。在文学的规范与评判问题上，美国长期以来都依赖英国和欧洲。

美国现代派诗人托·斯·艾略特（T. S. Eliot）在 20 世纪 30 年代曾经写了一篇文章，题为《苏格兰文学存在吗?》，探讨了英国文学和苏格兰文学中的中心与边缘问题，并把拜伦作为苏格兰作家加以贬低——在今天看来他的观点会显得政治不正确。但考虑到历史时期的局限，我们也不能过多责怪艾略特。直到 1945 年 F. O. 马蒂生（F. O. Matthiessen）出版了《美国的文艺复兴》（*American Renaissance*），美国人才意识到他们的文学可以作为一种不同于英国文学的独立传统来传授和学习。惠特曼（Walt Whitman）、狄金森（Emily Dickinson）、霍桑（Nathaniel Hawthorne）、梅尔维尔（Herman Melville）、爱默生（R. W. Emerson）和梭罗（H. D. Thoreau）成了美国文学传统的奠基者。

也就是说，只是在二战之后，在解殖民运动和美国的崛起后，曾经统一的“英国文学”才逐渐分裂成了七八种民族文学，我们现在才有可能去探讨若干英语国家的若干种“英语文学”（如美国、澳大利亚、加拿大、爱尔兰、新西兰以及加勒比海地区的前英属殖民地的英语文学），而不必去问诸如“什么是澳大利亚文学?”和“苏格兰文学存在吗?”之类的问题。

胡文仲教授认为，人们对澳大利亚文学的认知真正发生改变的时间是 1981 年，那年利奥妮·克雷默（Leonie Kramer）出版了《牛津澳大利亚文学史》（*The Oxford History of Australian Literature*）。当然在这之前，在 20 世纪 30 ~70 年代，也有人尝试构建澳大利亚文学史，但直到 20 世纪 80 年代，我们才见证了一个真正的改变，这时学术界才真正开始认真和严肃地对待澳大利亚文学。胡文仲教授的话之所以重要，是因为它提醒我们需要将澳大利亚文学放入其社会环境中来看待，需要特别注意作家撰写的澳大利亚内容，以及他们区别于英国作家的澳大利亚特色。澳大利亚文学与澳大利亚身份的想象特别相关，与澳大利亚作为一个亚太地区的多元文化国家特别相关。

二 澳大利亚经历

在这样的背景下，我们就能更好地理解李尧教授这 10 册《澳大利亚文学经典译文集》的意义。该译文集于 2018 年 1 月由青岛出版社出版。北京外国语大学胡文仲教授、悉尼大学的罗伯特·狄克逊教授（Robert Dixon）和时任澳大利亚驻华大使安捷思（Jan Adams）均为译文集作了序，帮助我们了解译文集出版的目的和澳大利亚文学取得的成就。

对澳大利亚文学来说，描写与澳大利亚这个国家相关的内容非常重要，因为要成为澳大利亚文学，必不可少的一点就是澳大利亚的经历。亚历克斯·米勒（Alex Miller）所著的《浪子》（*The Ancestor Game*）描述了不同种族的移民的祖先梦。其中的人物史蒂文·缪尔，奥古斯特·施皮斯和他的女儿格特鲁德，以及浪子（Lang Tzu）都表现出一种焦躁不安的文化错位之感，对澳大利亚的欧洲式文化表现出一种矛盾心态。年轻的时候离开英国来到澳大利亚的史蒂文多次尝试回归，但都没有成功。奥古斯特·施皮斯虽然不断念叨着要回家乡德国汉堡，却始终未能付诸行动，他的女儿也一样。浪子的名字决定了他的命运：这个词在中文中意味着漂泊不定的远方游子。

然而这场回归“游戏”中的人并不都是输家。尽管他们渴望祖先的家园，渴望归属自己真正属于的地方，米勒笔下的所有人物都没有离开澳大利亚，每个人都通过自己的方式意识到，归属与漂泊是澳大利亚籍的欧洲人共有的一个矛盾心态：在所有的欧洲文化中，这种矛盾的归属与疏离感都存在。

布赖恩·卡斯特罗（Brian Castro）的《候鸟》（*Birds of Passage*）的主人公是谢默斯·欧阳。他是一个澳大利亚籍的华裔，即“ABC”。他的父亲曾在中国清政府担任官职，在 19 世纪 50 年代的淘金热期间，他来到了澳大利亚。他的母亲是一个生活在澳大利亚的英国移民。从欧阳的家庭可以看出，他不完全是中国人，不完全是澳大利亚人，也不完全是英国人，就像小说作者一样。卡斯特罗出生于香港，他的父母有着葡萄牙、中国和英国的血统，后来，他成了澳大利亚公民。从此我们可以看出，身份问题是澳大利亚文学的一个突出特点。中国读者可能无法完全理解这个问题，因为中国没有类似的问题，或者这种问题在中国并没有那么突出。

在书中，谢默斯·欧阳对自己的边界身份感到极端困惑："是的，我是 ABC，字母表的前三个字母。这个身份跨越了两种文化。是的，ABC。我是一个难民，一个流放的人。我的心灵和头脑都放错了地方。我不来自任何国家，也无法回到任何国家。"这种疑惑感与迷失感相互叠加，使得他深刻地感受到自己身份分裂的不幸："我真的是一个没有国家的人。"卡斯特罗的小说将身份问题置于 19 世纪鸦片战争、农民起义以及华人海外移民的宏大巨变的历史背景之中。

身份问题一般存在于移民国家。因为在移民国家中，不同国家的人居住在一起，本地人和新移民会产生政治、经济和文化的冲突。亚历克西斯·赖特（Alexis Wright）的《卡彭塔利亚湾》（*Carpentaria*）便深入讨论了这种冲突的历史。书中的故事发生在昆士兰西北部卡彭塔利亚湾的一个虚构的小镇德斯珀伦斯。在那里，普瑞克尔布什的原住民与其他移民发生了激烈的冲突，包括与当地的白人居民、当地的执法部门、政府官员和一个在他们神圣土地上采矿的跨国公司。

故事讲述了卷入这场冲突的三个男人间的关系：睿智、务实、耿直的诺姆·凡特姆；虔诚的萨满教僧莫吉·费希曼，以及诺姆的儿子威尔·凡特姆。威尔抛下父亲的家，与费希曼一起踏上了横跨澳洲的心灵之旅，然后带着费希曼身上的一些特质回到了家乡。这本小说不仅记录了政治和种族的冲突，也描绘了澳大利亚土著人民异常丰富的文化传统。

在澳大利亚这样多元文化并存的社会中，历史和祖先是影响人们经历的重要因素。关于出身、移民和蔓延至澳洲以外的根，似乎每个人都有话要说。考琳·麦卡洛（Colleen McCullough）的《呼唤》（*The Touch*）一书以 19 世纪 50 年代的淘金热为背景，讲述了苏格兰出生的亚历山大·金罗斯和他的苏格兰新娘伊丽莎白·德拉蒙德，以及神秘的茹贝·考斯特凡和她具有中国血统的儿子李的传奇故事。金罗斯有一笔神秘的财产，他在苏格兰的亲戚以为这是他通过淘金获得的，但实际上这个谜团将由他刚刚踏上澳大利亚这片土地的妻子伊丽莎白一点点解开。

伊丽莎白将会发现，那位从前宣扬无神论的叛逆青年、懒惰的锅炉制造商的学徒现在已经成为一个重要人物，甚至有一个城镇以他的名字命名。但是她同样会发现，金罗斯还有一个情妇茹贝。并且，这不只是一个情妇，她还是金罗斯公司的合伙人。这家公司不断扩张，不再仅仅进行黄金交易。伊丽莎白将会发现，茹贝的儿子李的父亲是正处于困境中的华人社区的头领，而金罗斯打算把李培养成一个绅士，甚至还有可能让李接手他的公司。这本小说和《荆棘鸟》一样，是一部爱情小说和世家传奇，充满了悲剧、伤感、历史和激情，表达了一种身处异乡的人们的错位感，以及开始新生活的急切需要。

三　中国元素

《李尧译文集》10 卷本在某种程度上讲反映了他对澳大利亚文学的理解和看法。他的译文集不仅收录了著名作家帕特里克·怀特（Patrick White）、托马斯·基尼利（Thomas Keneally）和彼得·凯里（Peter Carey）的作品，而且还特别收录了描写中国移民在澳大利亚经历的作品。布赖恩·卡斯特罗的《萦系中国》（*After China*）就讲述了一个华裔建筑师和澳大利亚白人女作家在他设计的酒店里相遇的故事。内敛的建筑师被女作家深深吸引，但却小心翼翼地通过古代中国美妙的故事，编织着两人的罗曼史。他并不知道她已患癌症病危，即将离开人世，还讲述着道家经典中通过控制欲望以得永生的故事。最终他了解了她的困境，也意识到他要挽救她的行为多么具有讽刺意味。

建筑师设计的酒店像一个奇怪的迷宫，坐落在水面上，并不牢靠。由于酒店随时可能被海水吞没，我们和主人公都意识到，如果疾病有其时限，那么只有讲故事才能驱除时间。小说通过颂扬生命的故事建构了与西方不同的中国想象，与许多当代爱情故事中的矫情和吊胃口的做法也形成了差异，使读者重新思考与爱情和生存同样重要的问题。

在尼古拉斯·周思的小说《黑玫瑰》（*The Rose Crossing*）中，来自英国的园艺家爱德华·波普尔、他的女儿罗莎蒙德和一个水手在遭遇海难后被困于非洲沿海的一个岛屿。同样被困在岛上的还有一群中国难民，其中包括被流放的中国亲王太昭、老太监卢陆以及失事船上的船员。周思的另一部小说《红线》（*The Red Thread*）则是一部以现代上海为背景的爱情小说。小说中的上海被过去的记忆萦绕，有古代也有现代的记忆。澳大利亚的女画家茹丝·加勒特、其代理商沈复灵和“既是光耀女王，也是街头混混”的韩，一起编织出中国清朝作家沈复的《浮生六记》的故事。

作为《浮生六记》英译本的译者，周思在自己的小说里创造性地引用了这部中国古典作品。在沈复灵拿到用于拍卖的《浮生六记》初版残存的四记后，他遇到了茹丝，并且确信他和这位澳大利亚女画家就是沈复书中主角，即沈复和陈芸的化身。而且，当韩在夜店中遇到这一对爱人后，她感到自己与茹丝和沈复灵有着十分紧密的联系。于是这三个人在现代上海演绎出一种似曾相识的情节。《浮生六记》的残稿以陈芸的去世为结局，而在《红线》的最后，沈复灵得知茹丝身患癌症，这使他迫切地寻找《浮生六记》遗失的章节，希望这个悲剧的故事有一个不同的结局。

在这类作品中，中国元素发挥了重要作用，这大概也是译者李尧教授收录这些作品的一个重要原因。当然，译者应该考虑读者以及图书市场的特殊偏好，中国元素可能给中国读者带来一种亲切感。大卫·沃克（David Walker）教授的《光明行》（*Not Dark Yet*）把家族的历史和澳大利亚的历史联系在一起，追溯了沃克家族五代人的历史，从曾曾祖父母 19 世纪 50 年代在南澳大利亚定居开始，到 20 世纪 90 年代作者母亲的去世。回忆录的前半部分的许多章节的场景都在巴拉，这是阿德莱德以北 156 公里的铜矿小镇，沃克家庭是当地知名的商店店主。

对于中国读者来说，卢克·戴伊的故事对他们具有特别的吸引力。卢克·戴伊是巴拉的一个中国商人，因娶了沃克家的女孩而成为这个家族的一员。在这里，个人叙事与作者本人的学术兴趣互相交叉，沃克教授通过讲述戴伊的生活，重新审视了在种族歧视、民族主义和“白澳政策”盛行的时期，中国人在澳大利亚社会的地位。沃克教授透视了 20 世纪初澳大利亚小镇生活的实质，包括其优点、局限和狭隘的妒忌心理。

查·帕·菲茨杰拉德（C. P. Fitzgerald）的回忆录《我在中国的岁月》（*Why China*）记录了他从 1923 年来中国到 1949 年中华人民共和国成立这一时期的经历。在试图回答为什么他对中国有兴趣的问题之后，菲茨杰拉德回忆了他在中国从事的不同工作，在中国西南部的旅行（从昆明到重庆再到贵阳），在云南省与白族村民度过的时光，以及他对白族的历史、语言和文化所做的研究。正是在这一时期，他为人类学著作《五华楼》搜集了资料。

对于中国读者来说，这本回忆录吸引人之处在于它从另一个角度讲述了中国 20 世纪的历史。它从一个外国人的视角，讲述中国争取国家稳定的悲壮斗争和建立国家的艰难历史，包括特别令人感兴趣的历史片段，比如 1919 年日本在《凡尔赛和约》签订后接管德国在青岛的租界的阴谋，1924 年军阀冯玉祥将皇帝和皇室驱逐出紫禁城的故事，1925 年国民革命军的北伐以及对汉口的占领，1937 年日军进攻上海以及抗日战争的全面爆发。作者本人会说汉语，甚至能用汉语和黄包车夫就车费进行讨价还价，这让本书更具可信性。但是据菲兹杰拉德本人说，在 19 世纪 30 年代学习汉语的外国人都会被人视为“疯子”。

四　澳大利亚经典

李尧教授《澳大利亚文学经典译文集》中的 10 部作品是高度个性化选择的结果，自然无法全面呈现澳大利亚文学的丰富性和多样性。这些选择肯定带有李尧教授个人的偏好，比如他选择了《人树》（*The Tree of Man*）而不是《风暴眼》（*The Eye of Storm*），选择了《内海的女人》(*A Woman of Inner Sea*) 而不是《辛德勒方舟》(*Schindler's Ark*),选择了《呼唤》(*The Touch*) 而不是《荆棘鸟》(*The Thorn Birds*)。但是总体来说,这套译文集很好地呈现了澳大利亚文学的特点和宽度,可以帮助像我这样的新读者获得一个很好的指引。如果这套译文集将来有一天需要扩充,我认为一定要加上亨利·劳森(Henry Lawson)、班卓·帕特森(Banjo Paterson)、克里斯蒂娜·斯特德(Christina Stead)、大卫·马洛夫(David Malouf)、A. D. 霍普(A. D. Hope)、朱迪丝·赖特(Judith Wright)、莱斯·穆瑞(Les Murray)、大卫·威廉姆森(David Williamson)、蒂姆·温顿(Tim Winton)等人的作品。

帕特里克·怀特的《人树》讲述了一个虚构人物斯坦·帕克的一生。斯坦是一个农场主,在悉尼以外一块未开垦的土地上建立了自己的农场。从他青年时期直到生命终结的半个多世纪中,我们看到了一个早期的澳大利亚拓荒者的艰苦劳作:清理土地,种植作物,搭建居所;也看到他和艾米的婚姻,他们在大洪水中遭受的损失,他们和邻居欧多德太太和玛德琳的关系,二人的孩子雷伊和塞尔玛的成长,一战期间斯坦在澳大利亚陆军的服役,艾米和一个推销员的婚外情,雷伊的犯罪生活和在悉尼的服刑,塞尔玛和一个律师的婚姻以及她在悉尼的上流生活。

这部小说不仅写了一个男人与其家庭半个多世纪跌宕起伏的人生和历史,它也是一部记录了澳大利亚,尤其是悉尼地区历史变迁的史诗般的作品。早期开拓者在悉尼城外开垦荒地并定居的经历,是早期欧洲人来到这片广袤土地建立文明的缩影。在小说中我们看到其他拓荒者纷至沓来,使这个地区变成了村庄,并且出现了乡绅大宅格拉斯顿伯里庄园。但是,那场烧毁庄园的大火大概预示着特权阶级的没落和城市的兴起,年轻人们被城市里的商学院、律师事务所和剧院等深深吸引。最终,帕克农场所在的地区被分成了许多小块,在上面建起了房屋,悉尼郊区逐渐形成。在这些人物的人生背后,是他们生活的土地的历史。

托马斯·肯尼利(Thomas Keneally)的《内海的女人》讲的

是凯特·盖弗尼－科金斯基的幻灭的故事。凯特是一个漂亮的女继承人，从“监狱般的”悉尼逃到澳大利亚北部，过上了漂泊的生活。她的幻灭是因为丈夫保罗出轨，加上在一场大火使两个孩子失去了生命，她为孩子的死感到深深的自责。这让她舍弃了婚姻和遗产，逃到曾经是内海的澳大利亚内陆沙漠地区。在那里，凯特成了米亚姆巴小镇的铁路酒店的女招待，与像她一样的出逃者成了朋友，这些出逃者还包括一只雌性鸸鹋和一只叫奇夫利的雄性袋鼠。在与形形色色的人打交道的过程中，凯特经历了痛苦和挑战，这些人包括善良的罪犯詹莱和嘎斯·斯库尔波戈，还有她的丈夫保罗的邪恶亲信伯恩赛德。

故事对澳大利亚现代社会进行了一次全面探索，包括人物的善与恶，其矛盾复杂性令人无法解释，包括悉尼城市生活的腐败和遥远内陆生活的狂野和质朴。回到悉尼，凯特从她的叔叔弗兰克·奥布莱恩那里得知，是保罗放了那场大火，而且大火要伤害的目标原本就是她。尽管如此，她没有追究，依旧希望远离是非，在离婚协议中不要丈夫一分钱，甚至像对待朋友那样对待丈夫的情人。肯尼利用丰富的叙事塑造了一个复杂而令读者信服的女主人公形象，一个令人钦佩的幸存者。

彼得·凯里（Peter Carey）的《凯利帮真史》（*The True History of the Kelly Gang*）以浪漫的笔触描绘了澳大利亚历史上三位亡命英雄的传奇一生。小说再现了凯利帮的成员奈德，从他的立场上还原了凯利帮的故事。小说的内容就是奈德·凯利在被执行死刑之前，写给女儿的一封长信。据他所言，他的父亲生前是一名罪犯，被流放到塔斯马尼亚岛；他的母亲艾伦一家——奎因家族，也是惯犯。警察时时监视着他们家的一举一动，并且试图敲诈艾伦，想占她的便宜。警察以盗窃和宰杀别人的牛的罪名将凯利的父亲关押了起来，尽管实际上父亲是替他顶罪，而他的行为不是偷盗和杀害，而仅仅是偷盗和抹去了牛身上的烙印。在奈德·凯利的故事中，警察被描绘成了压榨和残害百姓的恶势力，而他所谓的罪行则是对统治阶级压迫的反抗。

在父亲死后，凯利与家人四处流浪、居无定所。在母亲奎因家人的资助下，他们最终在葛林罗旺一带定居下来，在那儿购买了一些土地，成了“有土地的农民”，或者定居者。他们遵纪守法，通过养马、驯马艰难维持生活。即使这样，他们一家还是成了当地警察的眼中钉。年轻的奈德给丛林大盗哈里·鲍威尔做了学徒，并且参与了几起犯罪活动。他因为偷牛和其他违法行为好几次入狱服刑。

小说被称作“真史”，是因为它试图颠覆过去的宣传对凯利帮形象的诋毁。凯利作为一名罪犯有可能被理解为一个叛逆者和反抗暴政精神的化身。在回忆过程中，凯里作为不可靠的叙事者可能粉饰或掩盖他的罪恶。他的故事结尾——他们与警察的最后一次冲突——不仅使凯利帮成了亡命之徒，也可能印证警察的压迫与暴虐。他们一家被控告持枪伤害了警察菲茨帕特里克，而实际上起因则是菲茨帕特里克试图强奸凯利的妹妹凯特。在逃亡的过程中，他们枪杀了追来的一群警察。最终，因为朋友的背叛，他们在混战中都被警察枪杀，只有奈德活了下来。

五　文学与读者

我相信，李尧教授作为一名翻译家在最大程度上做到了忠实原著。对于文化上不可翻译的因素，他为读者提供了脚注，而不像其他译者那样，为了读者的需求，对文本进行强行的本土化、归约化，或者删除其中的内容。李尧教授的翻译对原著及作者表示出高度的尊重。的确，所有的文学翻译都是再创造的过程。无论是选择行为还是翻译行为，都反映了译者和译入语读者的需求。

这一点引导我们来到我要讲的最后一个问题，即中国文学的英译，而不是英语文学的汉译。在澳大利亚乃至整个西方世界，外国人对中国文学的兴趣远不及中国人对英语文学的兴趣。在某种意义上讲，西方读者对中国文学感兴趣并不完全是出于文学方面的原因。他们更希望看到中国作家的作品充满了政治性含义，甚至持有不同政见，就像以前他们期盼苏联作家或者社会主义阵营的作家表现出的政治性和异见性。

莫言的作品早在2016年获得诺贝尔文学奖之前，就已经引起了西方的注意并被翻译成了英文。他的作品对独生子女政策的残忍性，以及芸芸众生中的个体在国家的巨大历史转变以及社会主义国家建国的过程中所经受的苦难，都进行了讽刺性的评论。莫言这个名字本身就可以进行政治化的解读，这个名字的意思是一言不发或者被迫沉默。在西方畅销的中国作家往往都是那些揭露祖国社会的阴暗面的作家，或者作者本身就是反政府的人士。

盛可以可能是另一个可以归为这个类别的中国作家。她的小说《北妹》（*Northern Girl*）呈现出一个激进的女权主义和反抗权威的立场，因此已经被翻译成英文在西方出版。故事讲述了一个到广东谋生的打工妹的故事，将经济剥削和性剥削的问题作为鞭笞政府和社会冷漠的武器。在西方的中国流亡作家有很大可能变成持不同政见的作家。他们的某些批判言论有时过于激烈，反而暴露了其不合逻辑之处。例如刘再复将一种政治解读强加于中国文学经典《水浒传》，猛烈批判古代中国文化对暴力的崇拜和反叛角色的赞美。激进主义可能会给这些作家带来一种生计，也可能给他们带来一种读者市场。

西方作者如艾伦·金斯伯格（Allen Ginsberg）和加里·斯奈德（Gary Snyder）在书写中国时也可能很政治化，他们会对西藏问题表现出担忧（斯奈德），对压制同性恋表现出愤怒（金斯伯格）。澳大利亚诗人詹妮弗·梅登（Jennifer Maiden）在诗集《液氮》（*Liquid Nitrogen*，2010）中，将澳大利亚、美国、印度、挪威、埃及以及中国的政治问题编织成一系列散文诗或对话。诗集关于中国的部分讲述了一个澳大利亚人和一个刚从监狱释放出来的持不同政见者在北京的一个咖啡馆的秘密会面，后者要向澳大利亚人提供关于监狱制造玩具的某种情报。整体的情景读起来就像是冷战时期的间谍电影，在他们穿过故宫和紫禁城的过程中，那些模糊不清的人物一直在跟踪他们。

这可能是西方读者群体喜欢的故事。如果一个澳大利亚编辑要出版一套当代中国文学作品的选集，就像李尧教授出版的这套译文集一样，我猜想或多或少会包含以上所提到的那种类型的文学作品。这不是因为这些作品更震撼人心，或者文学价值更高，而是因为它们可以投“市场”所好。西方图书市场的这种趋势可能反映了西方世界妖魔化中国的趋势，在意识形态上与升级版的“中国威胁论”一致，试图诋毁中国的全球影响力，贬之为“锐实力”，而将美国的霸权主义赞美为“软实力”。中国从未以如此尖刻的态度看待过西方！

参考文献

Carey, Peter. *True History of Kelly Gang*. New York: Vintage, 2001.

Castro, Brian. *Birds of Passage*. London: Allen & Unwin, 1999.

Castro, Brian. *After China*. London: Allen & Unwin, 1993.

Eliot, T. S. “*Was There A Scottish Literature?*” *Athenaeum*, 1 Aug. 1919, pp. 680 – 681.

Fitzgerald, C. P. *Why China*. Melbourne: Melbourne Univ. Press, 1985.

Heaney, Seamus. *New Selected Poems*: 1966 – 1987. London: Faber & Faber, 1990.

Jose, Nicholas. *The Rose Crossing*. New York: The Overlook Press, 1997.

Jose, Nicholas. *The Red Thread*. London: Faber & Faber, 2001.

Keneally, Thomas. *A Woman of Inner Sea*. London: Sceptre, 1993.

Maiden, Jennifer. *Liquid Nitrogen*. Sydney: Giramondo, 2012.

Miller, Alex. *The Ancestor Game*. New York: Allen & Unwin, 2003.

McCullough, Colleen. *The Touch*. New York and London: Simon & Schuster, 2003.

Walcott, Derek. *Selected Poems*, ed. Edward Baugh. New York: Farrar, Straus and Giroux, 2007.

Walker, David. *Not Dark Yet*. Sydney: Giramondo, 2011.

White, Patrick. *The Tree of Man*. New York: Vintage, 1994.

Wright, Alexis. *Carpentaria*. Constable, 2009.

胡文仲：《澳大利亚文学论文集》，外语教学与研究出版社，1994。

李尧：《澳大利亚文学经典译文集》，青岛出版社，2018。

莫言：《生死疲劳》，作家出版社，2012。

盛可以：《北妹》，浙江文艺出版社，2016。

会议综述

Conferences

“第十六届中国澳大利亚研究国际学术研讨会”综述

乌云高娃[*]

“第十六届中国澳大利亚研究国际学术研讨会”于2018年6月21日至23日在北京外语教学与研究出版社国际会议中心召开。北京外国语大学和内蒙古师范大学澳大利亚研究中心受中国澳大利亚研究会委托主办本届会议。今年是澳中理事会成立40周年和中国澳大利亚研究会成立30周年，来自中国和澳大利亚50多所高校、科研机构和政府部门的近200名专家和学者参加了本届学术盛会。

中国澳大利亚研究会会长、北京外国语大学副校长孙有中教授，澳大利亚驻华大使馆副大使董正德（Gerald Thomson）先生，澳大利亚国立大学副校长雪莉·利奇（Shirley Leitch）教授，内蒙古师范大学外国语学院院长兼澳大利亚研究中心主任武海燕教授在开幕式上致辞。本次会议还特别邀请澳大利亚研究前辈“九人帮”中的五位专家——胡文仲、胡壮麟、杨潮光、王国富和杜瑞清分享了澳大利亚研究历程中的经历——“我们的故事”。中国澳大利亚研究会常务副会长、华东师范大学澳大利亚研究中心主任陈弘教授、西悉尼大学梅卓琳（Jocelyn Chey）教授、哈尔滨工业大学刘克东教授和塔斯马尼亚大学韦恩·哈德逊教授（Wayne Hudson）分别进行了主旨发言。

---

* 乌云高娃，内蒙古师范大学外语学院副教授，研究方向是澳大利亚儿童文学。

本届会议的主题是“澳大利亚与变化中的世界”（Australia in the Changing World），旨在探讨澳大利亚在亚太地区的发展及其与亚洲、太平洋地区、美洲、欧洲和世界其他区域日渐重要的关系。

会议 150 多篇参会者的论文具有多学科和跨学科的特点，发言分成了政治与国际关系、经济与贸易、社会历史与文化、语言与教育、文学与翻译五个分会场，并且特设了国际澳大利亚研究协会代表专场、亚历克斯·赖特文学专场、硕士生论坛和博士生专场。中外专家学者围绕当今复杂的澳大利亚国内局势和国际关系，就澳大利亚政治、经济、贸易、国际关系、历史、社会、文化、教育、语言、文学、翻译、艺术等各个领域进行了探讨和交流。

政治与国际关系

鉴于澳大利亚近些年国内局势的不断变化，每届中国澳大利亚研究国际学术研讨会的一个热议的主题就是澳大利亚政治与国际关系。本届会议上，澳大利亚政治与国际关系依然是众人关心的话题之一。

在开幕式主旨发言中，华东师范大学的陈弘教授以“中澳关系背景下的澳大利亚与‘印太战略’”为题，从 2017 年澳大利亚外交政策白皮书中关于“印太战略”作为外交政策制定和国家安全发展的基础入手，阐述了澳大利亚政党与美国国家安全战略中体现的所谓“共同利益”，明显指向中国的和平崛起。从中国视角分析了此战略的潜在意图，指出澳大利亚在与美国分享共同利益的同时，也认识到中国在地缘政治经济中的重要作用。陈弘教授进一步探讨了澳大利亚对华政策可能的趋势与走向。他指出，由于该战略处于初级阶段，中国在推进“一带一路”倡议和构建人类命运共同体的同时，需要采取包容开放的态度，在亚太和印度洋地区和平发展进程中发挥自己的作用。

在题为“变化世界中的澳中关系：应对差异与不确定性之挑战”中，新南威尔士大学的张剑教授也指出，自 2012 年起，澳中关系经历了一系列的摩擦，随着“印太战略”的提出、国际局势的整体变化、中国的崛起和美国特朗普掌握美国政权，两国政府在有效应对差异的同时，将在保持持续稳定、互惠互利的重要双边关系上面临更大的挑战。

格里菲斯大学的马克林（Colin Mackerras）教授做了题为“2017 年以来的中美澳三角关系”的发言。发言指出：2017 年是中澳关系下滑的一年，澳大利亚政府因为南海争端问题重提“中国威胁论”，并通过大量媒体报道，宣传中国政府通过澳大利亚的华人社区来加强中国在澳的经济和政治影响，一些澳媒也指责中国留学生对澳大利亚学术的负面影响，也不乏澳大利亚学者提出“中国侵略论”。马克林教授认为，澳大利亚应当在外交政策上减少美国的影响，澳媒也应当减少不公平的报道，澳大利亚应当避免破坏中澳关系的不必要行为。

北京大学格里戈·麦卡锡（Greg McCarthy）教授也在题为“中国崛起的挑战：中国焦虑与澳大利亚”的发言中阐述了澳大利亚历史上由来已久的“中国焦虑”，如今中国作为澳大利亚最大的贸易伙伴，同时与澳洲在移民、旅游、商业、学术等方面保持不断的持续往来，中国依旧成了澳大利亚的“焦虑”。

这样的“焦虑”在悉尼科技大学的埃琳娜·考林森（Elena Collinson）题为“澳大利亚的中国论及其动机”的发言中也有所体现。发言主要强调了澳大利亚政府、学界和商业人士在澳中应保持怎样的双边关系上依然有很多分歧，但是当澳大利亚一贯“西方至上”的观念和做法受到挑战时，尤其是面对“中国崛起”和特朗普执政，澳洲出现了一些极端的观点。

针对澳大利亚政治、国际关系、外交政策等方面的问题，专家学者们各抒己见，现场讨论积极热烈。迪肯大学的大卫·沃克（David Walker）教授做了题为“美澳关系：百年伙伴关系?”的发言，将美澳伙伴关系的由来和沿革进行了介绍和分析，揭示了“百年关系”背景下的美澳关系实质；西悉尼大学梅卓琳（Jocelyn Chey）教授发表了题为“中国袋鼠：双边关系四十年的思索”的主旨演讲，图文并茂地梳理了从 20 世纪 80 年代至今袋鼠这一澳大利亚典型形象在四十年间作为软实力产物在中国的发展，并通过袋鼠的不同形象影射梅卓琳教授自 20 世纪 70 年代起在中国不同工作和生活的经历，从而进一步反映了中澳双边关系的不断变化和成熟；拉筹伯大学尼克·比斯利（Nick Bisley）教授的发言题为“焦虑盟友面前不断变化的世界秩序：澳大利亚多变的外交政策话语”，从历史的角度展示了关于澳大利亚的外交政策辩论，并提出四大主要辩论阵营及其对澳政府政策制定的影响；中国社科院韩锋教授在发言中精辟地总结了澳大利亚近期的外交政策，包括白皮书重心的转移，澳大利亚与美中关系如何平衡，澳国内政治如何影响外交等。

经济和贸易

经济和贸易也是本届会议热议的话题之一。发言人围绕受澳大利亚政治局势影响的经济变化进行了探讨，包括中澳贸易走向、中国在澳投资、货币政策、行业关系等。

华东师范大学陈曦在题为“2017 年 ~ 2018 年中澳贸易分析”的发言中分析了这个时期中澳贸易的发展状况，根据澳大利亚统计局提供的数据指出，澳大利亚针对中澳双边贸易增速减缓，分析了导致双边贸易产生变化的可能因素。

北京外国语大学胡丹在题为“基础设施投资、‘一带一路’倡议和国家安全审查：澳大利亚率先回应”的发言中，讨论了中国海外投资转向基础设施建设，连同“一带一路”倡议在海外的推广，引起了一些国家的质疑。当各政府还在考虑如何应对时，澳大利亚政府首先出台了一系列针对基础设施投资和建设的措施，来应对中国在澳的投资，从而进一步影响了两国间本就日益紧张的双边关系。

经济和贸易分会场的发言人还就澳大利亚的各个行业及其政策进行了深刻的剖析，如：澳大利亚当今货币政策的制定及其利弊

（吴茂国，上海大学）、中国在澳投资背景下的社会企业责任（Huw Slater，中国碳论坛）、中澳能源关系（Prachi Aggarwal，桑奇佛教与印度学研究大学），中澳服务行业产业内贸易现状及其影响因素（许梅恋，林丽清，厦门大学），中澳房地产市场关系（罗航，西华大学），茶叶出口反映出的中澳贸易结构发展（史逸林，北京外国语大学）等。

文学与翻译

文学理论和文学评论依旧是文学分会场的重要内容，尤其是在全球化和澳大利亚多元文化背景下的澳大利亚文学研究和跨文化研究，比如迪肯大学的林·麦克雷登（Lyn McCredden）教授对本土作家文化选择的探讨，文学评论家比尔·阿什克罗夫特（Bill Ashcroft）对澳大利亚文学中身份归属问题与后殖民话语联系的分析，香港大学的许道芝对澳大利亚文学中原住民和亚洲身份与归属的阐述，纽卡斯尔大学的大卫·马斯格雷夫（David Musgrave）对澳大利亚文学中的怪诞手法进行了梳理，并用文化自卑感的理论进行了诠释，武汉大学的黄忠通过华裔女作家的视角分析了华人男性的形象转变。部分发言人也利用文学理论对具体的作品进行了分析，如《凯利帮真史》中历史再现与回忆重建（方凡，浙江大学），《心中的明天》中澳大利亚土著身份的建构与道德冲突（冷慧，辽宁师范大学），《搬家》中的滥用权力（高萍，长安大学），《遥远的路》中乔治·约翰斯顿的跨文化写作（张丽丽，南通大学）等。

比较文学也是文学分会场的一个重要内容，包括埃迪斯科文大学格兰菲利普斯（Glen Phillips）对凯瑟琳·苏珊娜第一部和最后一部小说的比较与分析，清华大学王敬慧对日本诗人松尾芭蕉和澳大利亚小说家理查·佛拉纳根的比较，合肥大学朱乐琴对《洛丽塔》和《暗黑之地》中两位人物的对比，南通大学张加生对鲁迅和亨利·劳森作品和人物形象及特点的比较等。

上海外国语大学王光林教授在发言中强调了文学翻译不可译性

对世界文学边界带来的重新思考。安徽大学宋筱蓉与大家分享了李尧翻译作品反映出的中国澳大利亚文学研究发展历程。本届会议正值李尧教授从事澳大利亚文学翻译四十周年，对李尧教授的译作研究对澳大利亚文学研究来说可谓意义非凡。

本届会议上还突现了一系列针对儿童文学研究的发言，主要来自内蒙古师范大学，六位发言人（郭咏梅、何志英、姜鸿玉、刘海霞、乌云高娃、张宏燕）分别从动物形象、象征意义、文化研究、空间理论等角度探讨了六部澳大利亚儿童文学作品，为本届会议增添了文学研究的新生力量和新的视角。

社会历史与文化

社会历史与文化一直以来是澳大利亚研究必不可少的内容。本届会议有关澳大利亚社会历史与文化的发言主要包括文化研究（李景艳，哈尔滨工业大学）、跨文化研究（颜静兰、王慧，华东理工大学）、移民（Wenche Ommundsen，伍伦贡大学）、新媒体（陈贝贝，华东师范大学）、国家印象（Paul Pickering，澳洲国立大学；Denise Mountain，内蒙古师范大学）、体育文化（陈力全，牡丹江师范学院）、新科技（吴怡，上海大学）、跨国公民（Jatinder Mann，香港浸会大学）等主题。

本届会议中关于澳大利亚语言与教育的发言主要集中在对高等教育（马乃强，北京外国语大学）、国际教育（黄常钰，上海大学）、奖学金（王金贵，牡丹江师范学院）、语言政策（郭亚楠，内蒙古大学）、外语教育（胡钰翎，北京外国语大学）、教师教育（冯海佳，内蒙古师范大学）、比较教育（包红令，赤峰学院）等方面的讨论。

专场发言

本届会议特设国际澳大利亚研究协会和“亚历克斯·赖特文

学研究”专场发言。

国际澳大利亚研究协会专场由三位学者的发言组成。来自塔斯马尼亚大学的米歇尔·罗斯（Mitchell Rolls）在题为“如果土地是头”的发言中，从原住民“大地母亲”的视角，探讨了原住民的土地权利和土著社区文化的保护问题。阿德莱德大学史蒂芬·米克（Stephen Muecke）进行了题为“澳大利亚：脆弱的文明”的发言，探讨了澳大利亚历史上被政治所左右的两个文明——土著文明和西方文明，提出了自己对这两个文明受新世界秩序影响的反思。来自塔斯马尼亚大学的凯瑟琳·约翰逊（Katherine Johnson）在“人类动物园：一半故事”中，解构了闻名西方的“人类动物园：野蛮之始”展演中的“野蛮”视角，力争还原真实的澳大利亚原住民声音。

“亚历克斯·赖特文学研究”专场为三位研究亚历克斯·赖特的学者设立了专场发言，来自苏州大学的方红和内蒙古师范大学的魏靖分别从文学评论和语言学角度探讨了《卡彭塔利亚湾》，来自北京航空航天大学的邢春丽从土地的文化含义比较了《神秘的河》和《卡彭塔利亚湾》两部作品。

结　语

此次会议在主办方和参会专家学者的共同参与和互动中，形成了热烈、开放、启发式的学术氛围，展示了中国澳大利亚研究的高学术水平、求真务实和与时俱进的研究态度，以及中国澳大利亚研究的近期最新成果。本届会议为参会专家学者提供了便利的交流场所与进一步沟通与合作的平台，推动了中国澳大利亚研究向更深更广更新的方向发展。经中国澳大利亚研究会商议决定，第 17 届中国澳大利亚研究国际研讨会将于 2020 年在哈尔滨工业大学举行。

图书在版编目(CIP)数据

澳大利亚研究. 2018 年. 第 2 辑: 总第 2 辑 / 孙有中主编. -- 北京: 社会科学文献出版社, 2018. 12

ISBN 978 - 7 - 5097 - 7352 - 9

Ⅰ. ①澳… Ⅱ. ①孙… Ⅲ. ①澳大利亚 - 研究 - 文集 Ⅳ. ①K611 - 53

中国版本图书馆 CIP 数据核字（2018）第 281780 号

澳大利亚研究（2018 年第 2 辑/总第 2 辑）

主　　编 / 孙有中
副 主 编 / 陈　弘　韩　锋
执行主编 / 李建军　胡　丹

出 版 人 / 谢寿光
项目统筹 / 张晓莉　叶　娟
责任编辑 / 叶　娟　路子正

出　　版 / 社会科学文献出版社 · 国别区域与全球治理出版中心（010）59367200
　　地址: 北京市北三环中路甲 29 号院华龙大厦　邮编: 100029
　　网址: www. ssap. com. cn
发　　行 / 市场营销中心（010）59367081　59367083
印　　装 / 三河市龙林印务有限公司

规　　格 / 开 本: 787mm × 1092mm　1/16
　　印 张: 14. 75　字 数: 206 千字
版　　次 / 2018 年 12 月第 1 版　2018 年 12 月第 1 次印刷
书　　号 / ISBN 978 - 7 - 5097 - 7352 - 9
定　　价 / 89. 00 元

本书如有印装质量问题, 请与读者服务中心（010 - 59367028）联系